A Journalistic
Approach to
Good Writing

THE

CRAFT

OF

CLARITY

Second
Edition

A Journalistic
Approach to
Good Writing

Second
Edition

THE

CRAFT

OF

CLARITY

Robert M. Knight

Iowa State Press

A Blackwell Publishing Company

Robert M. Knight teaches journalism and English composition courses at Gettysburg College in Gettysburg, Pennsylvania. He earned his bachelor's degree at the University of Colorado at Boulder and a master's at DePaul University in Chicago. A veteran journalist, he has written for virtually all the news media. When he was a full-time freelance writer, Mr. Knight was published in more than 40 newspapers, magazines, and news services and contributed frequently to the *Chicago Tribune*, the *Tribune's Sunday Magazine*, the *Christian Science Monitor*, Reuters news service, and the *Washington Post*. He taught journalistic writing for 13 years at Northwestern University, was senior rewrite editor for the Chicago City News Bureau, and is a past president of the Chicago Headline Club (Society of Professional Journalists). His early career was spent at United Press International in Denver and Albuquerque; the *New Mexican,* Santa Fe's daily newspaper; and in New Mexico radio and television.

©1998 Iowa State University Press
©2003 Iowa State Press
A Blackwell Publishing Company
All rights reserved

Iowa State Press
2121 State Avenue, Ames, Iowa 50014

Orders: 1-800-862-6657
Office: 1-515-292-0140
Fax: 1-515-292-3348
Web site: www.iowastatepress.com

Back cover photo by Ray Miller, Gettysburg College

∞ Printed on acid-free paper in the United States of America

First edition, 1998
Second edition, 2003

Library of Congress Cataloging-in-Publication Data

Knight, Robert M., 1940-
  A journalistic approach to good writing : the craft of clarity /
Robert M. Knight.-- 2nd ed.
     p. cm.
Includes bibliographical references and index.
  ISBN 0-8138-1208-9 (alk. paper)
  1. Journalism--Authorship. I. Title.
  PN4783.K55 2003
  808'.06607--dc21
                          2003000541

The last digit is the print number: 9 8 7 6 5 4 3 2 1

Contents

Hold each moment sacred. Give each clarity and
meaning.
—Thomas Mann, *The Beloved Returns*

Culture is not life in its entirety, but just the moments
of security, strength and clarity.
—Jose Ortega y Gasset, *Meditations on Quixote*

Preface

This second edition of *A Journalistic Approach to Good Writing: The Craft of Clarity* keeps most of what has proven instructive for students who want to learn how to write honestly, directly and clearly, without writing down to their audience. For this edition, I have increased the number of writing examples (mostly of how not to write), updated and clarified some of the exercises. And I hope I've added some insights.

In addition, I've tried to eliminate a few sins that, for a journalist writing a book about journalism, come across as mortal sins—the dreaded errors of fact. For instance, it took a couple of alert students to tell me that a quote I used from Shakespeare's *MacBeth* was not "bubble, bubble, toil and trouble" but "double, double, toil and trouble;" that the Battle of Dunkirk occurred not in 1939, but in 1940, and that Dunkirk is in Belgium, not France. I am sitting in an imaginary corner with a dunce cap on my head and a deep shade of red on my face, as well I should.

When I finished the first edition in 1997, I was working full time as an editor for the City News Bureau of Chicago and teaching adults part time at Northwestern University's University College, now called the Continuing Education Division. Now I am an adjunct instructor of journalism and English at Gettysburg College in Pennsylvania. This experience has given me a better understanding of how young undergraduates learn—or successfully resist learning—how to write. I hope that understanding has led to a book that is better targeted to teachers of writing, journalistic or otherwise.

There is nothing like teaching with your own book to help you learn where the potholes are. I hope this second edition fills most of them.

One thing I've come to realize after teaching several semesters of regular college undergrads: I must be more careful with references to time. When I embarked on the first edition, most of my Gettysburg College students were nine or 10. This especially came to my attention when I wrote Chapter 6 ("On Being Original"), which included several pages of clichés, existing and about-to-become. But many of the clichés lived and died before my students had even approached college age. For example, I don't know how long "fish or cut bait" has been absent from everyday American conversation, but apparently it was long enough. The great majority of my students had no idea what it meant.

Sometimes, before we're aware of it, words die too. This became obvious when I used "dilapidated" in an exercise for one of my classes. Many of my students said they had never heard the word before.

Further, my reference to the Ayatollah Khomeini was lost on students who had not been born in 1980, the year he took over Iran and bedeviled the West, especially the United States. Student awareness has not been helped by the apparent disregard by many of them for history. A 2002 U.S. Department of Education study indicated that 57 percent of high school seniors could not perform even at the basic level on a history exam. Thirty-two percent did perform at the basic level and 10 percent at the grade level. Only 1 percent performed at the advanced or superior level.

As an instructor who now teaches nearly full time, I continue to help students struggle through the obstacle course known as the English language, semester after semester. I've paid particular attention to the links between journalistic skills and the art of writing. My students have learned to treat the often-peculiar rules of journalistic writing as a skills base for any kind of communication, from poetry to office memos.

Many students who take journalism courses (at least most of the students I've taught) have no thought of ever becoming journalists. They want no part of a business that demands strange hours and high stress levels, pays poorly, offers little job security and often provides the atmospheric warmth of a Siberian *gulag*. But they do want to learn how to write, and they guess–accurately,

I think–that skills training in journalistic writing can take them almost anywhere.

When I began teaching in 1983, I believed it to be my job to help my students reach that level of skill. I provided a 14-week course that combined concept and mechanics, encouragement and scolding, editing and rewriting. The end result should have been a student who could appreciate the whole of good writing and analyze, and often surgically remove, the parts.

The Student's Struggle

After several years, however, it was becoming apparent that my tactics were not working as they should have. No doubt I was becoming adept at taking some eager adults who knew little or nothing about the rigors of journalistic writing and teaching them something. A few actually learned journalistic writing, or at least they were well on their way. But for many others, the struggle at the beginning of the course simply was replaced by a struggle at the end of the course.

Certainly it wasn't their fault if they weren't immediately feeling confident and comfortable writing in a new medium. I couldn't expect them to know what, for many, was an entirely new way to communicate. That was what they had come into the classroom to learn. Yet I would question my own integrity if I failed to judge their work by professional standards.

I looked for a text that would provide the underpinnings they needed to know before I rapped their knuckles for failing to show that they knew them. There are plenty of good texts out there, and some of them are quoted liberally in this book. But regardless of whether the texts taught the philosophy of journalism or the philosophy of writing, when most of my students applied their fingers to keyboards, it became obvious the philosophy was not translating well.

Not that I expected much else. Writing can't easily be learned by reading about it; it must be done. Students need to make mistakes they don't even know are mistakes until an editor or instructor tells them. That's how I learned. That's how every veteran journalist I know learned.

But it wasn't fair.

What appeared to work best was sharing their mistakes with their classmates. I was careful not to name the authors of the mistake; egos are never more fragile than they are in a beginning journalistic writing course. I would grade papers and dutifully compile the most glaring examples of bad writing on two or three sheets of paper. Then I would photocopy them and go over them with the class, encouraging students to perform the edits themselves in front of the rest of the class. The examples seemed to make more sense if the students could see peer-level struggles with the English language and the in-class exercises made them more apt to say, "Oh yeah, I see what you mean."

My list of examples grew over the years, and each semester I abused more copy machines and killed more trees. Finally, it dawned on me that what I had might be the makings of a book— and maybe the book I was looking for. Although a text for journalists, such a book would be written in a style accessible to non-journalists who want to hone their communication skills. It would include concrete examples of how not to write, provided by students who were in the process of going through the often-painful experience of learning just that. Those examples provided the base for most of the first edition, and the augmented examples continue to provide direction for the student reading the second edition.

The first edition evolved from a big chunk of my 1996 master's thesis, or "Master Work," as the Graduate School for New Learning at Chicago's DePaul University calls it. The thesis and the book both needed some philosophical underpinnings, and that need was supplied in part by another project I had hammered together. A few years earlier, I had decided it was time that I share my writing wit and wisdom, for what it was worth, with people outside the classroom. What resulted was a three-part series, "What Pros Forget: Some Nearly Random Thoughts about What Makes Good Writing Good." The series ran in the *Chicago Journalist*, the award-winning journalism review of the Chicago Headline Club chapter of the Society of Professional Journalists (SPJ).

The series was received well enough that I put it together in a single document that became a second handout for my classes, as well as a handout for seminar sessions I occasionally participate in at SPJ gatherings and conferences of the Association of Educators in Journalism and Mass Communication (AEJMC). Combined with some fill-in handouts, the two documents appeared to work well for students who actually sat down and read them.

One note: Despite the horror displayed by some editors and academicians at my use of "lede" instead of "lead" to describe the introduction of a journalistic piece, I continue to use it in this second edition. I have worked with wire service and magazines editors who use lede, and a quick sampling of the subject on the Internet indicates it is used by at least the *New York Times,* as well as in dozens of journalism syllabi. The spelling is useful; it sets the intro apart from a police clue or something that comes out of a pencil.

A Larger Context

The theme of this book is the benefits of clear writing and how to write that way, but another theme might be implied. It addresses a rift that apparently has developed between those who teach journalism in the United States and those who practice it. Too often, especially in colleges that have no formal journalism or mass communication school or department, the teacher has little or no practical experience in the field. Too often, the practitioner has little or no grasp of the broader issues of journalism and its role in the democratic republic it's supposed to be supporting and protecting.

For reporters and editors who write the daily catalogue of fires, murders, drug wars, gang conflicts, child abuse, bank robberies, fluffy features, political intrigue, botched elections and sensational trials—for them, the role of journalism in society appears to be an issue without roots, one of only academic value. To be sure, the craft's professionals are concerned with journalistic ethics. They've learned it by rote, by poring over lists of thou-shalt-nots. And they are indeed concerned about something as conceptual as the First Amendment to the U.S. Constitution— anytime they are prevented from getting what they perceive to be the facts they need for the story they're working on at the moment. But many leave the nuances of ethics and freedom of information to the scholars whose job it is to address journalism as a vehicle that carries the material that will somehow alter a couple of amorphous concepts: the media and public opinion.

By the same token, some scholars who teach communication theory have a difficult time teaching journalistic writing. They might know, in theory, the importance of strong lead (or lede), the value of a direct quotation, the advantage of writing in the active voice, the concept of word economy, or why strong nouns and action verbs usually illustrate a story better than strings of adjectives and adverbs. But because such scholars have little hands-on newsroom training, many struggle to learn how to coach a student through the process of learning such skills. They have not themselves grappled with the concept that the journalistic style of writing is informal, yet "tight."

Thanks

Dozens of people helped me at every step of the project that resulted in the first edition of *The Craft of Clarity*. Many of them, especially the staff at the Iowa State University Press and my wife, Susan Knight, helped me—often pushed me—through the second edition.

The first person who comes to mind is Fiora Scaffi, a Chicago writer with whom I shared office space when I was a full-time freelancer. She would watch me compile student writing examples and say, "You could write a book!" Fiora was not one with whom it is easy to argue, so I wrote a book. And I owed, and still owe, some credit to Irene Macauley, no mean author herself, who helped convince me that I could write such a book. Similar encouragement came from two close friends who both happen to be graphic artists, Richmond Jones in Chicago and John Gebhardt in Denver.

As only a good friend can, writer and editor James Kepler, who with his wife, Ann, and son, Tom, runs Chicago's Adams Press, helped me decide what it was I really wanted to do with this thing. And when I was wondering if anybody would want to buy such a book, video producer Peter Greenbaum and ad agency creative director Gretchen Effler were there to say yes.

One entire group of people, the 15 other master's degree aspirants in my "cluster" at DePaul University, were free with cheery support and good advice. The other writer in the cluster, Marilyn Soltis, listened to me expound on what makes good writing good without once telling me she knew that already. And David Shallenberger, the cluster's faculty mentor, was most encouraging.

For their critiques of my work in progress and for helping me find stuff, I thank Michael Conlon of Reuters; Joseph Reilly, who was my boss at City News; and Susan Stevens and Jeffrey Finkelman, broadcast editors at City News. Susan provided a whole lot of moral support as well as technical support. Also on my list: Wendy McClure, a graduate of the Iowa Writers' Workshop at the University of Iowa; my old college friend John McLaughlin of Denver; the woman who defined the position of "writing coach" for newspapers, Paula LaRocque of the *Dallas Morning News*; Oliver Witte and Edmund Rooney of Loyola University of Chicago; Jan Whitt of the University of Colorado and Willard Rowland, a former dean of journalism and communication at the Boulder school; Louise Love, vice provost at Chicago's Roosevelt University and former associate dean at Northwestern University; and four former teaching colleagues at NU's University College: Terry Brown, George Harmon, Pierce Hollingsworth and especially Ray DeLong. Ray acted as my official professional mentor during the pursuit of my master's degree and, like a good instructor, provided encouragement as well as the occasional slap on the hand during the months it took for the master's thesis to spawn a book.

For their help on this second edition, I thank five colleagues in the English Department at Gettysburg College: Lani Lindeman, James Myers, Christopher Fee, Elizabeth Lambert and Robert Fredrickson. Lani applied the discipline of a classicist's mind to vetting what must have been some challenging chapters. Jim supplied some of this book's information on Celtic influences in English. Chris confirmed some of the information on Viking influences. Beth helped with Dr. Johnson, his dictionary and his club, which included her favorite Englishman, Edmund Burke. And Bob just seemed to be there whenever I needed moral support.

My friend from Essex, Massachusetts, and the founding editor of *Software* magazine, Ed Bride, brought me up to date on how corporate computing publications sort their audiences out. And Ed has offered great encouragement over the years.

A special thanks to Mark Barrett at Iowa State Press; this second edition simply would not exist without his efforts. And thanks also go to Tad Ringo and his crack staff of editors.

I must also point out that any errors in this book are mine alone; no blame should accrue to those nice people in Ames, Iowa.

My biggest thanks must go to my wife, Susan, the former high school English teacher who got drafted into reviewing manuscript pages. She has charitably refrained from saying, "Thirty-seven years of marriage and now this." Our daughters, Kelly Knight Douglas and Leigh Knight, made a heroic, and successful, effort at putting up with me too.

Finally, no one has worked harder at providing content for this book—just ask them—than the hundreds of students who have taken my journalistic writing and English composition courses at Northwestern University and Gettysburg College, and who continued despite the warnings of their better judgments.

A Journalistic
Approach to
Good Writing

THE
CRAFT
OF
CLARITY

Second
Edition

The best part of human language ... is derived from reflection on the acts of the mind itself.
—Samuel Taylor Coleridge, *On the Principles of Genial Criticism*

I got into my bones the essential structure of the ordinary British sentence—which is a noble thing.
—Winston Churchill, *Roving Commission: My Early Life*

1 What Makes Good Writing Good

He not only was an accomplished chemist, he was known as one of the most intelligent managers in the corporation. He worked with a combination of creativity, common sense and precision. But he hated to write reports. He had no confidence in his ability to communicate with words on paper or a computer screen. He was not alone.

Many Americans approach with dread the task of writing so much as a two-paragraph note. They view writing not as a means of communicating facts, concepts and ideas but as a survival course fraught with rules of grammar they tried, maybe not very hard, to learn in the eighth grade and have forgotten since.

This epidemic of unease with the English language has even reached those who make their living writing—in journalism, for instance. The more news I consume in broadcast, print or on the Internet, the more convinced I am that many writing professionals could use the same kind of rigor to which a journalism student should be routinely subjected. Such a rigor combines the reporting dictum of The City News Bureau of Chicago—"If your mother says she loves you, check it out"—with the writing dictum that "every word should pull its own weight. If it doesn't, throw it out."

Mainstream U.S. journalism and journalism schools have done a reasonably good job of teaching the ethics and craft of reporting, but often at the expense of providing practice in using precise writing skills. Granted, for the sake of accuracy, balance and fairness, ethics and good reporting should take priority. But does that mean we should forget about good writing? Must we make that choice?

Too often, today's newspaper, broadcast and magazine journalists are so intent on delivering the facts of a story—and beating their competitors to it—that the form in which the facts get delivered makes little difference. And often ideas and concepts don't get delivered at all.

In *Eyewitness to History*, a collection of reportage dating from medieval to modern times, British editor John Carey makes the point that what is reported cannot easily be separated from the reporting process. "Good reportage cannot, of course, get beyond the language," Carey writes, "because it is language itself." Good journalistic writing comprises a set of skills that makes the delivery of facts, concepts, ideas and emotions swift, easy and inevitable.

There is something here for the nonjournalist as well as the journalist. For the student of written expression who has no desire to get anywhere near journalism, journalistic writing can provide the rigor and framework needed to develop writing skills and measure the extent of that development. Its emphasis on word precision and economy, active voice, action verbs and robust nouns makes it good training for any kind of writing, unless the writer is intent on misleading the reader, viewer or listener with fog and confusion—a not uncommon intention.

The best journalistic writing combines skilled reporting and prose that communicates itself clearly, even passionately, without attracting too much attention to itself. As Michael Jordan used to glide by the basket, seemingly without effort, so the good writer seems to communicate without exertion. How simple it sounds; how hard it can be to do, even for the established writer.

Whether the writer is a professional or someone who writes to relatives or acquaintances once a year, the challenge is to take a fact, concept, opinion, feeling or idea that resides in the writer's head and transfer it to the head of the reader (or listener or viewer). When it arrives, the subject should look, feel, sound, smell and taste the same as it did when it lay unexpressed in the writer's head. It should have the same heft, the same mass.

The Writer as a Conduit

The writer—any good writer—should become a conduit, an unexciting word that describes exactly what a good writer is, regardless of mode or medium: reporter, novelist, poet, playwright, ad copywriter, lyricist, scriptwriter; even the writer of a computer manual. One way to become a good conduit is to use simple, declarative sentences.

It's the KISS principle: Keep it simple, stupid.

A writer, however, is no more restricted to stringing together short, prosaic sentences than a composer is restricted to writing, say, flute solos. If a full symphony conveys the emotions better than the solo, then compose a full symphony, even if you're a journalist. As does a good composer, though, a good writer knows when simpler is better. And knowing when simpler is better implies that you know your audience, the person or people to whom you are writing.

Sometimes a jargon test helps. If, for example, you use the term *writ of summons* for an audience other than lawyers, you most likely are going to have to explain what you mean. You would expect attorneys to know that a writ of summons is something that usually begins a civil action, but you wouldn't expect most readers of a metropolitan daily newspaper to know the term. If you're writing to a group of corporate software managers, you can most likely get away with using *MIS* or *IT* without explaining that they stand for management information systems and information technology. To talk about *diastrophism* without explaining that it is a force that deforms the earth's crust and creates mountains would be inexcusable unless you're addressing an audience of geologists or geophysicists.

Jargon words have special meanings that are appropriate when a professional talks to another professional. *Expenses* and *expenditures* might mean the same thing to a reporter. To a certified public accountant, however, getting them confused can guarantee a visit by the Internal Revenue Service.

It's when the writer writes jargon for a general audience that it becomes a problem. Jargon sounds pompous to unaccustomed ears. The reader is likely to receive messages the writer might not have meant to send:

- "I think you're stupid enough to be impressed with my use of pompous-sounding words that you obviously don't understand."

- "I am a sloppy thinker, and I am too lazy to take the time to provide a synonym that makes sense to you."
- "I don't know what I'm writing about, but I can fool you into thinking I do."
- "I am conning you."

Jargon puts the reader down. Unless you're a Marine Corps drill instructor, you won't gain much by putting down the people with whom you are trying to communicate. Instead of anointing themselves, the best writers create a dialogue with the reader. It's as if the reader is standing on the other side of the typewriter or computer, looking directly at the writer.

You ask, "Now, what do you need to know?" The reader or viewer or listener answers you. You write a paragraph or so in response and again ask, "OK, what do you need to know next?" and the reader tells you. You continue this stimulus and response with the imaginary audience until you've exhausted the subject and emotions you want to express, or you've reached the word limit the editor has assigned to you.

For most kinds of short writing (less than 3,000 words) such a dialogue might even eliminate the need to outline. It ensures that the copy flows as it's supposed to, that bridges appear to guide the reader from one paragraph to the next that the copy appears seamless.

Good Beginnings: The Lead (or Lede)

Fine. You've defined your audience, and you are prepared to create a dialogue with that audience. But first you need to get its attention. That's obvious, yet among the rules of good communication, this one seems to be one of the hardest to learn. If it's so obvious, then fewer reports would begin with something like "On July 4, 1776, a meeting was held in Philadelphia." Would such an announcement have inspired the 13 colonies to take on Great Britain, then the greatest military power in Europe? Not likely.

For any writer, getting the audience's attention is a good thing; for the journalist, it's imperative—especially if the audience includes an editor or an instructor. The device for doing so is the lead (or lede, as it's often spelled to distinguish it from a police clue or something that comes out of a pencil). A reporter rarely receives a greater compliment than "You got the lede right." Experienced journalists might differ on what makes up a good lede, but they almost always agree that a good lede is good. (See Chapter 3.)

The task is little different for a poet, novelist, speechwriter, playwright, copywriter or office memo writer. Each must accomplish the task with a headline or a well-crafted first line. Regardless of what kind of writing is involved, the principle is the same. The first words, the first phrases, the first sentences, the first paragraphs are critical:

Double, double, toil and trouble ...
When in the course of human events ...
In Xanadu did Kublai Khan a stately pleasure dome decree ...
Call me Ishmael ...
Drink to me only with thine eyes ...
In order to form a more perfect union ...
Fourscore and seven years ago ...
How do I love thee? Let me count the ways.

Such introductions need not summarize what is to follow, although they can. Most good ones don't. But each of those lines does accomplish what it was meant to accomplish. Each does get the reader's attention.

Lead with what is interesting, lead with what is newsworthy, lead with what is mysterious, lead with what is dramatic, lead with what is captivating. Inform the reader, tease the reader, anger the reader, challenge the reader, tickle the reader or prepare the reader for what is coming next. But don't bore the reader. There is almost never an excuse to be boring. (Unless it's to avoid dishonesty. See the introduction to Chapter 7.)

Picky, these readers. If your lede bores them, they retaliate. They refuse to read the rest of what you've written.

The most commonly stated reason for writing boring ledes is that the writers don't have time to fashion interesting ones. But they don't really have a choice. They must take the time. Ironically, if they take the time, they save time.

Here's how it works. You spend half the time on getting the lede right, so it feels just right. The word *feel* is used correctly here; the quality of a lede is measured more by the gut than the intellect. Once you have accomplished this, your beginning repays your caregiving by organizing the rest of the story for you, and that means you can write it twice as quickly. How? It sets up that dialogue I mentioned before, the one between the writer and the imaginary reader. First, a good, strong lede, then "What do you want to know next?" The story or report should flow without impediment—unless you start worrying about style, and clutch.

Many college and high school teachers seem to spend an inordinate amount of time trying to define style, to compare one writer's style with another, to inject style into the writing of their students. I wonder what the point is. How many students come away from such a class thinking they must have style because they have been exposed to so much of it?

I can count at least one. And I can tell you that the tortured, flowery, brittle style I developed only got in the way when I began to learn how to write for a living. Style can be as elusive and inscrutable as Lewis Carroll's Cheshire cat. That doesn't mean it doesn't exist. It's just that, when the aspiring writer tries to meet it head-on, it flutters away and becomes one with the ether. Instead of toiling to develop a "style," the beginning writer should concentrate on writing simply, honestly and directly to the reader. Style will develop on its own, organically.

Basic Guidelines for Good Writing

We'll explore those and some other guidelines in more detail in later chapters, but for now, here are some basic guidelines:

- Know who your audience is and write to it.
- Use strong nouns and verbs and cut down on your use of modifiers.
- Avoid clichés or, as someone blithely wrote, "Avoid clichés like the plague."
- Be specific. Use color when you can; color illuminates. But illuminate with detail.
- Beware of the murkiness of passive voice. Active voice sounds more honest. It accepts responsibility.

- When all else fails, write with energy. Convince the reader that you're convinced.

That reference to energy is especially important. You can commit a slew of writing sins in a story or report, but if you have managed to keep your energy level up, the sins will be forgotten. A century ago, William Strunk wrote about what he called "vigorous writing" in the compact writer's bible that the Cornell University professor wrote with the help of one of his brighter students, E.B. White. Here's what the book, *The Elements of Style*, has to say about energy:

> Vigorous writing is concise. A sentence should contain no unnecessary words, a paragraph no unnecessary sentences, for the same reason that a drawing should have no unnecessary lines and a machine no unnecessary parts. This requires not that the writer make all his sentences short or that he avoid all detail and treat his subject only in outline, but that every word tell.

All these criteria add up to the journalist's dictum, "Show, don't tell." No one to my knowledge does a better job of laying out information—describing in detail—than John McPhee. Here is his description of a neighborhood in Atlantic City, New Jersey, before gambling changed the way the resort looked—when it was best known for its boardwalk and its reputation as the birthplace of the Parker Brothers game Monopoly.

McPhee wrote this in 1972:

> *States Avenue, now a wasteland like St. Charles, once had gardens running down the middle of the street, a horse-drawn trolley, private homes . . . . Only an apartment building, a small motel, and the All Wars Memorial Building—monadnocks spaced widely apart—stand along States Avenue now. Pawnshops, convalescent homes, and the Paradise Soul Saving Station are on Virginia Avenue. The soul-saving station is pink, orange, and yellow. In the windows flanking the door of the Virginia Money Loan Office are Nikons, Polaroids, Yashicas, Sony TVs, Underwood typewriters, Singer sewing machines, and pictures of Christ. On the far side of town, beside a single track and locked up most of the time, is the new railroad station, a small hut made of glazed*

firebrick, all that is left of the lines that built the city. An authentic phrenologist works on New York Avenue close to Frank's Extra Dry Bar and a church where the sermon today is "Death in the Pot." The church is of pink brick, has blue and amber windows and two red doors . . . . St. James Place, narrow and twisting, is lined up with boarding houses that have wooden porches on each of three stories, suggesting a New Orleans made of salt-bleached pine. In a vacant lot on Tennessee is a white Ford station wagon stripped to the chassis. The windows are smashed. A plastic Clorox bottle sits on the driver's seat. The wind has pressed newspaper against the chain-link fence around the lot.

McPhee does much with simple brand names. Any urban dweller can sense what a neighborhood is like if it contains pawnshops and something called the Paradise Soul Saving Station, and I'm sure suburbanites and rural folk can use their imaginations and come up with the same picture that was in McPhee's head. Sticking a picture of Jesus in with all those typewriters, cameras and sewing machines provides a small jolt for the reader, which the author obviously intended but which he left without comment. McPhee paints pictures but he doesn't write the program notes. He draws no conclusions; that's the reader's job. He includes Monopoly properties—States Avenue, St.Charles, Virginia, New York Avenue, St. James Place, Tennessee—also without pointing out the obvious to the reader, that they are indeed Monopoly properties.

I might suggest that he backs away from explanation a little too much. He doesn't define *monadnock*, even though I would guess that not one in 100 Americans knows what it means, including me. I looked it up. A monadnock is a "residual hill or mountain standing well above the surrounding peneplain," according to *The Random House Dictionary of the English Language.* Maybe McPhee didn't bother to define it for his readers because then he would have to define peneplain, which is "an area reduced almost to a plain by erosion."

Even so, the reader should be able to infer what monadnocks are by how McPhee has described them. His allusion to a phrenologist refers to a study of the bumps on the skull, a pseudoscience that hasn't been popular or well known since Ralph Waldo Emerson dabbled in it. But McPhee has stuck to an apparent desire to not write down to the reader and not draw conclusions for the reader. Noble sentiments. And despite his inclusion of a reference to New Orleans, a city many readers would not have visited, most must have seen pictures of the French Quarter with its rows of wooden, three-story porches adorned with wrought iron.

A couple of additional ingredients need to be added to the mixture before it gets molded into good writing. Both have to do with attitude.

First, force yourself to fall in love with your subject. It saves a great deal of frustration for the writer who didn't want to write about the subject to begin with. Then, fall in love with the English language. It deserves it, and your writing will be better for it.

A Word about the English Language

Few who know and love the language would ever confuse the beauty of English with the smooth, sophisticated sound of French, the music of Spanish or Italian, or the seductive sibilance of the Slavic languages. At its base, English is a Germanic language, as are Dutch, Swedish, Danish, Flemish and Norwegian. And it shares much of German's reliance on athletic diphthongs, harsh consonants and guttural syllables.

We should not, however, make the mistake that because English carries the occasional dissonance, it is without rhythm, music or grace. To write or edit English well, the writer must listen to the tumble of words. Robert MacNeil, who for years co-anchored "The MacNeil Lehrer NewsHour" on the Public Broadcasting System, put it this way in his book *Wordstruck*:

> We forget perhaps that human language is primarily speech. It has always been and it remains so. The very word language means tongue. The ability to read and write is, at the most, five thousand years old, while speech goes back hundreds of thousands, perhaps a million years, to the remotest origins of our species. So the aural pathways to the mind—to say nothing of the heart—must be wondrously extensive. Like the streets of a big city, you have many ways to get there. By contrast, the neural pathways developed by reading are arguably less well established, like scarce roads in uninhabitable country.

Four qualities set English apart, even from other Germanic languages. Three of them are positive.

First, the structure of English is simpler and more direct than other Western languages, including the Germanic ones. English provides more emphasis on active voice, spends less time bothering with reflexive verbs and uses fewer verb tenses.

Second, English has dispensed with the need to match nouns and verbs by gender, so you don't have to know what sex a table is before you can correctly say what a table does.

Third, the vocabulary of English is greater, much greater, than that of any other Indo-European language, a group that involves a third of the world's population. The biggest reason is because English has imported the equivalent of two whole languages, Latin and Norman French, and large chunks of several more. But the size of the English vocabulary is not entirely a good thing, as we'll discuss shortly.

These three positive qualities derive from the fact that the language is such a mongrel. But its variety of pedigrees—or lack of pedigree—is responsible for its maddening inconsistency in spelling and verb forms. That inconsistency, however, also contributes to its richness, and its richness is the prime source of the beauty of the English language.

The Bane of a Big Vocabulary

Each new influence on English has added richness to the language, a fact that is both a curse and a boon. Not counting about half a million recent scientific, medical and technological terms, which often appear to have swamped the language, English contains more than 600,000 words—three or four times that of any other Western language.

Not that, as we write, we use them all. William Shakespeare got by with only about 34,000 words, and that's several thousand more than most modern writers use. The vocabulary of the King James Version of the Bible totals only about 8,000.

Being heir to a huge vocabulary might be akin to being heir to a great fortune. It is most tempting, and temptingly easy, to squander it, abuse it and create an artificial feeling of status with it. Somewhere in America there must be someone who went through 16 years of school without encountering teachers or textbook writers who took advantage of the English vocabulary to make themselves look superior—at least in their own eyes.

You can do that with English. The language can help you sound artificially important as few other languages can. The rules for such deception are simple: Never use one syllable when two or more will do; never use a simple sentence when a compound or complex sentence will do; never use a sentence when a paragraph will do—you get the idea.

This progression into verbal oblivion begins by using a greater choice of words than many people can handle. Writers or teachers who are inclined to enhance their self-importance will go for the big words first. They have traded the advantage of a large vocabulary—the ability to find the precise word that conveys the precise meaning and nuance they intended—for the pomposity that big words often carry with them.

The Beauty of a Big Vocabulary

The true beauty of English is its ability to make the writer or speaker sound honest. And the way the language works out, sounding honest means using the short, Anglo-Saxon words and usages that form the core of the language.

The language is fraught with latinizations, words that mostly end in *tion, sion, ous, ly, ate, ity, ence, ance, ent* or *ant*. Latinizations are not necessarily bad. For honest communicators, they come in handy when they strive for word precision. But latinizations should serve as accessories to the core language, not replacements for it.

That is the whole point. English gives the writer or speaker the ability to find *the* precise word or phrase to express the exact idea, concept or fact with just the right nuance.

When the executives of Ollie's Discount Outlet in Chambersburg, Pennsylvania, looked for a motto, they must have asked themselves who made up their clientele. If they had ever wondered if "Quality Merchandise at Reasonable Prices" might work, they discarded that notion. Instead they adopted "Good Stuff Cheap." By choosing Anglo-Saxon over latinization, they replaced 13 syllables with three.

In languages that lack the massive vocabulary of English, the writer is forced to derive precise meaning from context or from where the word falls in a sentence. In English, though, the task becomes a simple matter of selecting the exact color you want from the riotous palette available. But to accomplish that task, you must have a mastery of the vocabulary, you must refrain from abusing that vocabulary, and you must love the language enough to enjoy playing with each usage until the message comes out precisely right.

From such playfulness is poetry made. Robert Louis Stevenson played with the placement of the subject when he wrote his "Requiem."

> *Under the wide and starry sky,*
> *Dig the grave and let me lie.*
> *Glad did I live and gladly die*
> *As I laid me down with a will.*
>
> *This be the verse ye 'grave for me:*
> *Here he lies where he longed to be.*
> *Home is the sailor, home from sea,*
> *And the hunter, home from the hill.*

Stevenson didn't write "I lived gladly," "Engrave this verse for me" or "The sailor is home from sea and the hunter is home from the hill." He moved the subject around and, in doing so, added power to his poem. Strunk and White summed it up in their Rule 22: "Place the emphatic words of a sentence at the end."

We might wonder how much of the verse is the result of Stevenson's Scottish roots. He was not a Gael, but his rhythms most likely were influenced by Gaelic, the Celtic tongue of the Irish and the Highland Scots. (More about Celtic influences in English in the next chapter.)

It is the humble, Germanic idiom of the Anglo-Saxon peasant that gives the language its inherent power to communicate. Nowhere is that fact better illustrated than in an excerpt from a 1940 speech delivered by one of the language's great wordsmiths, who happened to be prime minister of England at the time. Winston Churchill's radio speech came after England had salvaged most of its army, and some of its French ally's army, from the Nazi invasion of northwestern Europe that ended in Dunkirk, Belgium. In that speech, Churchill threw Adolph Hitler what might be the most eloquent verbal gauntlet in the history of the tongue:

> *We shall fight on the beaches; we shall fight on the landing grounds;*
> *we shall fight in the fields and in the streets; we shall fight in the hills;*
> *we shall never surrender.*

As Robert McCrum, William Cran and Robert MacNeil point out in *The Story of English,* a highly readable companion to a BBC series of the same name, of all the words in that celebrated excerpt "only *surrender* is foreign—Norman French." Each of the remaining 32 words displays Anglo-Saxon (what we call Old English) roots.

The majestic structure that is the English language is built with small bricks.

The history of English is fascinating—to me, anyway. Knowing the roots of English helps writers appreciate the language and that, in turn, makes them better writers. The language's history is one of a number of subjects included in many thick books about English literature and British history. For those who agree with me, I have extracted some of that history and delivered it to the next chapter. Those who are instead more eager to get on with how to write clearly, concisely and directly to the reader may jump to Chapter 3.

The history of the world is the record of the weakness, frailty and death of public opinion.
—Samuel Butler, *Note-books*

The Celts certainly have [style] in a wonderful measure.
—Matthew Arnold, *On the Study of Celtic Literature*

2 The Beautiful Mongrel: Where English Came From

They came to what is now the British Isles in several waves from the mainland of Europe, from what is now France and Spain. Most of these Celts came not because they wanted to. They were forced to leave by folks who invaded Celtic turf, including the Teutons, who were the ancestors of later German tribes, and the Romans.

Apparently originating in the neighborhood of what we now know as Austria, northern Italy and Switzerland—some scholars now point to Ukraine—the Celts (from the Greek *Keltoi*) stretched from Western Europe to the middle of what is now Turkey. (Among the Turkish Celts were the "foolish Galatians" to whom Paul wrote an epistle that became part of the Christian Bible's New Testament.) Today's Celtic language comes in two varieties: *Goidelic* or *Gaelic*, spoken in the western fringes of Ireland and the Highlands and northern islands of Scotland; and *Brythonic* or *British*, spoken in the fringes of Wales and the Isle of Man as well as in Brittany, the westernmost peninsula of France.

Evidence suggests that, by 600 B.C., the Celts had migrated as far as the northeast coast of Scotland. Later generations of Celts in what is now Britain became known collectively as Britons. Several generations of Romans would fight them and finally conquer them. Twice, in 55 B.C. and 54 B.C.—with a little help from foul weather in the British Channel—they would prevent Julius Caesar from creating a permanent presence on their side. But contact between Romans and Britons continued, primarily through trade.

It took the Romans another 87 years to establish a permanent British province. Eventually all Britons south of Hadrian's Wall in Scotland and east of Wales and Cornwall would lose their independence to troops led by Emperors Hadrian and Claudius. Most upper-class Britons would blend in with their conquerors, and many would become citizens of Rome. They would adopt Latin but keep the Celtic language alive. Some would stay in the Scottish North, the Welsh West and the Cornwall Southwest, where they used Celtic variants for nearly two millennia. Despite four centuries of occupation, the Romans would have little effect on the later English language. Latin, the language of Rome, would come to England later.

It wasn't until about A.D. 450, after the Romans had abandoned their British subjects to fight in a vain attempt to stop Germanic incursions in Rome, that the Britons again found themselves forced to move. This time, the invaders were northern German tribes, tribes that had not been latinized as many of the southern tribes had been during Rome's expansion on the European Continent. Foremost among them were the Angles and Saxons from what is now northern Germany, and the Jutes, most of whom came from what is now southern Denmark.

Within a matter of a few years, England (*Angle-land*) became the realm of a people who spoke only Germanic dialects. Instead of mingling and intermarrying with the Celts, as the Romans had, they pushed the Celts into what is now Wales, Cornwall, Scotland and Ireland. Indeed, the gulf between the Anglo-Saxons and the Welsh Britons became a physical one. In 767, the English king, Offa, had a ditch built that spanned the entire border between England and Wales. Where "there had been no ethnic blending" now "there was deep and permanent division," writes Norman Davies in *The Isles: A History.* Offa's Dyke ensured that the Welsh would have almost no direct influence on the content of the English language. The isolation of Celtic tribes in not only Wales, but Ireland, Cornwall and the Scottish Highlands, also helped minimize the effect of Celtic dialects on English.

Today, the direct influence of the British or Gaelic idioms is reflected only by family names, place names and a handful of words, including *crag, tor, glen* and *loch*. Celtic roots also can be found through the French, including the words *car, carriage, chariot, carpenter* and *lance*. (By the way, *Celtic* is pronounced as if it begins with a *K*, not at all like a member of a Boston basketball team.)

The Celtic Influence

So why begin a discussion about the history of English with a people who had so little direct influence on the language? Because the Celts had what amounted to the last word. In Ireland, it is almost a cliché to say that "the English invented the language, but it took the Irish to show them how to use it." Some of the pithiest and most poetic writing in English comes as the result of the Germanic language being twisted into Celtic structures.

This is no small accomplishment. Some scholars credit 20th-century Irish writer James Joyce with establishing English as *the* language of modern Western literature. Without his help, they say, the most prominent Western literary language would have been French. And it was the likes of Joyce that gave much English prose its poetic expression. In his *Finnegan's Wake*, Joyce mixes Celtic rhythm, alliteration and pun in the following passage, one of his more comprehensible ones: "Hootch is for the husbandman handling his hoe. Hohohoho, Mister Finnegan, you're going to become Mister Finnagain."

Padraic Colum, in his *Anthology of Irish Verse*, points to a poem translated from the Irish Gaelic by Samuel Ferguson, "Dear Dark Head," which begins this way:

Put your head darling, darling, darling,
Your darling black head my heart above;
Oh, mouth of honey, with the thyme for fragrance,
Who with heart in breast could deny you love?

Colum writes that Ferguson's translation "makes one of the most beautiful of Irish love songs; it is a poem that carries into English the Gaelic music and the Gaelic feeling; the translation, moreover, is more of a poem than the original."

We need only imagine how the stanza might have come out un-aided by Celtic rhythms; something, I suppose like this (keeping in mind that in American English *blackhead* means something quite different than Ferguson's "black head"):

> *Place your head of black hair, my darling, above my heart,*
> *With your mouth of honey and its fragrance of thyme.*
> *Who with a heart in his breast*
> *Could deny loving you?*

The sentiments are no less noble in the more prosaic English; sure, but something is missing. The drumbeat of "darling, darling, darling" in the first line sets the whole verse to a rhythm that most likely would not be found in a more anglicized form of poetry. And where in normal English would even a poet write "put your head my heart above," with the preposition at the end? It's possible that such a structure was responsible for the practice of ending a sentence with a preposition, which my prim eighth-grade English teacher, Mrs. Falkner, told us we should never do.

(Winston Churchill had an answer for the Mrs. Falkners of the world. When he was criticized for ending a sentence with a preposition, he replied, "This is nonsense up with which I refuse to put." The retort is credited to him, anyway.)

Another reason Celtic rhythms sound poetic to proper English ears is that Celtic idioms have no real past tense. As scholar James Myers puts it: "'I went to the store' becomes 'I am after going to the store.'"

Even the present tense can feel different, and poetic, in a Celtic structure. John Millington Synge, in the journal and collection of sketches he entitled *The Aran Islands*, offers a Gaelic alternative to "we are":

> *A man who is not afraid of the sea will soon be drownded, he said,*
> *for he will be going out on a day he shouldn't. But we do be afraid of*
> *the sea, and we do only be drownded now and again.*

Synge scholar Declan Kiberd provides a further example of a "poetic" Celtic structure. He quotes a letter from the Irish novelist, poet and playwright to his German translator:

> *There is another form which occurs often, for instance, "I saw a man and he smoking a pipe" = I saw a man smoking a pipe. The idiom, of course, is a Gaelic one, and it has shades of meaning that cannot be rendered in ordinary English.*

Although most examples of Celtic influences on English seem to come from the Irish, they own no monopoly. We cited a 19th-century poem by Scotland's Robert Louis Stevenson in the last chapter; now we might address the 20th-century prose of a Welsh-man, Dylan Thomas.

> *Of what is coming in the New Year I know nothing, except that all that is certain will come like thunderclaps or like comets in the shape of four-leaf clovers, and that all that is unforeseen shakes a leg in the sky. And of what is gone I know only shilly-shally snatches and freckled plaids, flecks and dabs, dazzle and froth; a simple second caught in the coursing snow-light; an instant, gay or sorry, struck motionless in the curve of a flight like a bird or a scythe; the spindrift leaf and stray-paper whirl, canter, quarrel and people-chase of everybody's street; suddenly the way the grotesque wind slashes and freezes at a corner the clothes of a passerby so that she stays remembered, cold and still until the world like a night light in a nursery goes out; and a waddling cou-ple of the small occurrences, comic as ducks, that quack their way through our calamitous days; whits and dots and tittles.*

Like so much Celtic-influenced English, Thomas' passage may be called prose. I'm no scholar of literature, but I like to think of it as poetry trapped in the form of prose.

Old English: A Question of Pedigree

It has been the mongrel quality of English that has led to its simplicity of structure, its disposal of the need to match nouns and verbs by gender and its huge vocabulary. As one contributing tongue merged with another, it became easy to dispense with complications of grammar and adopt new words.

The true history of English rightfully begins in the mid–fifth century, when those Angles, Saxons and Jutes we mentioned ear-lier raided British coasts, taking over what is now England. The

Jutes landed in Kent on the southeast coast of England, near the Roman capital of Londinium (London). Centuries later, their accent would dominate the British nobility, producing what today is accepted as "Standard English." The plummy tones of Standard English are most associated with England's upper class and the British Broadcasting System, which the upper class has dominated.

What we know as "English" began as a mixture of the three Germanic dialects. Some scholars report that the first known usage of the word *Englisc* came from Alfred the Great, who consolidated the Angles, Saxons and Jutes into one nation. The Frisians, another Germanic tribe who resided in part of what is now mostly the Netherlands, provided some additional words. (Many of the profanities we now call "Anglo-Saxon" came from the Frisians.)

The second great influence on Anglo-Saxon, or Old English (old to them, not to us), came in the form of Latin, introduced in 597 by a Benedictine monk who would become known to history as St. Augustine of Canterbury. Augustine brought Roman Catholic Christianity and its language to the south of England just about the time that monks from Ireland, who had been cut off from Rome for centuries, were introducing Christianity and Latin to the North.

Seventy-five years later, the English were calling themselves Christians. Virtually all were illiterate, though, because literacy scarcely existed outside the church. The clergy's Latin, therefore, filled a need and began a strong, if not entirely comfortable, co-existence with English. But the two were to remain apart for several centuries.

The Germanic roots of English were strengthened and broadened in the 800s when the Vikings invaded, forcing proto-Danish words and usages on the language. Their influence was felt mostly in the northern and eastern half of England, which became known as the Danelaw. Indeed, the word *law* is of Scandinavian origin.

According to Otto Jesperson, an English speaker "cannot *thrive* or *be ill* or *die* without Scandinavian words; *they are* to the language what *bread* and *eggs are* to the daily fare."

We can see the similarity of Old English to the Old Norse of the Vikings by reviewing the days of the week, according to scholar Christopher Fee. Most are named after gods in the Germanic and Norse pantheons. *Tuesday* comes from the Old English god Tiw, who is equivalent to the Old Norse god Tyr. *Thursday* is the day of Thunor, the Anglo-Saxon god of thunder, among other things. His Norse equivalent is Thor.

Although Latin continued to nip at the edges of English, especially after the Danes became Christians, it wasn't until 1066 that English was presented with its greatest Latin influence. The Normans, a Viking group that had settled in northern France a century earlier, won the Battle of Hastings, an event that over the course of three centuries would render English incomprehensible to someone who had spoken it in 1065.

The Normans under William the Conqueror took over everything in what is now England—the administration, the courts, the economy, the military—but not the language. The Normans clung to the language they had begun to learn a century earlier, a French hybrid with Latin roots. After the Conquest, three distinct languages—not dialects, languages—lived together in not much harmony. The Normans and their descendants, now the nobility of England and large chunks of France, spoke Norman French. The high clergy continued to speak Latin, and the commoners spoke Old English.

Middle English and Geoffrey, Will and the Boys

It took a while, but the three castes did begin to talk with one another so that by the time Geoffrey Chaucer (1340?–1400) was ready to write in Middle English, the singular language of English was ready for Geoffrey Chaucer. Chaucer, the best known of the English poets of the time, was among the first to write with the mixture of English, French and Latin that is known to us as Middle English. And that is one of the main reasons his *Canterbury Tales* take up so much space in high school English literature texts today.

This fusion of three languages can be seen today in the way that most words seem to have at least two synonyms. For example, *happy* has Anglo-Saxon roots, *content* comes from the French and *satisfied* has a Latin ancestor.

Anglo-Saxon	French	Latin
frightful	hideous	horrible
go	continue	proceed
gathering	society	community
hereafter	future	posterity
loveliness	beauty	pulchritude
mill	plant	factory
show	present	demonstrate
small	petite	minute

Richard Lederer, who for years has written about the vagaries of English, offers this list of synonyms:

Anglo-Saxon	French	Latin
ask	question	interrogate
dead	deceased	defunct
end	finish	conclude
fair	beautiful	attractive
fear	terror	trepidation
help	aid	assist
rise	mount	ascend
thin	spare	emaciated

A quick look through a dictionary and thesaurus indicates that most of these words carry more than two synonyms, none of them exact. In virtually every case, shades of meaning separate them. That supports the point that English provides more word precision than any other Indo-European language. With English, you don't have to worry so much about a word's context or where it lands in a sentence. Its 600,000 word vocabulary—not counting recent scientific, medical and technical terms—is broad enough that you can find *the* precise word to say exactly what you want to say with just the nuance you intend.

Less than a century after Chaucer died, the next great influence on English came in 1476 when William Caxton (1422–1491) brought the first printing press to England from Holland and set it up in Westminster. He did so at a time when the language was still sorting itself out and few spelling guidelines existed. Many of Caxton's spellings were Dutch, and while they made sense in Dutch, they did not in English. Instead, they played havoc with English spelling, and they still do today. Take the word *people*, for example, or the fact that two U.S. presidents of Dutch descent, the Roosevelts, pronounced their first syllables with a long *O*. It was Caxton who first printed Chaucer's *Canterbury Tales* in 1478.

Since Chaucer and Caxton, English has been heir to many additions, modifications and codifications. When scholar Sir Thomas Elyot published *The Book Named Governour* in 1531, he incorporated some new usages that he admitted he was uncomfortable with. The authors of *The Story of English*, Robert McCrum, William Cran and Robert MacNeil, tell us that Elyot introduced words, including *education, dedicate* and *maturity*, for which he apologized, calling *maturity* "strange and dark." (But he said that soon these words would be as easy to understand as "other wordes late commen out of Italy and Fraunce" and such borrowings from Latin contributed to "the necessary augmentation of our language.") Latinizations have proved to be great auxiliaries to basic English and essential to word precision, but in no way should they take the place of the language's Anglo-Saxon core.

A couple of hundred words were imported from ancient Greek by a group of scholars known as the Oxford humanists: William Grocyn, Thomas Linacre, John Colet, William Lyly and Thomas More—he who lost his head in a dispute with Henry VIII. Among the Greek borrowings: *agile, capsule* and *habitual.* Francis Bacon added to the Latin influence on English by adding words, including *catastrophe, lexicon* and *thermometer.*

The efforts of these Renaissance scholars soon were matched by those of six committees averaging eight men apiece. King James I directed them to write an English version of the Christian Bible that both the Church of England and the Puritans could agree on. Although Latin and Greek sources were to be consulted for accuracy, the committees were to translate from half a dozen English Bibles that had been published in the 16th century. In 1611, after seven years of work, the leaders of this group of scholars accomplished what committees almost never do. They made the Bible clearer—and more poetic.

When the King James Version was published, the man who more than any other individual altered the English language was still alive. In addition to his other contributions, William Shakespeare (1564–1616) added dozens of words and phrases to the language. (Well, maybe not all by himself. There still exists a fringe of scholars who insist that many of Shakespeare's works were written by others, including Bacon.) Here's how a British journalist, Bernard Levin, looks at the Shakespearean influence:

> If you cannot understand my argument, and declare "It's Greek to me," you are quoting Shakespeare; if you claim to be more sinned against than sinning, you are quoting Shakespeare; if you recall your salad days, you are quoting Shakespeare; if you act more in sorrow than in anger, if your wish is father to the thought, if your lost property has vanished into thin air, you are quoting Shakespeare; if you ever have refused to budge an inch or suffered from green-eyed jealousy, if you have played fast and loose, if you have been tongue-tied, a tower of strength, hoodwinked or in a pickle, if you have knitted your brows, made a virtue of necessity, insisted on fair play, slept not one wink, stood on ceremony, danced attendance (on your lord and master), laughed yourself into stitches, had short shrift, cold comfort or too much of a good thing, if you have seen better days or lived in a fool's paradise—why, be that as it may, the more fool you, for it is a foregone conclusion that you are (as good luck would have it) quoting Shakespeare; if you … clear out bag and baggage, if you think it is high time and that that is the long and short of it, if you believe that the game is up and that truth will out even if it involves your own flesh and blood, if you lie low till the crack of doom because you suspect foul play, if you have your teeth set on edge (at one fell swoop) without rhyme or reason, then—to give the devil his due—if the truth were known (for surely you have a tongue in your head) you are quoting Shakespeare; even if you bid me good riddance and send me packing, if you wish I was as dead as a doornail, if you think I am an eyesore, a laughing stock, the devil incarnate, a stonyhearted villain, bloody-minded or a blinking idiot, then—by Jove! O Lord! Tut, tut! for goodness sake! what the dickens! but me no buts—it is all one to me, for you are quoting Shakespeare.

(I did mention that Levin was a British journalist, didn't I? I can't think of an American journalist who could get away with a sentence like the one above.)

To the possible detriment of the language, we can't get away with some of the inventiveness that Shakespeare did. His freewheeling no longer is an option for the serious writer. Today, people like me have set down a flurry of rules for students and writers. We might accept his transformation of a conjunction into a verb and a noun—"but me no buts"—but we turn our collective noses up at business bureaucrats who turn verbs into nouns—*impact* or *access*. We do so in the name of communication—clarity, craft and crispness.

Obviously I think we're usually right or I wouldn't have written this book. There's no question, though, that our rules of communication have killed much of the creativity a writer might display. Inventive and imaginative writing still exists, but it requires some skill to write that way and still stay within the bounds of the rules, especially journalistic rules. The language continues to change, but only after an elaborate process. A nugget of inventiveness from, say, an American rap artist, a pidgin speaker in the Pacific, a Rastafarian from Jamaica or a London Cockney—usually someone not considered part of the mainstream—makes its way into English slang. If it is particularly imaginative or particularly apt, it might survive a decade or two and become part of the conversational style used by most English speakers. Once it stops being apt, it might die like an old cliché; but if it hangs on, it might make it into the dictionary.

It was the dictionary that began this infringement on inventiveness in the English language.

Dr. Johnson and the Beginnings of Modern English

It was Samuel Johnson (1709–1784) who, more than anyone else, began the process of formalizing the language, its usages and its spellings. He did it with the 1755 publication of his *Dictionary of the English Language*. It is worth noting that even 250 years ago, Johnson was aware that the language does not stand still, that even then the acceptance or rejection of a word or phrase depended on a living process. In his preface to the dictionary, he put it this way:

> Who will consider that no dictionary of a living tongue ever can be perfect, since, while it is hastening to publication, some words are budding and some fallen away?

This sentiment earns a resounding "amen" from the American wordsmith H.L. Mencken, who wrote in *The American Language*:

> A living language is like a man suffering incessantly from small hemorrhages, and what it needs above all else is constant transfusions of new blood from other tongues. The day the gates go up, that day it begins to die.

By that measure, English isn't about to die anytime soon. The codification of the English language that began with Johnson was continued in the United States by Noah Webster (1748–1853), who brought out his dictionary in 1828. Exactly 100 years later, the first edition of the *Oxford English Dictionary*, known as the *OED*, was published in 12 volumes.

Certainly, none of these efforts have stanched the flow of new words into the language. The United States and Canada, especially, have benefited from a slew of words from Native Americans and the Spanish. And the French language of Quebec and northwestern New Brunswick has enriched the vocabularies of Canadians and New Englanders. But this process had begun long before either the United States or Canada became independent of the British.

The Oxford Companion to the English Language lists dozens of words that came directly and, by necessity, from Native Americans. Most named things that could not be found in the Old World: *chipmunk, hickory, moose, parka, pecan, raccoon, squash,* and *tomahawk*. Many terms arrived by way of the Spanish, who dominated most of the New World when the English founded its first permanent colony, Jamestown, Virginia, in 1607. These terms include *avocado, barbecue, cannibal, chili, chocolate, cocoa, coyote, guano, hammock, hurricane, jerky, potato, tobacco, tomato* and *savanna*. The book also lists several words that began with island peoples (including the Caribs), got filtered through French, then Spanish, and finally made it to English. Among them are *buccaneer, cashew, cayenne* (pepper), *cougar, jaguar, petunia* and *tapioca*.

Most of these words came into the language when Americans still lived in colonies. By the 1900s, an entirely new set of Spanish words had entered the language, mainly from Mexico and through the western U.S. territories and states. Many were adopted by cowboys from their Mexican counterparts, the *vaque-*

ros. They include *bronco, desperado, lariat or lasso, maverick, mustang, poncho, ranch, rodeo, stampede* and *vamoose.*

(It must be said that we have given as good as we've gotten. Many English words have entered the Spanish vocabulary, creating an idiomatic condition, especially in Mexico, that has not been entirely appreciated.)

The United States isn't alone in its ability to absorb words from other cultures. The British borrowed many words from Hindi, the official language of northern India—*bungalow, dinghy, dungaree, shampoo*—and passed them on to us. We can thank the Malays and the British for *amok, bamboo, caddy, camphor, gong, kapok* and *sarong,* and we can thank Tamil-speakers from southern India and Sri Lanka, as well as the British, for *cheroot, curry, mango and pariah.* Australians have adopted many words from that continent's Aborigines, and New Zealanders have taken some of their vocabulary from the Maoris, the Polynesians who occupied New Zealand long before the British showed up.

Since the middle of the 19th century, English has been bombarded by new scientific, medical and technical terms, a process that has only accelerated as we have entered the 21st century. Think of some of the computer and communications terms we use in ordinary conversation that would have baffled most people in, say, 1975. If you were to tell me then that you were going to *email* me, I would wonder which part of my body was being threatened. Today, we *fax* people, but only if we have a *modem.* Back then, we wouldn't have dreamed of doing such a thing, nor would we have talked about it in public—or even on our *cell phone.* Of course, 25 or 30 years ago, the cellular telephone hadn't been developed. In 1975, *software* was in its infancy. Now it is carried on *disks* or *diskettes,* neither of which has anything to do with the *discs* humankind has lived with for centuries or the discus of the Olympics.

Electronic computing has taken a number of existing terms and redefined them: *Monitor* used to be a verb or an ironclad vessel used in the American Civil War. *Enter* used to be a command to open the door and walk in. A *laptop* was where a sweetheart or a grandchild sat, and a *mouse* was an unwelcome houseguest. Computer people also has been responsible for introducing technical terms, including *scalable, turnkey* and *access* (as a verb), and then making them part of the language of business and commerce. (See Chapter 8.)

On rare occasions, a word from old technology enters the modern vocabulary. *Chad* has been best known as a man's name, but since the 2000 election most Americans know that chads are the rectangular pieces of cardboard that dangle from a punch-card system; in this case, a voting system.

Regardless of how many new words enter the language or how many we lose through cliché and decay, the language *at its base* has not changed since the time of Chaucer. It bears repeating that that base remains the most influenced by Germanic words and usages. And the power of the language continues to come from the humble idiom of Anglo-Saxon peasants.

Sure it does, but only with some wee help from their Celtic cousins.

A bad beginning makes a bad ending.
—Euripedes, *Aeolus*

Of a good beginning cometh a good end.
—John Heywood, *Be Merry, Friends*

Things are always at their best in their beginning.
—Blaise Pascal, *Lettres Provinciales*

3 Leading with the Lede

It's simple. Or so it seems.

The single most important element in an article written for a print medium is the lead (or *lede*, as many editors now spell it); it is important to the reader as well as the writer. When we talk about the lede, we most often refer to the first paragraph of a story. But "lede" can easily refer to the conceptual beginning of the story, the first three or four paragraphs.

There aren't many communication sins that cannot be forgiven if the lede is written well. Mechanical problems, overblown sentences, too many modifiers, passive voice, linking or "being" verbs, too many complex and compound sentences, monotonous rhythms, clichés—if the lede is right, that's what's most important. If the lede is right, the piece is going to communicate, to create an environment.

Notice how the lede helps set a mood for this newspaper travel story about the pirate Edward Teach—Blackbeard—and the North Carolina coast.

> *Here he was known as Mr. Thatch, a merchant from England by way of Jamaica and the Bahamas, a good friend of the colonial governor. Aye, a good friend indeed.*

If, however, the words roll out as Shakespeare's did, if the sentences are lean, if the copy speaks in active voice with strong nouns and verbs, if it uses compound and complex sentences sparingly to provide rhythmic counterpoints to basic, simple declarative sentences—if all that is in place and the lede is flat, you might as well have stayed home.

Some editors and teachers demand that the lede always be short, no more than, say, 25 words. Such a demand is arbitrary, and it often reflects the cynical assumption that the reader doesn't have the intellectual power to handle anything greater. But the dictum does have some value. It makes the point that shorter ledes usually have more impact.

For the reader, the lede can provide a fact, it can summarize, it can tease, it can entice. But somehow it sets up the rest of the story. For the writer, the lede helps organize the story. Even if you are writing under deadline, you will save time.

The most common lede in newspaper reporting, historically, is the summary lede, which shoehorns the *who, what, where, when* and *how* into the first two or three paragraphs, with the *why* being picked up in the rest of the story, if at all. Breaking news stories lend themselves to summary ledes. The first paragraph—or graf, as reporters and editors call it in shorthand—of a breaking story almost always tells what happened and, if possible, what its effect is on the reader. For example:

> *A barge on the Monongahela River near Pittsburgh ran into a bridge piling Monday, collapsing the bridge and stranding motorists. No one was reported hurt, but drivers are likely to be forced to rely on alternative routes for weeks or even months.*

In one paragraph, we have the *what* (the collision), the *where* (near Pittsburgh), and the *when* (Monday). But the writer has waited until another paragraph to provide the *who*, the *how* and the *why*, some of which might be covered with a good quote in the second graf. Not too many years ago, the reporter might have tried to stuff the answers to all these questions in the first graf, which would become the lede in an *inverted pyramid* story.

Why? When copy editors prepared stories for typesetting, the lazier ones saved time and effort by cutting the story from the bottom. If the story had to be cut drastically, even to a one-paragraph newsbrief, the reader would still get the gist of the story. The problem: inverted-pyramid ledes get cluttered and become nearly unreadable. They are responsible for more than a few reader naps, and they might have something to do with the fact that most people get all their news from television.

> *A 39-year-old man, identified as John Graham, was killed Wednesday morning when his car was struck by a van in the 600 block of Muriel Street NE in Albuquerque, according to police.*

Although this type of lede is usually adequate, it displays a mass-produced quality to it that tends to sap the reader's energy. Spreading this information over two or three paragraphs would make it more comprehensible and allow the reporter to add some interesting information, including the *how*, an apparent *why*, and a good quote (nor does it hurt to use active voice):

> *A 39-year-old man is dead today, the victim of a two-vehicle crash on the 600 block of Muriel Street NE in Albuquerque, according to authorities.*
> *The Bernalillo County medical examiner's office identified the victim as John Graham of the 300 block of Eubanks Avenue SE.*
> *Police said the driver of the other vehicle, a van, was being held on charges of vehicular homicide. He was identified as Carlos Williams of Tucumcari.*
> *"We have evidence that Mr. Williams was talking on his cell phone when he ran a stop sign and rammed the driver's side of the car Mr. Graham was driving," said Albuquerque police officer Julia Garcia.*

What I mean by a lede with a mass-produced quality is that it invites the writer to fill in the blanks in what has the look of a template. In one two-day stretch recently, a wire service offered these ledes:

> *An 18-year-old Lockport woman dies late Sunday of injuries suffered hours earlier when her car struck a car-hauling semitrailer truck head-on in the far southwest suburb.*

> *A 50-year-old South Side man was killed when his car ran into the back of a semitrailer tractor truck in Elk Grove Village early Monday morning.*

> *A 15-year-old boy died early Wednesday after being critically wounded in a gang-related shooting on the West Side.*

A 35-year-old man was charged with sexually assaulting an 8-year-old girl in Englewood who had been left home alone in squalid conditions by her mother.

Such ledes not only wear out the reader, they foster sloppy thinking on the part of the reporter. Look at the last two ledes. One says the shooting was gang related; the other says the girl's mother left her alone, but neither answers the question, "Who says so?" The shooting might well have been gang related, but that characterization is not the reporter's to make. Only a quote, direct or indirect, of a law enforcement officer, should reveal that. The mother might well have abandoned her daughter in what the reporter can justifiably report are squalid conditions— if the reporter actually saw them. But the "left home alone" part of it must come from a police officer or a prosecuting attorney, and that must be included as a quote with an attribution.

Unlike most inverted pyramid ledes, summary ledes do not have to be tired, cluttered or unreadable. That's one reason they are now usually spread over two or three paragraphs. They can invite the reader's attention as they summarize a couple of pertinent points, leaving other points to later paragraphs. Take this example from a feature story in a museum magazine about a survey of Nobel Prize winners:

DNA charms them. The human brain challenges them. The bomb frightens them. And they expect to be profoundly influenced by computers and robots.

At this point, the readers have no idea who "they" are, but that's all right. The readers are sufficiently enticed to read on. ("They" were a congregation of Nobel laureates.)

Here is another summary lede applied to a news feature, this one capturing a little irony. (Irony usually makes a good lede better.)

Memphians will mark the Christian celebration of Easter today in various parts of the city by dressing up as rabbits, rolling Easter eggs with their noses—and turning in illegal guns.

Another type of lede, which many editors and reporters call a "creative lede" or a "coming-out-of-left-field lede," can be the exact opposite of a summary lede. It informs the reader of almost nothing, but that doesn't mean it isn't effective.

> *He did not know that the moment he stepped off the curb, his whole life*
> *would change.*

Who? What? Where? When? How? Why? This lede answers none of these questions. But the readers don't feel cheated just because they haven't learned anything yet. They will learn, they know that and, meantime, they're eager to read on.

I mentioned irony. Few techniques work as well as its skillful application. It's a great way to make instant friends with your readers. You're sharing a subtle joke with them and you're putting a fine point on what actually happened. For example:

> *The mayor of one of China's most exotic cities today visited the fertile flat-*
> *lands of northwest Ohio to sample some products of a Chinese-Ameri-*
> *can food factory. He pronounced the fare good—for American tastes.*

Sometimes you can set a tone or mood by manipulating time. The most common way to do this is in a breaking news story, which involves something called the *today angle.* In its simplest form, the today angle inserts the word *today* in the lede. Or, if the newspaper uses weekday designations for yesterday, today and to-morrow, it means inserting *Thursday* into the lede if indeed today is Thursday.

The use of time in a lede doesn't have to be restricted to breaking stories, though. Witness this wire service story that appeared on the anniversary of the plane crash that killed three popular rock and roll stars: Buddy Holly, Richie Valens and J.D. Richard-son, who was known as the Big Bopper:

> *Twenty-five years ago on a wintry February morning, a search party*
> *found the wreckage of a single-engine plane on a farm nine miles*
> *northwest of the Mason City Municipal Airport.*

Despite the lede's importance, however, it need not be em-bellished. Anecdotal ledes simply tell a story and, without using any kind of setup, bring the reader into it, as does this business magazine article on product tampering:

The phone rang at Robert Walker's suburban Denver home one Saturday in October. At the other end of the line was John White, the company's South Carolina broker.

Not much information so far; we don't even know what the company is. But chances are the reader will read on to find that information.

For the reader, if the lede hasn't done its job, the rest of the story represents wasted time and effort. If the lede has not convinced readers that the rest of the story will merit their continuing time and effort, they will get even with you. The readers simply will move on to another story, another publication or another medium. Or find something else to do.

For the writer, if the lede hasn't done its part, the rest of the story will be difficult to organize. It will suffer from a lack of focus, factual or emotional, and will provide no starting point to develop a dialogue with the reader. We'll talk more about building the story in the next chapter.

As we noted in Chapter 1, that dialogue can set up the organization of the story. After each paragraph, the writer asks, "OK, what do you need to know next?" The imaginary reader answers and the writer responds with a new paragraph, after which the writer again asks what the reader needs to know next. The dialogue continues until the story plays out or the writer has reached the space maximum dictated by the editor or instructor.

Without a good lede as an anchor, however, such a dialogue is difficult if not impossible.

Avoiding Dull Ledes; Avoiding Generic Ledes

If a story is worth telling, it is the writer's responsibility to make it interesting. And that is impossible if the lede is dull. Even if the readers are generous enough to make the effort to read the rest of the story, their perceptions of its subject will be skewed. They will have been robbed of the focus a good lede provides, and they will greet ledes like the one that follows with a resounding "Yes, that's nice," or "Who cares?"

SACRAMENTO—An assistant in the California secretary of state's office made a statement at a news conference today.

"But but but," the reader sputters, "What did the assistant say? In reference to what issue? And what does the statement mean to the reader?" The reader isn't looking for a direct quote here, for reasons we'll discuss shortly, but some reference to the story's impact. We might try this:

SACRAMENTO—California drivers will now be able to register to vote when they renew their drivers' licenses, according to an assistant secretary of state.

Leaving the possible impact out of the lede often sounds ludicrous:

MIAMI—Mechanical difficulties with some punch-card voting systems were reported Tuesday by Miami-Dade County election officials.

That's like saying, "As its band played on deck, the Titanic nudged an iceberg." Here are some other ledes that the reader is liable to greet with a "so what?"

Education is an important issue. Local, state and federal taxes are used to support our education system.
(I think the reader knew this already.)

Prof. Lani Guinier, the assistant attorney general for civil rights designate in 1993, gave a lecture at Gettysburg College last Monday. The Office of Intercultural Advancement in celebration of Black History Month invited Guinier, who usually teaches at the University of Pennsylvania Law School.
(But what did she say? And why is Guinier newsworthy? [The Clinton appointee failed to be confirmed because most Senators considered her views too radical.] And her sponsorship does not belong in the lede; it might even be appropriate in the last paragraph.)

Jack Gonzales studies journalism at Highlands University to expand his communication skills.

(Good for Jack. Now tell us something interesting about him.)

Ray DeLong is a guest lecturer at Northwestern University's Fall 2325 B01 Journalistic Writing Practice class. He is also the focus of the class assignment today.

Since 1999, Ron Jackson has been a student at the University of Wyoming. He is seeking a bachelor's degree in anthropology.

Some ledes are dull because they are hackneyed. (The following lede might also fit in Chapter 7 under the heading "Avoid Empty and Trite Statements.")

Fall is a wonderful time of year. It indicates the end of summer and the beginning of a new season. Seasons are part of city living.

Too many ledes look as if all they require is that the writer fill in the blanks. Pick a person, pick an issue, and the rest of the lede will apply.

Ardith Johnson daily struggles between her concerns for financial and career security and her grander commitments to make significant contributions to the community.
(There's nothing particularly wrong with this lede; it speaks of the human condition. But to make it effective, the writer should deal with Johnson's specific condition.)

The moral issue of abortion is being argued everywhere.
(Yes. So? And if I want to pick a nit, the use of *everywhere* is inaccurate. See "Red Flag Words" in Chapter 9.)

It can be said that a name suggests just as much about a person as does, for example, mannerisms and appearance.

Obstacles are what you see when you take your eye off the goal.

A little sincere praise is often all people need to discover a new direction to take with their lives.

Philosophical commentaries on the travails of life usually make lousy ledes. Be specific.

One note, though. Many journalists find themselves reaching as they try to avoid generic ledes. But they try too hard, as the author of these two paragraphs did:

> *Burglary and plumbers have not been commonly associated since President Richard Nixon's henchmen coined that nickname for themselves—and those guys weren't even real plumbers.*
> *But police say they believe the burglars who stole nearly three tons of copper tubing this week from a suburban company really are in the plumbing business.*

Leading with a Question or Quotation

Many editors are adamantly opposed to leading with a question. Others say it's OK sometimes. I am among those who do not like the practice. Here's why:

Leading with a question demands an answer that the reader might not want to bother with. Readers might feel they are being interrogated or forced by guilt to provide an answer. If they don't want to respond, the writer has made them feel as if they are being impolite. No writer with scruples wants readers to feel that way.

> *Who among us would deny that life is fraught with problems—with missed opportunities, missteps, bad decisions and bad luck?*
> *How would you like to do your own job and almost half of someone else's work every day?*

Paula LaRocque, a writing seminar star who is writing coach for the *Dallas Morning News*, puts it this way in an article in *Quill* magazine:

> Among the questions to avoid are those that evoke a "no," a "who cares?" or a "beats the hell outta me":
>
> • Want to be a midwife?
> • Ever wonder how Fortune 500 company execs start their day?
> • How many times do you suppose Rob Willis has remembered the crazy '60s?"

LaRocque does not, however, place a blanket prohibition on question ledes. She cites a story by Neil Strauss in the

New York Times that she says makes a good use of a question lede:

> How many people have you killed in your lifetime? Have you shot them with a cap gun or a cocked forefinger in a game of cops and robbers? Have you blown them up with a laser or torn their heads off in a video game?
>
> Simulated murder has become an acceptable form of play in American culture. Such games are the only way we're allowed to live out our destructive impulses without crossing moral or legal boundaries.

"Strauss' lead shows us that in certain hands, almost anything can work—even devices that in uncertain hands have become trite or worn," LaRocque writes.

Leading with a direct quotation also gets a "no" from people like me. As much as editors and journalism instructors like direct quotes, the lede is too important to leave to the subject of the story. A quote in the lede is the mark of a lazy writer who is telling readers they are not worth the writer's efforts.

> *"You must think I'm crazy," Doris Jones said as she began the interview.*

A better lede might be this one, which returns control of the story to the writer.

> *Doris Jones says she understands anyone who might think she's crazy.*

Making Sure Your Ledes Make Sense

We'll be talking more about eliminating wordiness and convoluted sentences in later chapters, but nowhere is it more important to have lean, clean prose than in the lede. Here are a couple of examples that did not make it.

> *A 21-year-old woman died Thursday afternoon of injuries suffered in a three-car accident five days ago that injured five others, including two children, on the South Side.*

Officials and village President Betty Madison found themselves under a
  federal corruption probe after they were secretly taped inside the town
  hall to investigate suspected political fund raising.

Murkiness of a different sort is appearing at an alarming frequency in many newspapers. Their editors have made a conscious decision not to tell their readers what the story is about, seemingly forever.

Their thinking is this: "We can't compete with the immediacy of radio and television news. So the best way for us to survive in the journalism marketplace is to get behind the breaking stories and concentrate on the story's environment and its 'why.'"

An admirable goal, especially today, when most Americans get all their news from television, and most TV newscasts use a headline-and-soundbite style that doesn't provide the viewers much depth.

Often, however, instead of illuminating with background, the editors encourage their reporters to write long, slice-of-life ledes that can extend to eight or 12 paragraphs. Instead of providing solid description or unbiased analysis, they manage to create a mini soap opera before they ever get around to telling the reader what the story is about.

The editors of such newspapers defend their practice, saying that what they're doing is "magazine style." Perhaps, but I would guess most well-written magazines would reject it. Here's an example that begins well enough:

The Women's Affairs Boutique struck some neighboring merchants as
  odd.
Opened only a few months ago, the nondescript storefront with "Oy Vey"
  painted on the window had Michigan Avenue prices and Rush Street
  hours.
Yet it was located in a frayed North Side neighborhood with pockets of
  run-down apartments and drifters on the streets. The store, at 5613 N.
  Ridge Ave., purported to sell African-style clothes, shoes and bags.
Raul Castillo, who runs V&S Print-Plus across the street, said he didn't
  see too many customers at Women's Affairs Boutique and "figured
  they must be losing a bundle." He said the staff was "businesslike"
  when his wife stopped in a few days ago.

"One of the outfits was $185, and she said, 'Are you crazy? This isn't Michigan Avenue,'" he said.

By now, you can hear the readers drum their fingers and exhort the writer to please get on with it.

Sargon Gilliana, who owns the Quicker Printers a few doors down, said he thought it was strange that the store was usually open at night. Even then, it was packed not with customers, but with family members, children and friends.

"They had more parties than they had business," he said.

The few exchanges he had with the store's employees were equally bizarre. One woman dropped off an order for copies at the Quicker Printers, but when a colleague of Gilliana's called back with a question, another employee at Women's Affairs Boutique said the woman didn't exist.

But wait, there's more. Not that what is being reported isn't interesting. And it's reasonably well written. But the reader still doesn't know what the story's about. This approach might work in what Truman Capote called a "nonfiction novel," but it doesn't seem to work well in a newspaper story.

Also, employees of the clothing store stopped by frequently to send items on the fax machine—to Nigeria.

"My brother asked me what I should charge, and I said '$10 a page,'" Gilliana said. "He said, 'Isn't that a lot?' And I said, 'Yeah, but they're probably smuggling drugs anyway.'"

At a news conference Friday with U.S. Atty. Gen. Janet Reno, federal authorities announced that the tiny clothing store was a front for a massive heroin smuggling ring, a worldwide operation that was run mainly by Nigerian women.

"Aha, finally," the reader says. The drumming fingers stop and the reader notices a cuticle that needs repairing.

In all, 24 people were arrested in Chicago and its suburbs, while others were arrested in locations as scattered as Bangkok, Pakistan, New York and Detroit.

The last two paragraphs lend themselves to becoming a power pair of lede paragraphs. But it took 10 other paragraphs to get there. Such are the demands of the would-be magazine formula.

Using the "Nut Graf" Approach

If students must follow a formula, they might do well to review how newspapers known for the quality of their writing, including the *Christian Science Monitor,* the *Wall Street Journal* and the *Washington Post,* craft their ledes. The *Journal* in particular has formalized what its editors call the nut-graf approach.

Here is a broad interpretation of what *Journal* editors tell their reporters to do: Go wild with your lede paragraph, or "graf." But make sure that by the third or fourth graf, the reader gets a payoff. By then, they should know what the story's about and what's in it for them. That third or fourth paragraph is the nut graf. It contains the "nut," the seed, the core of the story.

Take this example written by the *Journal*'s Amy Dokster Marcus in the late 1990s during a period when the Middle East was relatively peaceful:

> *CAIRO, Egypt—Four years ago, when Egypt first began seriously trying to attract foreign investors, Owens Corning sent a group of executives here to look into setting up a factory. They soon reached a decision: Egypt was no place to do business.*
>
> *"We couldn't even get a firm date to the next meeting of the government commission that was supposed to approve our investment," says Kleovoulous Leondaris, a Middle East regional general manager at the Toledo, Ohio, maker of glass composites and building-material systems. "We were told it could be six months, or a year, or maybe 18 months." And even if Owens Corning did build a factory, it couldn't own the land beneath it.*

Now, the nut graf.

> *Mr. Leondaris went to Cairo again last week, but this time to sign a joint venture between Owens Corning and its Egyptian and Saudi partners setting up an $11 million factory for making fiberglass-reinforced*

plastic pipes in an industrial area on the outskirts of the city. "Egypt,"
Mr. Leonardis says, "has changed."

How does a newspaper with the reputation of the *New York Times* handle a lede? Well, many journalists believe that while the *Times* can be brilliantly written, but it is often overwritten. It considers itself the nation's newspaper of record ("All the news that's fit to print"), so it is averse to cutting out detail that normal strictures of newsworthiness would keep out of a story.

The *Times'* writers do know better than to drag out an anecdotal lede forever. Here's an example from reporter Alan Cowell:

SARAJEVO, Bosnia and Herzogovina, April 24—Dragana Seferovic tells
her story in the sort of jumbled haste that 7-year-olds are prone to, full
of disjointed images and leaps in time. "My mother was shot," she said.
"She was all red. So I had only my Daddy." In other words, at the mo-
ment she found herself abandoned, her father could run fast, but her
mother could not. So her mother was shot in what she called Sarajevo's
"little war" and now she has only a father, whom she does not know.
But she was 2 or younger at the time, so no one can be sure what parts of
the story are true. It may, in fact, be only a version of reality designed
to make sense of a short life that has been incomprehensible so far
and is likely to remain so.
Dragana was one of a group of orphanage children bundled out of Sara-
jevo under sniper fire that killed two of the children in August of 1992,
to take refuge in Germany.

Now, the *New York Times* version of a nut graf:

Just over three weeks ago, under pressure from Bosnian authorities, she
was one of 30 children five years or older who reversed that journey,
returning to a land so ruined that, in some parts of this town, shell-
struck homes stand like rows of black teeth in bad gums.

Getting to the Point

Many academic appraisals of journalistic writing dwell on the classification of ledes. They identify various subcategories of ledes: blind ledes, delayed-identification ledes, creative ledes and imperative ledes; they spend paragraph after paragraph defining each and providing examples.

Most people in the business, however, have at best a fuzzy definition of the various types of ledes. In a newsroom, you might hear the term *inverted pyramid* to describe the bulkiest version of a summary lede. Or you might hear talk about a "feature lede" or a "lede that comes in from left field." But these pragmatists of daily journalism are more interested in finding a lede that works. And, pragmatic though they might be, they know that a good lede is fashioned as much by the heart or the gut as it is by the head.

Hence the advice that if you spent half your time on the lede, even under deadline, you haven't wasted time. If that lede feels good—not just looks good or informs well, but feels good—then it can be counted on to do its job in organizing the rest of the story for the writer.

For all our talk about the lede setting up the story for the reader, of providing a payoff by the fourth paragraph, of leading with irony when you can, the most common lede is the one you use for a breaking story. And that usually turns out to be a summary lede, if not a true inverted pyramid.

No matter how many questions you answer in the lede paragraph, the most newsworthy part of the story usually is what happened last, and that becomes the lede. Often, a story grows what we are fond of calling "legs"; it lasts days or weeks or months. And their ledes still concentrate on what happened last. For example, here are four paragraphs that began an earthquake story by Luis Cabrera of the Associated Press:

> SEATTLE—*A powerful earthquake shook the Pacific Northwest yesterday, shattering windows, showering bricks onto sidewalks and sending terrified crowds into the streets of Seattle and Portland, Ore.*
> *At least 25 people were injured. At press time, CNN was reporting that at least one person died.*
> *The strongest quake to hit Washington state in 52 years temporarily shut down the Seattle airport, knocked out power to hundreds of thousands of people, cracked the dome atop the state capitol in Olympia and briefly trapped about 20 people atop a swaying Space Needle in Seattle.*
> *"Everyone was panicked," said Paulette DeRooy, who scrambled onto a fire escape in a Seattle office building.*

This first paragraph is almost a classic summary lede. It has the *who* (terrified crowds), the *what* (the earthquake), the *where* (Pacific Northwest) and the *when* (yesterday), and the *how* is implied (shook). Cabrera managed to pack all that into one paragraph and still provide a lede that is graceful and moving. He doesn't answer an obvious question in the first paragraph: "Was anyone hurt or killed?" But he does answer it right away in the second paragraph.

Now, read how the same day's edition of *USA Today* led into the story. The reporter, Patrick McMahon, covers the four *W*s and the *H* over two paragraphs.

> *SEATTLE—This business capital of the Pacific Northwest has been preparing for a big earthquake for more than 10 years. But when it finally struck Wednesday, it still jolted the city's psyche.*
>
> *A midmorning 6.8-magnitude earthquake made skyscrapers sway, damaged overpasses, knocked out power, jammed cell phones and injured at least 25 people. One man died of a heart attack.*

By avoiding a standard summary lede, McMahon has been able to inject a little color into his story, reminding readers that Seattle is a commercial capital for the region and dealing with more detail in the second paragraph.

By anyone's standards, both Cabrera's and McMahon's ledes work. Cabrera's reflects the professional caution that a wire service must use to satisfy the diverse demands of the hundreds of newspapers that make up the membership of the Associated Press. (See "Writing for Wire Services" in Chapter 10.) McMahon has a little more leeway. His lede reflects the bright, lean prose for which *USA Today*—"McPaper"—is known.

Notice that both reporters mentioned a fatality. By quoting the Cable News Network, Cabrera saved himself the possible embarrassment of reporting the death himself and possibly getting it wrong. McMahon wasn't so careful and, as it turned out, no deaths were reported.

Now, let's see how the AP and *USA Today* handled the second-day lede.

Another AP reporter, Gene Johnson, wrote the first few paragraphs of the next day's story from Seattle. It follows the dictum that, in a breaking story, what happened last is usually your lede.

SEATTLE—The damage estimate from the earthquake that rocked the Northwest climbed to $2 billion yesterday as engineers inspected bridges, buildings, dams and roads. But the region congratulated itself for escaping far worse damage.

Most people went about their lives as usual, swapping stories about close calls during the most powerful quake to hit Washington state in 52 years. Few people noticed two minor aftershocks yesterday, and no additional damage was reported.

State emergency officials counted 272 injuries directly linked to Wednesday's magnitude-6.8 quake, but most were minor and none critical.

"The biggest news is that there is no news," Seattle Mayor Paul Schell said. "There aren't any fatalities. The damage, while serious, is not anything like what people would have expected."

McMahon continued covering the quake for *USA Today*. Here is how he handled the second-day lede, again concentrating more on writing a lede that would involve the reader and less on a traditional "what happened last" approach:

SEATTLE—City historian Walt Crowley made it sound like a good martini. "Seattle," he said, "is shaken, not stirred."

His upbeat assessment captured the general mood in the Pacific Northwest on Thursday, a day after the region's worst earthquake in 52 years. People mostly went back to work, back to school and back to normal.

Still lingering were questions about when to expect a larger earthquake— one perhaps 1,000 times as powerful as Wednesday's 6.8-magnitude temblor. But there were few answers.

There are no inviolable rules for writing a breaking story that extends beyond its first day. In this case both versions, one traditional and one not, were effective. And as we read the first few paragraphs of each, it isn't difficult to figure out what went through each reporter's mind and how he addressed the needs of his audience.

Avoiding Lede Intimidation

All this emphasis on the importance of writing ledes can be daunting. It's easy for the writer, who has spent effort and time trying to craft a quality lede without yielding results, to panic. For that, the veteran journalist can offer a couple of pieces of advice.

The first has to do with attitude. Despite all the characterization of journalistic writing as an aggressive, direct, active form of communication, the pursuit of a good lede usually works best when it is the result of a passive process. There is nothing wrong with sitting back, relaxing and letting the lede come to you.

Many journalists find it helpful to tell themselves to write the lede the way it wants to be written. They have faith that the lede is already there somewhere. It's just waiting to come out. But trying to force it will only make it more stubborn.

My writing instructor at the University of Colorado, Robert Rhode, said he would try this trick: As he drove back from covering a story, he would mentally compose the lede as he "saw" it on the visor at the top of his windshield. I've tried this, and often it works.

What has worked for me equally well several times is to lead with the weather. In a feature, the weather can set up the environment of the story about as well as anything. Even in a breaking story, describing the weather in some detail and weaving it in with what happened last often works—as long as it helps move the story along. (See Chapter 4.)

Failing all else, the best advice might be to write something—anything—just to get the story started. Then plow through the rest of the story before returning to the lede.

Now, take a look at the second paragraph. Often your real lede, or the core of the real lede, is there. All you need do is tweak it and you've made it your lede. You can dump the false lede you began with. (Computers are wonderful tools for accomplishing such a task. You can make a false start and just wipe it out; no penalty.)

Lede writing goes back to basics. The story should, if nothing else, communicate. If the story is going to communicate, it must be introduced by a lede that illuminates, somehow sets up the rest of the story, convinces the reader to read on—or all three. If the lede is going to accomplish its job, it requires more of the writer's craft than any other part of the story. And that usually means paring.

We'll talk about wordiness and how to surgically remove excess words in Chapter 5.

Exercises

The following exercises are jumbles—news stories that have been separated into their parts, and their parts mixed.

A. Find the lede paragraph. Keeping in mind that the most news-worthy part of a breaking story is usually that which happens last, find—or write—the most likely lede paragraph from among these series of facts and quotations. Then choose the two paragraphs that should follow the first one. For simplicity's sake, "today" is Saturday.

1. Bridge collapse

"A bus has fallen into the river," Gisela Oliveira, spokeswoman for the National Civil Defense Service said.

According to local media reports, the bridge collapsed after one of its support pillars gave way under the pressure from river waters swollen by prolonged heavy rain.

As many as 67 people were feared dead after a bridge in northern Portugal on which a bus was traveling collapsed late Sunday, officials said.

Oliveira said two other cars had also fallen into the river Douro near the town and that one body had so far been recovered.

"We don't believe there are any survivors," Castelo de Paiva Mayor Paulo Teixeira told SIC television news.

Civil defense officials said a bus fell into the river near the town of Castelo de Paiva and that a local bus company reported one of its coaches with 67 passengers aboard was missing.

The town's mayor told SIC television he did not believe anyone could have survived the accident, which occurred at about 4 p.m. EST.

2. Prostitutes gathering

A member of the forum, Bachchu Dutta, said that prostitutes would use the occasion to demand they be given workers' rights so that they could form unions to fight against harassment.

West Bengal, whose capital is Calcutta, has around 60,000 prostitutes, many of whom are minors, volunteers said.

The women say they will take part in music and dance programs to display their talents in these arts at the three-day Millennium Milan Meta (Gathering of the Millennium).

"The gathering will act as a bridge between common people and prostitutes and remove some of the stigma attached to their profession by making clear that it is like any other job," said Smarajit Jana, adviser to the forum.

Twenty-five thousand Indian prostitutes will gather in a Calcutta football stadium on Saturday to demand official recognition for their profession.

Prostitutes seeking a more dignified life will seek recognition as sex workers during the three-day carnival, a statement of Durbar Mahila Samanwaya Committee, a forum for sex workers, said Friday.

The committee would not ask the government to legalize the profession by granting licenses to prostitutes, Jana said. "All we want is that prostitutes be treated better."

Dutta said prostitutes were like any other service industry workers and were doing a service for men who sought relief from stress and depression.

3. Storm warning

Experts said the brewing storm may not be the biggest blizzard in decades, but very well could become the biggest of its kind—a merger of two storms into a single massive one—in 35 years.

A meteorologist with the National Weather Service, Michael Eckert, called the late-winter storm highly unusual. It represents the combination of two mighty weather systems. "It's very rare. We just don't see things like this happen very often," he said.

Local officials from Virginia to New England faced the task of preparing for the approaching storm, while people flocked to stores to buy food and supplies. The storm had the potential to wreak havoc for air travelers and motorists, with the possibility of businesses, schools and government offices being closed on Monday.

Two major storm systems—a wet one trekking through the South and a frigid one moving down from Canada—were on a collision course on Saturday, threatening to spawn a massive snowstorm in northeastern and mid-Atlantic U.S. states the likes of which have not been seen since 1966.

"Just be ready," he said. "All you can do is be prepared for how this thing will evolve. Fortunately, we've got a lot of time. It's not like it's something that's jumping up at us from the middle of nowhere."

The National Weather Service said heavy snowfall could begin on Sunday afternoon and evening, blanketing an area from Washington, D.C., to southern Maine with at least a foot of snow, with some areas getting even more.

"What's going to happen is they'll eventually merge into one main system," he said. "You combine the extreme wetness of the system coming up from the South with the really deep, cold air of the north and you've got the ingredients there for a major storm."

The rain could begin to turn into snow toward evening on Sunday near Washington—and perhaps as far south as Richmond, Virginia, Eckert said. The storm then is expected to track slowly northeastward up into southern New England through Monday and into Tuesday, dumping heavy snow all the way to Portland, Maine, he said.

4. The 4,000-year-old man

Professor Konrad Spindler of Innsbruck University in Innsbruck, Austria, says the corpse's teeth are well worn, consistent with those of a Bronze Age man.

Spindler and his colleagues flew by helicopter Wednesday to the 10,500-foot glacier. Scientists from Mainz University in Mainz, Germany, were to join the investigation.

The Iceman, as Austrian newspapers have dubbed him, lay undisturbed for about 40 centuries in a pass between Austria and Italy, mummified by the wind and preserved by the ice.

The exact age of the body is to be pinpointed using carbon-14 dating techniques. Scientists believe the man's age to be between 20 and 40. He was dark brown and measured five feet.

Scientists say the Iceman had been nibbled by animals, but only slightly.

Climbers on the Similaun glacier in the Tyrolean Alps between Austria and Italy last week found the frozen corpse of a Bronze Age man believed to have died 2,000 years before the birth of Jesus.

Spindler, who dated the body from a crude Bronze-Age ax clutched in a hand, says the remains, clothed and remarkably well preserved, were of "extraordinary scientific significance."

Scientists, worried that their find might rot before detailed examinations can begin, were busy Friday preserving the remains of a man believed to be 4,000 years old. They were using special chemicals for storage in a low-temperature container.

"The man wore weatherproof clothing of leather and fur, lined with hay," Spindler said in a written statement. "The fine leather is tanned, the pieces stitched together with fine thongs. His equipment consisted of a sort of wooden backpack, a leather pouch hanging from his belt with a fire flint, probably a bow, a stone necklace and a knife with a stone blade.

"But the most important discovery is an ax with a bronze head attached to a clef shaft," Spindler said.

The scientists' tests over the next few months are to include an examination of the contents of the Iceman's stomach to provide clues to the Bronze Age diet.

B. Lede drills. Give yourself a minute to read each of the following stories. Then give yourself three minutes to write a lede paragraph for each.

1. Job fair

Summer jobs pay $7.46 to $13.12 per hour. Applicants can partici-pate in on-site interviews for city positions at the job fair.

The city is seeking qualified job applicants for summer job positions that include lifeguards, lifeguard instructors, track and tennis coaches, parks workers, youth program leaders, youth program directors and as-sistant youth program directors for day camps, mobile playgrounds and the Youth Volunteer Corps program.

A city Summer Job Fair will be from 10 a.m. to 3 p.m. Saturday at the Civic Center, 950 Broadway.

Information about the job fair can be obtained by calling the Human Resources Department, 303-555-7245.

2. Postal rates

T.J. Robinson, an assistant postmaster general, issued a statement at a Washington news conference today.

He said the cost of running the postal service is constantly in-creasing.

"Further attempts must be made to cut costs," he said." One of the plans under consideration is twice-weekly home mail delivery and thrice-weekly deliveries to businesses."

Nothing is definite yet, pending further examination of options, Robinson said.

3. Shooting

Bernice Joyce, 32, who lives in San Marino, was arrested Friday evening at the home of her mother in New Dublin.

She was taken to criminal court and charged with shooting her hus-band, Coleman Joyce, during an argument Friday morning, according to New Dublin police.

Police officer J.N. Snodgrass said the two had quarreled over her plans to divorce him.

A fight ensued and he was shot.

Coleman Joyce is in critical condition at Kerry County Hospital.

The charge was attempted homicide.

4. Drive

Sharon Ann Gordon, president of the Brigham Estates chapter of the American Civil Liberties Union, has announced a new membership drive.

The chapter usually solicits members by mail and telephone.

Next month, the drive will be made person to person. The goal is to gain 50 new members.

Members and volunteers will be asked to invite friends to their homes to acquaint them with the goals of the ACLU.

"The chapter hopes to increase its membership to replace those who have dropped out or moved away," Gordon said. "If we cannot do so, we must discontinue the chapter."

Suggested Rewrites

A. Find the lede paragraph.

1. Bridge collapse

As many as 67 people were feared dead after a bridge in northern Portugal on which a bus was traveling collapsed late Sunday, officials said.
"A bus has fallen into the river," Gisela Oliviera, spokeswoman for the National Civil Defense Service said.

Civil defense officials said a bus fell into the river near the town of Castelo de Paiva and that a local bus company reported one of its coaches with 67 passengers aboard missing.

"We don't believe there are any survivors," Castelo de Paiva Mayor Paulo Teixeira told SIC television news.

2. The prostitutes gathering

Twenty-five thousand Indian prostitutes will gather in a Calcutta football stadium on Saturday to demand official recognition for their profession.

Prostitutes seeking a more dignified life will seek recognition as sex workers during the three-day carnival, a statement of Durbar Mahila Samanwaya Committee, a forum for sex workers, said Friday.

"The gathering will act as a bridge between common people and prostitutes and remove some of the stigma attached to their profession by making clear that it is like any other job," said Smarajit Jana, adviser to the forum.

3. Storm warning

WASHINGTON—Two major storm systems—a wet one trekking through the South and a frigid one moving down from Canada—were on a collision course on Saturday, threatening to spawn a massive snowstorm in northeastern and mid-Atlantic U.S. states the likes of which have not been seen since 1966.

The National Weather Service said heavy snowfall could begin on Sunday afternoon and evening, blanketing an area from Washington, D.C., to southern Maine with at least a foot of snow, with some areas getting even more.

A meteorologist with the National Weather Service, Michael Eckert, called the late-winter storm highly unusual. It represents the combination of two mighty weather systems. "It's very rare. We just don't see things like this happen very often," he said.

4. The 4,000-year-old man

Scientists, worried that their find might rot before detailed examinations can begin, were busy Friday preserving the remains of a man believed to be 4,000 years old. Using special chemicals, they prepared the body for storage in a low-temperature container.

Climbers on the Similaun Glacier in the Tirolean Alps between Austria and Hungary last week found the frozen corpse of a Bronze Age man believed to have died 2,000 years before the birth of Jesus.

Professor Konrad Spindler of Innsbruck University in Innsbruck, Austria, dated the body from a crude Bronze-Age ax clutched in a hand. Spindler said the remains, clothed and remarkably well preserved, were of "extraordinary scientific significance."

B. Lede drills

1. Job fair

A city Summer Job Fair will be from 10 a.m. to 3 p.m. Saturday at the Civic Center, 950 Broadway.

2. Postal rates

A U.S. Postal Service official said Friday the agency is considering a plant that would make mail delivery more effective—by eliminating most deliveries.

3. Shooting

A San Marino woman was arrested Friday evening in New Dublin and charged with shooting her estranged husband, who is in critical condition at Kerry County Hospital.

4. Drive

The president of the Brigham Estates chapter of the American Civil Liberties Union says the chapter must get 50 new members, or perish.

There are only two or three human stories, and they go on repeating themselves as fiercely as if they had never happened before.
—Willa Cather, *O Pioneers!*

... not that the story need be long, but it will take a long while to make it short.
—Henry David Thoreau, *Letter to Mr. B*

4 Building the Story

It was a warm but crisp day, not unusual for north central New Mexico in late summer or early fall. The sun glanced off Air Force One as it taxied down the runway and approached some bleachers that had been set up for the local news media. Half an hour later, and less than 100 yards away, on a tarmac at the Albuquerque Sunport (now Albuquerque International Airport) a reporter found himself standing alone.

The reporter had driven down from Santa Fe, where he normally covered state government. Years later, as he thought back, he could not remember how or why he was separated from the rest of the local media. But there he stood, with a tape recorder strapped around his left shoulder and a microphone in his right hand.

A white Cadillac limousine drove down the tarmac. It stopped in front of the reporter and its right rear window rolled down. A familiar face appeared, and the reporter found himself facing the President of the United States.

Thinking quickly if not well, the reporter turned on the recorder, placed the microphone near the face of the president and said, "Uh. Uh. Uh, welcome to New Mexico, Mr. President."

"Thank you," replied the president. "Thank you very much."

Up rolled the window, and the Cadillac made its way to another part of the airport.

The year was 1973. The president was Richard Nixon, a Republican. He was in the middle of his bid for reelection against what appeared to be an anemic and badly organized campaign on behalf of South Dakota Senator George McGovern, a Democrat.

Many were the questions the reporter could have asked. The president had recently returned from China, where he had opened up a government that had been closed to most of the outside world since 1949. Americans had just begun to hear about a "third-rate" burglary (as the White House called it) that took place in Democratic headquarters in a Washington complex called The Watergate. The Vietnam War was consuming more and more of the resources and spirit of the United States. There was the campaign itself—Why was Mr. Nixon so eager to gather New Mexico's four electoral votes, when it appeared all but certain that he would win reelection by a record landslide? (Which he would go on to do.)

But the reporter didn't ask any of these questions. In fact, he ended up with about the same campaign news that every other reporter, local or national, did. And he kicked himself all 60 miles back to Santa Fe.

I know. I was the reporter. To my credit, it took me only about half a second to realize how dismally I had failed to do my job. But I had violated a basic principle of fact-gathering; I ended up with no more information than I absolutely needed to file a story.

Why? Because I had allowed myself to be intimidated by a public official—another basic principle violated.

Gathering Facts and Interviewing People

The average reporter gets at least 90 percent of his or her information by interviewing people. When the reporter sits down to type out the story, that information had better be good, in quantity as well as quality. No matter how strong or enticing the lede might be, if the reporter doesn't have more than enough information to develop the story, the reporter is in trouble.

There is no attempt here to cover interviewing techniques; the world of journalism and writing is awash in books and articles that address them. But I can say this: The attitude, the mind-set, the reporter brings to the interview is as important or more important than the techniques themselves.

The reporter can act meek or flustered, as I did in my single encounter with a U.S. president, and miss getting the facts. The reporter can act arrogantly and miss getting the facts. The reporter can act bored and miss getting the facts.

Years of experience have convinced me that a good reporter approaches an interview subject the way a good reporter approaches a reader: with respect, humanity and a modicum of professional distance. Unless you are digging in to "get" a public official who you suspect is violating a trust with the voters—as perhaps I should have done with Mr. Nixon—you are going to want to gain the confidence of the interview subject.

You do that by meeting the subject at eye level, just as you meet the reader, listener or viewer. You do this not with arrogance—"I am so erudite and you are such scum"—nor with abject humility—"Oh, dear and gentle interview subject, please excuse me while I ask for a moment or two of your precious time."

No.

You approach the interview subject as one human being to another, one capable of sharing some experiences with you that will be of legitimate interest to your audience. There's nothing wrong with liking the person; most people like to be liked, and that's OK. It's no crime, not a journalistic crime. But do keep that hint of professional distance. It is not the reporter's job to cheerlead any more than it is to pass judgment and mete out a sentence to the accused.

Another basic of interviewing: Ask open questions, questions that cannot be answered with only a "yes" or a "no," that force interview subjects to expand on their answers. Good interview questions often begin with "why" or "how" and a pair of follow-up phrases that are basic to good journalistic interviewing: "What do you mean by that?" and "Give me an example."

Oh yes. One more thing. Listen. Listen hard. Don't make the mistake many novice television reporters make. Don't concentrate so hard on fabricating the next question that you forget to hear the answer to the last one.

So, first, gain the confidence of the subject by approaching him or her as one human being to another. Second, be friendly but keep a little professional distance from the subject. And third, listen.

Follow these principles and the finer techniques of interviewing will work themselves into position. And you will have more than enough quality facts and information with which to build a solid news story.

Bringing the Story Together

We'll be spending much of the rest of this book talking about what to take out of a clause, sentence or paragraph to ensure a well-written story. But for now, let's talk about what to put into it.

Remember that little formula we talked about in Chapters 1 and 3: Start with a strong lede, try to get a direct quote as high as the second paragraph and establish a dialogue with the reader? Well, to someone unfamiliar with journalistic writing, it might not be as easy as I made it sound. Walter Fox puts it this way:

> If the most important aspect of the story appears in the main clause and less important information is in the subordinate clause, the writer simply follows that order. Yet many beginners start to waver at precisely that point. Having written an acceptable lead, they tend to fall back on organizational devices learned in composition classes, such as chronological or climactic order.

In fact, some newspaper features do thrive on chronological or climactic order. But in a breaking news story what Fox calls the "order of importance" amounts to the about same thing as asking the reader "What do you need to know next?" The reader will establish the order of importance, so it behooves the writer to keep listening. The important thing is to keep concentrating on that imaginary dialogue that follows a strong lede.

One writer and teacher known not as a journalist but as a writer of good nonfiction, William Zinsser, agrees. He put it this way:

> Most of us are still prisoners of the lesson pounded into us by the composition teachers of our youth: that every story must have a beginning, a middle and an end. We can still visualize the outline, with its Roman

numerals (I, II and III), which staked out the road we would faithfully trudge, and its subnumerals (IIa and IIb) denoting lesser paths down which we would briefly poke. But we always promised to get back to III and summarize our journey.

That's all right for elementary and high school students uncertain of their ground. It forces them to see that every piece of writing should have a logical design that introduces and develops a theme. It's a lesson worth knowing at any age—even professional writers are adrift more often than they would like to admit. But if you're going to write good nonfiction you must wriggle out of III's deadly grasp.

I say something similar to my students: "If I can visualize Roman numerals in your copy, then something's wrong." Usually what is wrong is that the student writer has provided no bridges between some paragraphs. The reader might as well see stop signs. Remember the dialogue method with the reader that we talked about in Chapters 1 and 3: You ask the reader what he or she wants to know next, and the answer to that becomes your next paragraph. That dialogue method ensures that no stop sign will appear unless the writer wants one to. Such a story might begin like this:

> *The pilot went through her checklist the way she always did. Soon she knew that the propeller, the elevators, the rudder all worked; that the oil pressure was at a level it was supposed to be; that the fuel gauge was on "F."*
> *But she didn't know about the bomb under the back seat.*

There. The readers are stopped dead. But that's exactly the effect the writer wanted. Once they recover, they will read on and the dialogue will continue.

In the following 1998 story from the Reuters wire service, the lede paragraph brings history into play and the second paragraph brings the reader up to date. A thread does exist between the two. It takes the form of numbers—the number of young men who fought the Battle of Gettysburg compared with the number of tourists who visit the battlefield each year. The shorter third and fourth paragraphs include quotes. Now the writer and the reader are on their way.

GETTYSBURG, Pa. (Reuters)—On one July day, more than 160,000 men, mostly very young men, faced each other under a relentless mid-summer sun, across rolling hills, piles of rocks, wheat fields, meadows and peach orchards. Here they began a three-day confrontation that would decide if the United States of America would remain united. Two days later, at the end of the biggest battle ever fought in the Western Hemisphere, nearly one in three was unable to answer muster.

Now, 135 years later, about 1.8 million visitors visit the site annually to walk across what Abraham Lincoln called the "hallowed ground" of the battlefield—about 50 square miles, depending on who's counting. The outdated facilities of the Gettysburg National Military Park can scarcely keep up.

Park Superintendent John Latschar has spent the past four years trying to do something about it. He made note of a Congress unwilling to fund the National Park Service's charter, "to preserve our historic resources and to make them available, unimpaired, for all future generations."

The entire National Park Service, Latschar recently told an audience in Harrisburg, Pa., "is bankrupt. If the NPS were a Fortune 500 corporation, we would be filing for Chapter 11 protection right now." ...

Now, what does the reader need to know next? The reader replies, "What has the superintendent done about it?" The reporter provides an answer, using the adverb *so* as a transition between paragraphs.

So in November, Latschar announced a public-private agreement with a York, Pa., developer, Robert Kinsley, which turned out to be as fraught with politics as anything Congress ever did. Kinsley set up a non-profit corporation, the Gettysburg National Battlefield Museum Foundation, to raise $27 million in donations, grants and corporate sponsorships. The remaining 31 percent would be borrowed.

The new complex would revert to NPS ownership after the mortgage is paid. Latschar estimates that will be in 20 years.

Aha. I suspect the reader sees complications ahead. Complications are apt to appear in most stories dealing with politics and political motivations, and this story provides no exception. "What do other folks think about this 'public-private agreement?'" the reader asks.

The plan has been assailed by competing developers. It has been assailed by amateur historians averse to changing so much as a blade of grass on the hallowed ground. It has been assailed by dozens of merchants lined up along Gettysburg's Steinwehr Avenue, many of whom object to the implied competition of gift shops and cafeterias on National Park property not far from them. ...

By now, the reader is entitled to some background about and history of the controversy.

A local family, the Rosensteels, built the existing center in 1921 as a private museum. It can exhibit only 8 percent of the artifacts from the battle. When the National Park Service bought the center in 1971, its officials planned to raze the facility and replace it, but Congress never approved the funds to do so. ...

The writer then added some detail on what has been going wrong for years, including the deterioration of the park's Cyclorama and the lack of storage space and conservation conditions for thousands of battlefield artifacts.

After the story has provided an adequate amount of background, a copy editor short on space can reasonably end the piece. This reporter built the story so the copy editor or the reader could bail out at this point.

But the writer created a dialogue of quotes, in this case, a debate. In more complex stories, a good reporter can weave together six or eight points of view and let the interview subjects carry the story, matching quote for quote. But the writer should never relinquish control. Using short explanations and paraphrasing, the writer can continue to maintain the flow of the story.

A copy editor short on space can end the story at this point. But in case space remains, the writer provided a final two paragraphs that refer back to facts in the lede, and provide irony, a valuable commodity in news stories or stories of any kind.

Journalism isn't, or shouldn't be, blindly optimistic. About two-thirds of good journalism is demonstrating what's wrong with the world and what some people think can be done about it. That's our job. But because the world is imperfect, some interesting, and sardonically funny—ironic—things happen. Report them.

Use them in your lede if you can. And maybe you can use irony to tie up the ending of the story.

> *The battle 135 years ago marked as far as the South ever got. But it would take nearly two years, a score of battles and thousands more lives to determine that the United States would remain united.*
> *The battle over how to mix scarce public revenues with private funds, to preserve and enlighten, continues.*

Even though many copy editors will cut a story from the bottom, it doesn't hurt to end a story with a little rhetorical flourish like this one. That's what the irony in this story provides. And by referring back to the lede, the reporter has given the story unity.

When to Stop Describing

Bringing detail and description into the lede, as the Gettysburg story's did, can be effective—as long as it moves the story along. But take it from a well-established writer of fiction, Barnaby Conrad: Too much description can kill a story. The journalist can borrow freely from his admonition. Here, in shortened form, is a list of what Conrad called the "Four Deadly Sins of Description" in an article for *The Writer* magazine:

> Don't let your description, no matter how beautifully written, bring your narrative to a halt.
> This must be kept in mind by the writer of fiction: Do not overdescribe anything, whether it be the Grand Tetons or the sunset or zebras on the beach at Waikiki; your narrative thrust will suffer for it, and you will put your readers' attention in jeopardy. ...
> Don't spend too much time describing nonessential surroundings. [A journalist should spend no time on nonessential surroundings.] ... It would be a waste of space to include it in a novel, much less a short story. ...
> Don't squander the reader's attention by focusing on an inconsequential action. This is a more common fault among beginning writers than you might think. ...
> Don't generalize—be specific. ... Not a drink but a martini; not a dog but a poodle; not a flower but a rose; ... not a cat but an Abbyssin-

ian; not a gun but a .44 Colt on a frontier frame; not a painting but Manet's "Olympia."

About all I can add to that is to suggest that you read "A Passion for Accuracy" in Chapter 7.

Developing the Breaking Story

When you're reporting breaking news, you often find yourself using a summary lede. You might even revert to the inverted pyramid, which summarizes at the top and then recounts the facts of the story in descending order. For a story that's already broken but is still too newsworthy to ignore, you can use the *second-day lede*, as Ben Fox of the Associated Press did in this story:

> *EL CAJON, Calif. (AP)—An 18-year-old student accused of shooting five people at his high school made a reference to the Columbine High massacre in class earlier this year and simulated guns with his hands, a classmate said yesterday. …*

Now the dialogue with the reader begins. The reader wants to know who the student and classmate were. And "How have the authorities learned about the reported reference to Columbine High?"

> *Bernadette Roberts, 18, said girls were making noise in a classroom in January when [Jason] Hoffman appeared to become frustrated, put his hands in the shape of guns and stated, "I wish I could do Columbine all over again." …*

"What did she do about it?" the reader might ask.

> *Roberts said she told her teacher and met in February with Vice Principal Dan Barnes, who asked if she needed protection. She said she declined and did not know what steps the district took. …*

Well, what steps did district officials take?
Fox indicated the officials didn't respond to questions about a breaking story. Often, this means they haven't yet talked with

their lawyers. This is not a cynical remark; in this case, it might not even be true. But in a society in which people put lawsuits among their top priorities, it behooves officials to put their lawyers near the top of their priority list. Regardless, a no-response can be frustrating for the news media as well as the public they are supposed to serve.

The prosecutor did respond concerning the target of the attack and the motive, and Fox was able to include a direct quote. It showed how carefully the prosecutor had couched his own statement. The prosecutor's legal language doesn't enlighten the reader much, though. Let's go on.

> *Barnes was not harmed, but three students and two teachers were hit by shotgun pellets, none seriously. ...*

The victim count was new at this point; the total count was three on the day of the shooting. So the reader might be asking why the current count wasn't inserted higher in the story.

On this, the second day after the shooting, very little detail about Hoffman had been released. But Fox was able to come up with an interesting item of his own. We might wonder why it didn't go higher in the story.

> *The Associated Press learned yesterday that Hoffman assaulted a middle-school classmate several years ago and was ordered to attend an anger management class.*
>
> *Hoffman was 14 when he struck the student in the head with a racquetball racket, according to a source familiar with the case who spoke on condition of anonymity. ...*

Too bad that's the only way Fox could get that item, from an anonymous source. But anyone who has covered a story that even hints at politics knows that anonymous sources can sometimes be the only source. For example, the *Washington Post* requires its reporters to get at least two anonymous sources who independently verify the facts before printing the information. Bob Woodward and Carl Bernstein did just that when they broke the Watergate story that doomed the Nixon administration. Anyway, using a technique proven quite effective, Fox ended the story with a good quote:

"Nobody picked on this kid because he was so intimidating," student Sean Connacher said.

When many reporters winnow through their notes, they look for a bright, pithy or ironic quotation to end with. Even though many lazy copy editors cut from the bottom, it's worth a try, because it gives readers quite a send-off. They are much more likely to think about the story as they walk away from it.

Developing an Issue with Specifics

We mentioned the *Washington Post*. Let's turn to a story by a member of the *Post*'s Foreign Service, Rajiv Chandrasekaran. It starts with a lede that might be considered long, except that it does a great job of setting the story's environment and its length provides a counterpoint for the terse second paragraph.

> *SINGAPORE—The tree-encircled park designated as the first Speaker's Corner in this tightly controlled city-state has almost everything necessary for lively public oration: Shady spots to place one's soapbox. A spacious patch of manicured grass for crowds to gather. Benches for rest. Even the occasional ice cream vendor.*
>
> *Everything, that is, except speakers.*

The reader now is wondering what Chandrasekaran is getting at. That's all right. He has generated the reader's interest.

> *Many view the corner, which opened six months ago, as the most significant step toward free expression here in years, the first place where ordinary people can speak out in public without a permit. But after an initial flurry of activity, and flattering headlines around the world, the park has largely gone back to what it always was—a hangout for retirees, a lunching spot and a shortcut for office workers on their way home.*

Here comes the crux of the story, in the form of a quote:

> *"It's not just pretty quiet, it's totally quiet," said a policeman patrolling the park on a recent afternoon. "People in Singapore aren't interested in speaking in public."*

> *Only two or three speakers regularly use the corner, largely to complain about the same few issues: government ministers' salaries, care for the elderly and a law that allows authorities to imprison landlords who rent to illegal immigrants. Even when there is a speaker, there have rarely been more than a handful of listeners.*

And now, some background; why the reader should care. (Note a local reference for the *Post*'s hometown audience).

> *Free speech has long been a thorny issue in this country of 4 million people that has transformed itself in just a few decades from a Third World backwater to one of the most prosperous and modern nations—a place where the subway is cleaner than the Washington Metro and grade-schoolers regularly outrank the rest of the world in math and science tests. Lacking in natural resources, Singapore has fashioned itself into a global financial center and maritime transportation hub.*
>
> *But to squelch any discord that might disrupt the emphasis on development, the government places restrictions on many forms of public expression. In particular, it targets any individual or group it feels might promote communal violence in its multi-ethnic society, composed mainly of Chinese, Malays and Indians. Ethnic rioting has rocked the island at a number of points in its history.*
>
> *Speaking in public requires a permit from the police. Even staging a play needs governmental approval. Books, movies and television programs are censored. It is illegal to have a residential television satellite dish. Access to the Internet is restricted.*

Good. Chandrasekaran was not satisfied simply making a general statement: "… the government places restrictions on many forms of public expression." He gives examples. Here are some more specific ones:

> *The government has not been shy about enforcing the laws. An opposition politician, Chee Soon Juan, was jailed for 12 days in 1999 for speaking in public without a permit. During one speech that resulted in the charges, he read parts of Singapore's constitution and said such things as: "It's time to break the atmosphere of fear, to say it's all right to criticize the government, to hold it accountable for its actions."*

And now, back to our story.

So now that Singapore finally has a place where people can speak out, why aren't more residents flocking there?

"We are too busy with our jobs and our families," says Cindy Li, a secretary who was walking across the park on a recent afternoon. "Nobody has the time to stop here and listen."

Sociologists say Singaporeans are not accustomed to ranting in public, "It's not like America, where people say, 'Let's get a community group going. Let's change things,'" said Gillian Koh, a research fellow at the Institute of Policy Studies, a research organization here. "People in Singapore are not interested in mass mobilization. They would rather write a letter to the government in private."

Now, at the reader's request, the writer brings in the view of the opposition.

Free-speech advocates contend the government has placed too many restrictions on the park. Speakers must register with the police. They are prevented from using amplification devices. They must speak only in one of four official languages. And people believe security officials closely monitor the speeches.

There are strict rules about what cannot be said. Wooden signs warn speakers to refrain from any topic that "may cause feelings of enmity, hatred, ill will or hostility between different racial or religious groups."

The speakers are not exempt from the country's Internal Security Act, which allows the government to jail without trial people deemed to be a threat to national security. They also can be charged under libel and slander laws, which have been aggressively used by the government party.

A little scary, the reader might be thinking. Why so many restrictions? Chandrasekaran provides an answer:

Government officials contend the rules are reasonable and are aimed at ensuring social harmony. "Just because someone is at the Speakers' Corner doesn't mean they can say whatever they want," one [anonymous?] official said. "They can't use it as a forum to slander someone with impunity."

Again, the reporter takes the reader from the general to a specific example.

Police are investigating one event at the corner to determine whether organizers held a rally without a permit. On Dec. 10, almost 100 people gathered to commemorate International Human Rights Day. Eight speakers urged the government to abolish the Internal Security Act. One person read a letter from U.N. Secretary General Kofi Annan about human rights.

Chandrasekaran ends the story with an effective quote:

"What's the point of a speaker's corner if you can't gather there and listen to people speak?" said James Gomez, the executive director of Think Centre, an organization that promotes free speech in Singapore.

We've spent several pages talking about what to put in a story. Now we're going to concentrate on what to take out. Chapter 5 looms. The process involves a great deal of word surgery that is required in good journalistic writing, especially newspaper writing.

Exercise

The following story by Mary Klaus of the *Patriot-News* in Harrisburg, Pennsylvania, begins with a lede paragraph and three short grafs. Two paragraphs contain direct quotes. The rest of the story is jumbled; the paragraphs are not in the order they appeared in the story. See if you can put them in an order that responds to a dialogue with the reader.

Here are the lede grafs:

It's called The Best Little Cat House in Pennsylvania.

But lately, this feline hospice in West Hanover Twp., also a home for abandoned domestic rabbits, has seen an overflow of bunnies.

"And it's not even Easter," said Lynn Stitt, owner.

"I am swamped with rabbits," said Stitt, walking among cages of white, brown and black rabbits. "Last year, a lot of people got rabbits who shouldn't have. We've had poor adoptions this year."

Now, here are the jumbled paragraphs:

The Best Little Cat House, the final home for many terminally ill and handicapped cats, began accepting rabbits a few years ago. Now, rabbits and cats coexist peacefully, the rabbits in individual, roomy cages and the cats freely roaming the facility.

Occasionally, the center gets an abused rabbit, Stitt said, pointing to Zeus, a 3-year-old rabbit whose owner, she said, would fight with his girlfriend and then beat up Zeus.

On a recent morning, all 31 domestic rabbits seemed peaceful, a variety of Dutch, New Zealand, Fuzzy Lop, Red and Californian, along with several mixed breeds.

These days, Stitt is busy planning an 18-by-22-foot rabbit addition to the shelter. She hopes to break ground for it this fall.

Meanwhile, she keeps accepting unwanted domestic rabbits from some people and adopting rabbits out to others.

Tammy Paull of York Springs, president of BunnyPeople, said that rabbits aren't for everyone. BunnyPeople is a Harrisburg-area organization promoting responsible ownership and care of rabbits.

"Rabbits don't follow commands and may not be as affectionate as dogs or cats," she said. "You can't pick them up like you do a cat, although most like to be petted."

Long considered a popular symbol of Easter and spring, rabbits take center stage this time of year. Some parents put a real bunny in their child's Easter basket and, a few hours later, realize that the cute, warm and cuddly gift is a lot of work.

"People see rabbits as cute, cuddly, cheap pets," said Sandy Nevius, BunnyPeople capital campaign coordinator. "People often buy rabbits on impulse, without knowing that the maintenance of a rabbit is as much or more as a dog or cat."

Sometimes, she said, parents buy a rabbit to teach their kids responsibility. Once the novelty wears off, the rabbit is neglected "and either ends up here or is let loose in the woods, where it can't survive because it isn't fast and doesn't camouflage easily."

Domestic rabbits live an average of 10 years, are sexually mature by six months and can have litters of eight every several weeks.

"We start getting calls by Easter afternoon from people who decide they don't want to keep their rabbits," said Stitt. "Most people should buy stuffed rabbits for Easter baskets. Rabbits are not disposable animals."

Stitt said that pet rabbits should be spayed or neutered to control the population and to calm them down.

The center also has Tack, a white 1½-year-old New Zealand rabbit experimented upon in an animal laboratory. "We had Tick, Tack and Toe from that lab," Stitt said. "Tick and Toe were adopted, but we still have Tack."

What the Original Looked Like

It's called The Best Little Cat House in Pennsylvania.

But lately, this feline hospice in West Hanover Twp., also a home for abandoned domestic rabbits, has seen an overflow of bunnies.

"And it's not even Easter," said Lynn Stitt, owner.

"I am swamped with rabbits," said Stitt, walking among cages of white, brown and black rabbits. "Last year, a lot of people got rabbits who shouldn't have. We've had poor adoptions this year."

Long considered a popular symbol of Easter and spring, rabbits take center stage this time of year. Some parents put a real bunny in their child's Easter basket and, a few hours later, realize that the cute, warm and cuddly gift is a lot of work.

"We start getting calls by Easter afternoon from people who decide they don't want to keep their rabbits," said Stitt. "Most people should buy stuffed rabbits for Easter baskets. Rabbits are not disposable animals."

The Best Little Cat House, the final home for many terminally ill and handicapped cats, began accepting rabbits a few years ago. Now, rabbits and cats coexist peacefully, the rabbits in individual, roomy cages and the cats freely roaming the facility.

On a recent morning, all 31 domestic rabbits seemed peaceful, a variety of Dutch, New Zealand, Fuzzy Lop, Red and Californian, along with several mixed breeds.

"People see rabbits as cute, cuddly, cheap pets," said Sandy Nevius, BunnyPeople capital campaign coordinator. "People often buy rabbits on impulse, without knowing that the maintenance of a rabbit is as much or more as a dog or cat."

Sometimes, she said, parents buy a rabbit to teach their kids responsibility. Once the novelty wears off, the rabbit is neglected "and either ends up here or is let loose in the woods, where it can't survive because it isn't fast and doesn't camouflage easily."

Occasionally, the center gets an abused rabbit, Stitt said, pointing to Zeus, a 3-year-old rabbit whose owner, she said, would fight with his girlfriend and then beat up Zeus.

The center also has Tack, a white 1½-year-old New Zealand rabbit experimented upon in an animal laboratory. "We had Tick, Tack and Toe from that lab," Stitt said. "Tick and Toe were adopted, but we still have Tack."

Tammy Paull of York Springs, president of BunnyPeople, said that rabbits aren't for everyone. BunnyPeople is a Harrisburg-area organization promoting responsible ownership and care of rabbits.

"Rabbits don't follow commands and may not be as affectionate as dogs or cats," she said. "You can't pick them up like you do a cat, although most like to be petted."

Domestic rabbits live an average of 10 years, are sexually mature by six months and can have litters of eight every several weeks.

Stitt said that pet rabbits should be spayed or neutered to control the population and to calm them down.

These days, Stitt is busy planning an 18-by-22-foot rabbit addition to the shelter. She hopes to break ground for it this fall.

Meanwhile, she keeps accepting unwanted domestic rabbits from some people and adopting rabbits out to others.

Many a poem is marred by a superfluous verse.
—Henry Wadsworth Longfellow, *Elegaic Verse*

The difference between the almost right word and the right word is really a large matter—'tis the difference between the lightning bug and the lightning.
—Mark Twain in *The Art of Authorship*, edited by George Bainton

5 The Craft

It wasn't a big story, and when it appeared, it carried no byline. Apparently it received only passing attention from the editors who handled it. The story passed through two respected news organizations, one known for the integrity of its reporting and the other for the brightness and economy of its writing. Yet the reporting apparently was not thorough. I say "apparently" because the murky way it was written camouflaged any good reporting that might have been accomplished.

The lede of the *USA Today* story, which was picked up from the Associated Press, became a murky start to a murky story. One sentence was followed by a dependent clause that carried a dependent clause of its own.

> *The U.S. transplant network has agreed to share with Mexico its experience in distributing organs, opening an information exchange that officials hope will boost Mexico's less developed system and give the U.S. system insight into increasing Hispanic donations.*

Let's see. The network that distributes organs—I assume human organs—in the United States is going to share the results of its experience with officials in Mexico. OK, that makes sense. Enough information there to comprise a sentence all its own.

"Now, why would they do that?" the reader asks. And the writer responds as the writer should—"to help boost Mexico's less developed system and" (here comes the murk) "give the U.S. system insight into increasing Hispanic donations."

What the heck does that mean?

"Insight." The U.S. system wants to understand why Hispanic donations are increasing? I don't think so. What, then?

Ah. Maybe the writer meant that an increased understanding of Mexico's system would help increase the number of donations coming from Hispanic countries. If that's true, it's too bad that isn't what the writer wrote. Well, at least now we're ready for the second paragraph.

> *The formal agreement, signed Friday in Mexico City, was not necessary from the American point of view, given that the U.S. network regularly shares information with other nations. ...*

"From the American point of view." "Given that." Oh my, a band of bureaucrats has stolen some reporter's ability to write in English. Why not say something like: "Officials from the two countries signed the agreement Friday in Mexico City. Americans said it would be of no direct benefit to the United States. The U.S. network regularly shares information with other nations anyway."

All right. Let's move on.

The next paragraph explains that Mexican authorities might want to do more than simply share information. In an indirect quotation of Mark Rosenker, a spokemsan for the United Network for Organ Sharing (UNOS), says the Mexicans are seeking a formal relationship with the U.S. transplant network, whose system distributes donated hearts, lungs, kidneys, livers and pancreases.

Nothing particularly wrong there. A direct quote from Rosenker would have worked better, but the paragraph is understandable. Next?

> *"We have much to teach and much to learn through this exchange," says Walter Graham, executive director of UNOS.*

Good. A direct quote. Next?

> *The agreement is not expected to lead to the exchange of actual organs. Rather, the agreement is meant to help Mexico's National Trans-*

plant Council develop a nationwide system for distributing organs. For
example, the agreement calls for an information exchange on how to
certify transplant centers and professionals.

Why is the reporter filtering all the information in this para-graph? We might as well believe that the reporter has made all this up. No quotes, direct or indirect. And the fog factor—the ab-stract quality of the copy, enhanced by so many latinizations—is great. And what is the second sentence an example of?

Graham might have been a source. If so, the reporter could have written: "Graham said no one expects the agreement to lead to an actual organ exchange between the two countries. But it is meant to help Mexico's National Transplant Council build a na-tionwide organ distribution system. The agreement calls for the United States to give Mexico information about how to certify transplant centers and professionals."

This is what happens when a reporter or writer or editor gets lazy and stops demanding the most direct English available. The story makes up for the fact that it is dull by being mostly incom-prehensible.

Direct English calls for the skills of a craft. This chapter dwells on many results of good craftsmanship.

Separating the Craft from the Profession of Journalism

Journalism often is called a profession. And so it is, I suppose, sometimes. It's a profession when we talk about journalism in the society in which it is practiced, the U.S. Constitution that governs its practice and the academic atmosphere in which it is taught.

When the term is applied to newspapers, magazines, newslet-ters and radio and television newscasts and documentaries, though, journalism is much more a trade, a craft, than a profes-sion. The best drafters of English are those who make the most economic use of language, especially words, without losing mean-ing or flavor. And that means eliminating many of them.

For journalists, regardless of medium, craft means pare, pare, pare. Getting rid of even a two-letter word if it fails to carry its weight should represent a tiny triumph. If writers don't pare, they risk inflicting sentences such as this one on their audiences:

At the end of the alley, there were two construction workers surrounded by orange cones wearing brown overalls and gloves drilling a hole from the end of the alley to the middle of the street.

Let's think about this 35-word sentence for a moment. We can't fault the writer for poor observational skills, but the sentence is wordy. It's needlessly complex. It portrays cones wearing overalls and gloves drilling a hole.

Now, let's try again:

Orange cones surround two construction workers wearing brown overalls and gloves. The workers are drilling a hole from the end of an alley to the street.

There. Twenty-six words split into two sentences. We've pared nine words, 26 percent, of the original sentence with no meaning lost, no flavor changed, nothing of value left out. In other words, we've eliminated some wordiness. And we've clarified the meaning by getting rid of dangling modifiers.

Avoiding Wordiness and Using Plain English

It is one of the leading corporations connected with the Internet and, during 2000, it was one of the darlings of Wall Street. In 2001, though, executives at Cisco Systems Inc. saw much of their business and profits evaporate. That's when they announced they would eliminate the jobs of 8,000 employees. But in a story by Steve Rubenstein of the *San Francisco Chronicle*, a spokesman "declared that the employees were to undergo 'normal involuntary attrition.'" (See "Be Honest: Avoid Euphemisms" in Chapter 7.)

Rubenstein quoted an emeritus professor of English at the University of California at Berkeley, Julian Boyd, who called the phrase "comical. It's someone trying to avoid blame. It's someone trying to say this thing is doubly not my fault."

A spokeswoman for the California Employment Development Department said she didn't know what it means. "Each one of the words I have heard before," said Suzanne Schroeder. "They're English. Put them together, I'm not sure."

English it might be, but plain English—good, solid, clear, unambiguous, forceful English—it isn't. The phrase should be taken out and shot.

Not that journalistic plain speaking originated from someone's loving attention to clarity and honesty. The often brutal emphasis on brevity and word economy that characterizes much journalistic writing began not so much from a desire to improve communication as it did to save money, time, ink and trees.

In the United States, the Civil War is credited with inspiring much of today's spareness of copy. Americans on both sides used the world's first wire service, *Agence France Presse* (AFP), as a model. AFP showed journalists how to cover the war for dozens of newspapers that were members of the wire service. The only link the reporter had to the member newspapers was an expensive telegraph wire, and the only language the wire recognized was Morse code.

To get the story out about, say, the Battle of Shiloh in Tennessee (Union generals called it the Battle of Pittsburg Landing) required that the reporter find an authorized telegrapher and wait impatiently while his deathless prose was translated into dots and dashes. The fewer the words, the shorter the wait and the less the expense.

The tradition continued through at least six more wars, with publishers devoting much of the time in between worrying about the price of paper, called newsprint, which even now comes from expensive trees in faraway places like northern Canada. Regardless of their motives, however, there is little question that in the process they enhanced the ability to communicate in English. Avoiding wordiness and using plain English has become an art form as well as a mechanical writing and editing function.

Sometimes getting rid of an unneeded word is simply a matter of changing an adverb into an adjective; in this case, the word *not*.

Police have not found any witnesses.
Police have found no witnesses.

Here are some more examples in italics, followed by edited versions, with any comments in parentheses or brackets:

He considers himself a supporter of the Republican Party. He did not, however, support its choice of George W. Bush.
He says he is a Republican, but he did not support George W. Bush.

People were sitting in the restaurant, eating and conversing.
People sat in the restaurant, eating and talking.
Or
In the restaurant, people ate and talked.

She is hoping to organize a service project.
She hopes to organize a service project.
Or (to make sure the writer isn't making it up):
She said she hopes to organize a service project.

Our footsteps fell lifeless, and void of synchronosity.
Our footsteps fell lifeless, out of step with each other.

We had an ample supply of time to get to know each other.
We had ample time to get to know each other.

The budget plan will stem the skyrocketing deficit by $496 billion through raising taxes on individual and corporate income.
Raising individual and corporate income taxes will reduce the deficit by $496 billion.

People become disoriented from their friends due to their preoccupation with their significant other when they should be preoccupied with relationships with friends, it shifts to concern about their significant other's happiness as well as their own happiness.
(I have no idea how to edit this. I do wish someone would come up with a less cumbersome synonym for "significant other." See "Clichés to Avoid" in Chapter 8.)

I find myself zipping up my leather jacket and struggling with cold hands to fasten the metal snap at its neckline.
(Sometimes you can achieve word economy by using a more direct verb form.)
I zip up my leather jacket and struggle with cold hands to fasten the metal snap at its neckline.

He spends the majority of his time with his girlfriend.
He spends most of his time with his girlfriend.

When high school coaches encourage this atmosphere of free agency,
they are endorsing the sense of randomness in teenagers that leads
some of our city's youth to drop out of high school to join gangs in-
stead of remaining committed to their schoolwork.
By encouraging free agency, high school coaches contribute to a sense of
randomness among teenagers. This lack of direction can lead them to
drop out of school, even to join gangs.

She competed in the Olympic swimming trials and just barely missed a
spot on the team.
She competed in the Olympic swimming trials and just missed a spot on
the team.

Neither of them saw it as a permanent move, they said.
Neither saw it as a permanent move, they said.

With the patents, inventions and discoveries she has developed for the
pharmaceutical business, it seems that the ideas and planning have
been great, however the rewards have not been equivalent to the
effort. She says she wants to find a way to improve her job or remu-
neration both financially and personally.
She appears proud of the patents, inventions and discoveries she has developed for the pharmaceutical business. She says she wants to improve her job financially and personally.

One way to avoid wordiness is to replace a string of adjectives
or adverbs with a noun or a verb. For example, the writer can
look up into a summer sky in the Southwestern United States and
describe a *big, black and gray, anvil-shaped cloud,* or the writer can
define it with a single noun familiar to Southwesterners—*thun-
derhead.*

The journalist can write that police believe the suspect *beat the
victim repeatedly over the head with a blunt object.* Or the journalist
can write that police believe the suspect *bludgeoned* the victim.

As we mentioned in Chapter 1, English is at its base Anglo-
Saxon. The Anglo-Saxon gifts to the language usually are shorter

and punchier than their latinized equivalents. In *On Writing Well,* William Zinsser points out that paring often means working on the size of a word as well as the number of words. He asks why people insist on using *assistance* when *help* will do nicely. The same for *facilitate* instead of *ease, numerous* instead of *many, individual* instead of *man* or *woman, remainder* instead of *rest, initial* instead of *first, sufficient* instead of *enough, attempt* instead of *try* and *referred to as* instead of *called.*

"Beware of all slippery new fad words for which the language already has equivalents," Zinsser warns. He includes "*overview* and *quantify, paradigm* and *parameter, optimize* and *maximize, prioritize* and *potentialize.* They are all weeds that will smother what you write. Don't *dialogue* with someone you can *talk* to. Don't *interface* with anybody." (Italics added.)

Eliminating Redundancy

Redundancy is a wonderful thing to have in a space vehicle. One computer system goes down, another takes its place; the mission lives and so do the astronauts. Redundancy might keep a space vehicle aloft, but it can sink a sentence.

Redundancy is defined in the dictionary as the quality or state of exceeding what is needed or normal. Redundancies in English do serve a couple of useful purposes, though. They provide fodder for a chapter in a book that talks about how to write better. And often, they provide comic relief.

I saw a slight hint of light.
(How slight can a hint get?)
I saw a hint of light.

... the Catholic pope.
... the pope.

He was promoted in the organization to handle the newspaper's layout, design and photography.
(Unless "the organization" is a group dedicated to organized crime, we can safely assume that he works for the newspaper.)
He was promoted to handle the newspaper's layout, design and photography.

The smell of burnt charcoal loomed in the air.
(Where else? Also, in the United States the preferred usage is "burned."
"Burnt" is more of a British usage.)
The smell of burned charcoal loomed.

Remember the old adage.
Remember the adage.

The beating victim can now dress himself and brush his own teeth.
(Before he was the victim, he must have been able to brush other peo-
ple's teeth as well.)
The beating victim can now dress himself and brush his teeth.

... a private school which is located in Simsbury, Conn.
(More often than not, "located" is redundant.)
... a private school in Simsbury, Conn.

*He continued on in the tradition of DePaul University, where he
has obtained both a BS as well as an MBA from the School of
Commerce.*
(This sentence isn't big enough for both "both" and "as well" as well. In
addition, "earned" is a more precise word than "obtained." [See "Writing with Precision" below.] And when did DePaul University get a
patent on this tradition?)
He earned a BS and an MBA from the School of Commerce at DePaul
University.

*Besides pursuing an internship in the field of journalism, he is in a
band.*
(Also, change to an action verb: "... he plays in a band." See Chapter 6.)
Besides pursuing an internship in journalism, he plays in a band.

... 5 a.m. in the morning.
... 5 a.m.

*Bond was set at $900,000 Wednesday for an 18-year-old man charged
with killing two men dead and wounding another.*
(How dead can they get?)
Bond was set at $900,000 Wednesday for an 18-year-old man charged
with killing two men and wounding another.

His desire to get better and improve is a major reason for his success.
His desire to improve is a major reason for his success.

The mayor says she wants to talk about the town's poverty-stricken slums.
(Slums are, by definition, poverty-stricken.)
The mayor says she wants to talk about the town's slums.

Police said drug paraphernalia was found on the body. They said they believe the shooting was drug-related.
("Gosh, I never would have thought of that," the reader says ironically. This sentence falls under the heading of telling the reader what to think. See Chapter 7.)

He moved like an unstoppable tornado.
(I have never heard of a stoppable tornado.)
He moved like a tornado.

In addition, he also edits the yearbook.
(A very busy guy, no doubt.)
In addition, he edits the yearbook.

In school, he says he enjoyed history the most out of his subjects.
In school, he says he enjoyed history the most.

He is an avid traveler who has, in the past, written a number of travel stories.
(Guess he didn't have time for them in the future.)
He is an avid traveler who has written a number of travel stories.

The temperature in the barn had reached a smoldering 115 degrees.
(Most would agree that 115 degrees is smoldering.)
The barn's temperature had reached 115 degrees.

Among her most favorite destinations is London.
Among her favorite destinations is London.

I feel the majority of people want to be well liked and popular.
Most people want to be well liked.

Not only has she competed in Chicago, but also around the nation.
("Also" simply takes up space. Here you might be tempted to over-edit and
    reduce the sentence to "She has competed around the nation." But you
    would lose some of the rhetorical flavor of the sentence if you did so.)
Not only has she competed in Chicago, but around the nation.

Photography has also become another of his passions.
Photography has become another of his passions.

*Pennsylvania Hall stands among the large trees, casting its own unique
    shadow.*
Pennsylvania Hall stands among the large trees, casting its unique shadow.

Compounding the Sentence with Complexity

A quick grammar review: What is a compound sentence, what
is a complex sentence and what is the difference? A compound
sentence is two sentences joined by a conjunction (*and, but, for,
or, nor*). A complex sentence contains at least one clause that acts
as an assistant to the main part of the sentence. Clauses aren't
supposed to stand by themselves.

There is nothing particularly wrong with a compound or complex sentence. Often the ideas don't get across without their
help. It is when they are not needed that they create problems for
the conscientious writer, journalistic or otherwise.

Extra sentence elements (words, phrases, clauses) should carry
red flags to wave in front of the writer. When these elements appear, the red flag should go up, reminding the writer to ask, "Do
I really need this?" If you do need it, fine, keep it in. But more often than not, it just gets in the way.

The easiest way to break up complexity is to divide the sentence and transform it into at least two sentences. Take this one,
for example:

*Her Wednesday playwriting course will have a direct impact on this
    class, as some of the basics can easily be transformed from journalism
    to theater writing, she believes.*
She says journalism will have a direct impact on her Wednesday play-
    writing course. The basics will transfer easily.

Sometimes you can simply boil down the sentence by rewriting it. In this example, the rewritten sentence still fits the definition of "complex," but it's much less complex than the original:

> *She explained that, although she was afforded the chance to travel throughout Europe during her semester abroad, there are many places she has not yet visited, but there are still many places there she wants to see.*

(Notice the use of passive voice—"she was afforded" [see Chapter 6]—and the needless "there are" [see Chapter 9]. Both contribute to bogging down this sentence.)

She says she saw much of Europe during her semester abroad, but she still wants to see more.

Here are some additional examples:

> *The price of gas and a Whopper can be discerned by gazing at the corner of State and 12th, where an Amoco gas station with a Burger King restaurant stretches out a quarter of a block.*

An Amoco gas station and a Burger King restaurant take up a quarter of a block. One displays the price of a gallon of gasoline; the other, the price of a Whopper.

> *Residents in the subdivision have formed an action group called AWARE (Amber Grove—We're Against Road Expansion) and they have spent the last three weekends picketing the developer's sales office at Amber Grove, carrying signs that read "Ask before you buy" and "Trucks + Traffic = Tragedy" in below-freezing temperatures.*

(Apparently they believe road expansion is all right during the summer.)

Subdivision residents formed an action group, AWARE (Amber Grove—We're Against Road Expansion). They have spent the past three weekends in freezing temperatures, picketing the developer's sales office with signs: "Ask Before You Buy" and "Trucks + Traffic = Tragedy."

> *The icy wind, making itself felt through my mittens, reminds me of the lake's incredible power over this city at all times.*

The icy wind makes itself felt through my mittens. It reminds me of the lake's incredible power over this city at all times.

Whole chapters have been written about what a sentence is and what it isn't. Actually, a few principles should suffice. Here, so far, we've seen simple sentences and those adorned with extra phrases and clauses. But because good newspaper writing can be informal and conversational, sentence fragments are often allowed. However, they must make sense and the reader must sense that the writer wrote the fragment on purpose, not by mistake.

What you should not see in newspaper writing are run-on sentences—two sentences that, because they were not separated by a period, resemble a head-on train wreck. Like this one:

There was no one who could help me, I was devastated.
(Also note: We do not need the "there was." We can take it out and turn a being verb into an action verb. See Chapter 9.)
No one could help me. I was devastated.

In this case, the writer supplied punctuation in the right place, but it was a comma, not a period.

Football immediately caught his eye, filled with desire and self-discipline, he knew he would excel.
("Caught his eye" is a cliché, and an inapt one at that. See Chapter 8.)
He took to football immediately. With desire and self-discipline, he knew he would excel.

Correctly Using That, Which *and* Who

It's a bigger problem than grammatical hairsplitting might indicate. Not many discussions veer so closely to grammatical pedantry as a review of *restrictive* and *nonrestrictive* clauses. For this reason, the editors of *The Associated Press Stylebook and Libel Manual* have chosen instead to use the terms *essential* and *nonessential clauses*. This grammatical banter would not be necessary if more writers used *that* or *which* correctly to begin with. But many don't. The problem affects meaning, so it's real.

In its simplest terms, restrictive or essential clauses use *that*, without a comma. Nonrestrictive or nonessential clauses use *which*, with a comma. And either type of clause can use *who*, with the comma rules intact.

In *When Words Collide,* Lauren Kessler and Duncan McDonald use these examples to explain the difference between restrictive and non-restrictive clauses:

> Restrictive: *Construction bonds that are issued by local governments generally carry tax-free interest.* [Only those bonds issued by local governments carry tax-free interest.]
>
> Non-restrictive: *Construction bonds, which can be a dependable tax-shelter, carry different interest rates according to the credit standing of the local government.* [Nothing here implies that only construction bonds can be a dependable tax shelter.]

As we indicated, the *AP Stylebook* editors refrain from using *restrictive* and *nonrestrictive,* but their *essential* and *nonessential* refer to the same things. Here are a some of their examples using *who* instead of *that* or *which*:

> Essential: *Reporters who do not read the stylebook should not criticize their editors.* (… Only one class of reporters, those who do not read the stylebook, should not criticize their editors. [The implication is that other reporters may criticize editors if they want to.])
>
> Nonessential: *Reporters, who do not read the stylebook, should not criticize their editors.* [What a difference a pair of commas makes. Not a single reporter has read the stylebook, so none of these reporters should criticize their editors.]

Now, let's talk about *who* versus *whom.* Strictly speaking, if the word is the subject of the sentence—if it is doing the action or portraying a state of being—it is *who.* If the word is receiving the action, it is *whom*: "*Who* is throwing a baseball at *whom?*" the announcer asked. But in American English, using *whom* can sound awkward, even pompous: "Who do you know?" really should be "Whom do you know?" By that measure, the famous reference books that appear under the title of *Who's Who* should actually be entitled *Who's Whom.*

Suppose you and a friend arrive at a party. You are invited in and, as the door closes behind you, you looked over the crowd, then at each other. "With whom are you acquainted here?" You ask.

No you don't; not if you're an American living in the 21st century. We don't talk that way. Maybe 100 years ago we did, but not since the World War I era has such stuffiness entered the conversation of any but the most pedantic of Americans. What you most likely asked was, "Who do you know here?"

What many Americans do to avoid sounding pompous is replace *who* with *that*. Unfortunately, though, they have forced a choice between pompous and sloppy. Doing so places human beings in the same category as chair legs, as things.

I know it was Jackson that had just been shot.
I know it was Jackson who had just been shot.

A person that excels in academics is not necessarily interested in other areas.
A person who excels in academics is not necessarily interested in other areas.

Writing with Precision

It is true that precise writers avoid being wordy; wordiness does imply the use of extra words. But imprecision implies the use of the wrong word. We talked in Chapter 1 about what an asset the huge English vocabulary can be when the writer is looking for the precise word to convey the precise idea to the reader, nuances intact. And yes, it does work the other way. The best way to appear to be a sloppy thinker is to write and speak without precision.

Think of Mark Twain's quotation at the top of this chapter, comparing the use of almost the right word with getting *lightning bug* and *lightning* mixed up. Then look at each of the following examples. Each is imprecise enough to make the reader wonder what the writer is writing about. On occasion, the reader is simply tempted to respond with a "Huh?" And sometimes, as with the following example, the reader simply laughs.

The house displayed peeling pants and weathered roofs.
The house displayed peeling paint and a weathered roof.

The next example illustrates one of the most misused words in the English language, especially among those who would impress people with their vocabularies.

Most bugs are hideous and make me nauseous.
(The correct word, the precise word, is "nauseated." If you are "nauseous," you make other people feel sick.)
Most bugs look hideous. (Note the change to an action verb. See the next chapter.) They make me nauseated.

Here are some more examples:

He had a chance to run through the various vendors.
(But better judgment overtook him and he kept his sword in its scabbard.)

The father's gait is unusually large.
(Huh?)

A walk down the sidewalk revels large black and gray garbage cans.
(Party on, garbage cans.)
A walk down the sidewalk reveals large black and gray garbage cans.

The proposal would allow residential permit parking on streets with businesses and residences after 8 p.m., and on streets and residences on one side and business on the other after 9 p.m.
(Again, huh?)

People finished all there gossiping.
People finished all their gossiping.

A flock of yellow cabs soar north like vultures looking for passengers late for work.
("A flock of yellow cabs" is apt; not bad imagery. But the reader has a hard time believing they soar.)

A few cars with curious passengers drove past us.
(The cars were driving themselves?)
Curious people drove past us in cars.

With election day upon us, and many Republican incumbents unsure of winning back their congressional seats, Democrats are firm in their plan to undo the George W. Bush administration.

As election day nears, Democrats are trying to increase the uneasiness many Republican congressmen feel about their ability to win back their seats. The Democrats say they are firm in their plan to undo the George W. Bush administration.

There were many nights were I had a lot of work to do.

(I had to look at this sentence a couple of times before I figured out what the writer was trying to say. That's something the reader should not be forced to do. The writer wrote "were" when he meant to write "where." But when you correct that, the sentence just looks sloppy.)

On many nights, I had much work to do.

... a seemingly congruous addition to the area already redolent of elitism and the pursuit of knowledge.

(Huh?)

I was excepted to a few different schools.

(Also, use active voice. See next chapter.)

A few schools accepted me.

He is embarked on himself being first from now on.

(Embarking is something you do to a boat or a ship. Unclear.)

He is not a person who is often taken serious.

He is not a person who is often taken seriously.

There is much more to life then academics.

There is much more to life than academics.

The car suffered minor damage.

(People suffer injuries. Cars usually "sustain" damage.

As new generations are coined, those claimed to be a part of them may feel the urge to rebel.

(How do you coin a generation? In addition, "might," not "may," implies probability. "May" implies permission.)

As new generations grow up, some of their members might feel the urge to rebel.

His ideal predicament would find him employed in the research and de-
   velopment area of the pharmaceutical industry.
(A predicament is a difficult or trying situation. I don't think that's what
   the writer meant.)
The ideal job for him would be to work in pharmaceutical research and
   development.

After Boston, she attended Northwestern University.
(Is Boston no longer with us?)
After she left Boston, she attended Northwestern University.

Fallen leaves adorn the lawn, doctoring it with their beauty.
Fallen leaves decorate the lawn.

In the following example, the problem is not with word precision, but with staying in the same tense.

Not only did he devote himself to music and politics, he has also excelled
   in athletics.
(Also, note the redundancy of "also.")
Not only did he devote himself to music and politics, he excelled in athletics.

You wouldn't think that too many people would get the words
ancestor and *descendant* confused. But apparently many do. James
J. Kilpatrick, writing for the Universal Press Syndicate, found six
articles that brought someone's ancestors back to life.

In Olympia, Washington, a newspaper headline reads, *"Geronimo's
ancestors face a million-dollar question."*
In Columbia, South Carolina: *"Ancestors of Civil War veterans
protested the removal of the Confederate flag from the state capitol."*
("A haunting story," Kilpatrick says.)
In Salmon, Idaho: *"A century after prospectors prowled the mountains looking for gold, their ancestors walk the same trails."*
In St. Augustine, Florida: *"An ancestor of Christopher Columbus
canceled a speech here and returned to Spain."* (Kilpatrick: "And high
time, I'd say.")
In Dearborn, Michigan: *"Founder's ancestor named Ford executive."*
In the dairy industry, making a living can be impossible *"for Ameri-
can farmers 100 years ago"* and *"their ancestors today."*

In another article, Kilpatrick pointed to a story in the *Las Vegas Sun* in which the reporter wrote, "… here is a synthesis of what happened."

"Synthesis?" Kilpatrick asked. "Maybe, to synthesize is to combine various elements into a single entity, but … I suspect the reporter wanted 'synopsis.'"

In the same article, written during the Clinton presidency, the veteran columnist cited a Cox News Service story on a Chicago homecoming by Hillary Rodham Clinton, which said, "Indeed, the first lady was palatably more popular there than is the president."

Kilpatrick again: "Palatably? There are times when Mrs. C. looks like a bonbon, but 'palpably' was the adverb the writer needed."

Or maybe the writer meant to say "patently."

Using Parallel Structures; Making Your Numbers Agree

When you write a sentence that features a series of clauses, make sure they start and end the same way. If you don't, you destroy whatever rhythm you've tried to establish. More important, if you use parallel structures your readers will have a more enjoyable time absorbing and understanding your facts, ideas and concepts.

Look at the following sentence. The writer used the same verb form, present participle, in three clauses but switched to straight present tense in the final clause. The writer also has implied that Peru is in Europe.

Note that the rewritten sentence eliminates all reference to Europe without sacrificing meaning or content.

> *She has spent time in Europe participating in programs to benefit people in need, which included working with Albanian refugees, working in Peru as part of a community development program and in Greece, where she studies anthropology.*
>
> She has spent time working with refugees in Albania, taking part in community development in Peru and studying archaeology in Greece.

Sometimes it's a subject switch that confuses the reader. In this series of commands, the subject, "you," is implied, but then it is replaced:

Take 12 paces to the north, take 20 paces to the east, dig a four-foot hole and the treasure will be there waiting for you.

Walk north 12 paces, go east 20 paces, dig a four-foot hole and discover the treasure.

If you can't seem to find a lede that works, sit back, take a deep breath and the lede will come to you.

If you can't seem to find a lede that works, sit back, take a deep breath and let the lede come to you.

News people cite something they call "the rule of threes" to explain how best to communicate with the reader. The writer or a news source makes an assertion, then backs it up with three examples. Not *two;* it sounds funny. Not *four;* it sounds funny. *Three.* For some reason either mystical or deeply psychological, three works well. The same appears to be the case with parallel structures. They are most powerful and persuasive when they come in threes.

When you read your copy aloud, you make sure your rhythms are right, your words are necessary and your sentences are direct.

First, look up the police records; second, pick out those that appear newsworthy; third, set up interviews to flesh out possible stories.

Driving through New York City can be frustrating, frightening—and thrilling.

Agreement of a different sort becomes an issue when writers try to match singular nouns with plural pronouns or vice versa. Take an example supplied by Lauren Kessler and Duncan McDonald in *When Words Collide:* "One of the biggest problems in grammar are maintaining harmony among sentence elements." *One* is singular; *are* is plural. They correct the sentence to read: "One of the biggest problems in grammar *is* maintaining harmony among sentence elements."

As obvious as this problem appears to be, it seems to have taken over American speech and writing patterns. The problem only gets more subtle when the subject of the sentence is followed by a prepositional phrase:

The group of students spent their second week on an educational excursion to the Sea Islands off the coast of Georgia.

The sentence seems OK; after all, *students* is plural, so is *their*. But *students* isn't what *their* is referring to. The real subject of the sentence is *group*. It is followed by the prepositional phrase of *students*, which is acting not as the subject, but as a modifier of the subject. A group? What kind of group? A group *of students*.

Now let's make the sentence grammatically correct.

The group of students spent its second week on an educational excursion to the Sea Islands off the coast of Georgia.

All right, it's grammatically correct, but it sounds strange. Where once you had several students sailing off the coast, now you have a clump, an *it*. I don't think students like to come in clumps any more than anyone else does.

Aha. We have found a solution. Why not change the subject?

Several students spent their second week on an educational excursion to the Sea Islands off the coast of Georgia.

But have we changed the meaning? Have we left something out? *A group of students* implies that the students were members of something: a class, an assembly, a team. Now we have some students who might have come together only by chance.

Well, as far as I'm concerned, all we've succeeded in doing now is prove that a grammarian can split hairs that would send a lawyer screaming. The answer to whether or not the students have become part of a greater whole is most likely covered somewhere else in the story anyway.

As we shall see, however, making words agree in number can create problems elsewhere.

Sexist Language versus Good English

One excuse for violating the agreement-in-number rule is that you must to avoid committing sexism in your writing. For example:

A student can spend his week on an educational excursion to the Sea Islands off the coast of Georgia.

But here we can apply the most universal antidote to sexist language, *pluralization.*

Students can spend their week on an educational excursion to the Sea Islands off the coast of Georgia.

Why is sexism apparently such a problem? For nearly 200 years, Americans have acquired the habit of taking a noun representing a person or a number of persons, and referring to that noun with the pronoun *he, him* or *his.*

Everyone in school knows when it's his time to deliver his senior thesis.

Each manager in the bank knows what he has to do in case of a robbery.

He who laughs last laughs loudest.

Sentences like these reinforce the stereotype that women have been relegated to the positions they once were forced to occupy, like teacher, librarian, nurse or airline stewardess (now flight attendant). And those occupations seemed to automatically attract the pronouns *she, her* or *hers.*

After a while, it became apparent that the use of sexist language was helping to keep women from high-level positions in business like supervisor, manager or executive and keeping them from professional jobs like physician, lawyer or engineer. Today, more women have entered all these positions, but the use of sexist language has tended to retard the willingness of people to hire them.

It's pretty easy to change the above sentences to remove the sexism. In the first, you simply eliminate the *his*'s.

Everyone in school knows when it's his time to deliver his senior thesis.
Everyone in school knows when it's time to deliver the senior thesis.

In the second example, get rid of *he has*, and you have not changed the meaning of the sentence at all. In fact, you've improved it.

Each bank manager knows what he has to do in case of a robbery.
Each bank manager knows what to do in case of a robbery.

And in the third example, all you need do is pluralize this old and stale proverb.

He who laughs last laughs loudest.
They who laugh last laugh loudest.

One way to eliminate sexism in old proverbs is to simply ax the *he* without replacing it. Doing so can add a poetic feel to the phrase. One person who long ago apparently thought so was George Norlin, whose name adorns the library of the University of Colorado at Boulder. Beneath the carved letters identifying the Norlin Library is an equally impressively carved "Who knows only his own generation remains always a child."

Unfortunately, old George didn't get rid of the *his,* but he lived in a time when sexist language had not yet become much of an issue. Let's see what we can do with the pronouncement. First, let's try it his way:

Who knows only one's own generation remains always a child.
(One problem: We don't know whether old George would be referring to his generation or somebody else's. Another problem: The use of "one" as a pronoun, although quite acceptable among the British, sounds needlessly stiff in good conversational American English.)

Now let's apply another cure-all for sexist language:

Who knows only his or her own generation remains always a child.
(I don't know about you but, even though I'm forced to use "his or her" or "he or she" or "him or her" once in a while, I would rather spend the time shooting myself with a staple gun. "His or her" does nothing if not stop the reader dead in his or her tracks.)

All right. Now let's pluralize.

They who know only their own generation remain always children.
(Lost some of the poetry, didn't we? Nor do we know if "they" all belong
   to the same generation. If not, we might have to say, "They who know
   their own generations.")

Oh well. I haven't visited Boulder in a while. By now, the administration (I almost wrote *they* instead of *administration*) might
have erased the whole thing. Nice sentiment old George had,
though.

There appear to be times when, because of the peculiarities of
American English, you are forced to use *he or she* or *his or hers* or
him or her—or reverse them if you want—*she or he*. For example:

Everyone had the identical expression on their face.

Here, pluralizing simply doesn't make it, because *everyone* (and
everybody) is treated as a singular pronoun. If you want to see
lovers of the language cringe, just stick *their* into a sentence that
begins with *everyone* or *everybody*. We could use *his or hers* or *her or
his* but the usage would be awkward enough to interrupt the flow
and rhythm that keeps the reader with us. What we cannot do,
not anymore, is use *his* by itself.

So we're left with two choices: *their*, which is bad English, and
his or her, which kills any elegant usage of the language. Other
countries don't seem to have this problem. It seems to be acutely
American.

The British, for example, have an easier time pluralizing (or
as they would write, pluralising) than we do. The reason is that
they treat collective nouns as inherent plurals. We might find it
awkward to say, "The government has come out foursquare in favor of motherhood" because what we really mean is "the people
in the government." The British, however, would say, "The government have come out foursquare in favor of motherhood and
they say they will continue to do so"; it's already understood that
the government is—excuse me, the government *are*—made up
of a bunch of people who, apparently in this case, all agree. Sim-
ilarly, a corporation takes the verb are and the pronoun *they*. In

the United States, such constructions would be considered poor English.

Like Americans, British do treat *everyone* and *everybody* as singular pronouns, but maybe because of the way they treat collective nouns, *everyone ... are ... they* doesn't sound so jarring to them.

Other Germanic and Romance languages don't seem to have a problem with gender specification because their languages are so riddled with gender references already. In Romance languages, nouns take on genders regardless of how manly or ladylike they might appear. In Spanish, the table (*la mesa*) is female even if it is made of the heavy masculine-looking woods for which much Spanish and Hispanic furniture is noted. In French, the table (*le table*) is masculine, as it is in German (*der Tisch*). German includes a neuter gender as well as a male and female, but none seem to carry any psychological weight.

So the restrictions on American English appear to be just that, American. Here, then, the formula has to be this: Pluralize whenever you can, use *he or she* or *him and her* or *his and her* when you must, but do not use sexist language because it is, after all, sexist. (See Chapter 8, toward the end of the "Business Jargon" section.)

Your Antecedents Are Showing: Avoiding Dangling Participles and Misplaced Modifiers

As the section on redundancy demonstrates, it isn't difficult to use the English language in a comical way, but writers usually prefer that they do not become the subject of the laughter.

When writers violate rule 20 in Strunk and White's *The Elements of Style*—"Keep related words together"—they risk falling into the most ludicrous pitfall in the English language. In a complex sentence, if the subject does not closely follow the *antecedent* (the word, phrase or clause that begins the sentence), strange things can happen.

What the writer can end up with is a *dangling participle* (a participle is a word that can function as a verb or an adjective, and it usually ends in *ing*) or some other form of misplaced modifier. Some well-known examples of dangling participles come from Strunk and White, this time as examples of how to violate their rule 11: "A participial phrase at the beginning of a sentence must refer to the grammatical subject."

As I have been known to tell my students, "If you don't understand the humor in these examples, you really are missing a basic point of good English." Here are three famous examples from Strunk and White:

> *Being in a dilapidated [or run-down] condition, I was able to buy the house very cheap.*

> *Wondering irresolutely what to do next, the clock struck twelve.*

> *As a mother of five, with another on the way, my ironing board is always up.*

Here are some examples loosely translated from some of student papers, with a little advice on how to make them come out right.

> *Once defrosted, we add pumpkin to the other ingredients.*
> (We couldn't have done it when we were frozen.)
> Once the pumpkin is defrosted, we add it to the other ingredients.

> *Looking to the left is Sears Tower, tall, shiny, black and powerful-looking.*
> (Sears Tower is looking left?)
> I look to the left, and there stands Sears Tower, tall, shiny, black and powerful-looking.

> *Police said a patrol officer was issuing tickets when he noticed a Jeep Cherokee with Minnesota license plates wanted in a double homicide.*
> (Killer Jeep Cherokee.)
> Police said a patrol officer was issuing tickets when he noticed a Jeep Cherokee with Minnesota license plates, apparently driven by a suspect wanted in a double homicide.

> *Lighting a cigarette, a small prop plane passed overhead.*
> (Good thing it didn't stop to light the cigarette.)

> *Since the age of three soccer has been a favorite hobby.*
> (How old is soccer now?)
> Since he was three, soccer has been his favorite hobby.

After graduating, the editor of the paper offered him a position as a beat reporter.

(Who graduated? By the way, here's a case in which the writer must go into passive voice to be accurate.)

After he graduated, he was offered a position as a police reporter by the editor of the paper.

She could be found on the rugby field, a sport that she has recently picked up.

(The field is a sport?)

She could be found on the rugby field, practicing a sport she had recently picked up.

Occasionally, you hear a car drive by. Could be another bad muffler.

(That is one macho muffler.)

Occasionally you hear a car driving by. Could be another one with a bad muffler.

Admitting that there were many questions concerning the body that would never be answered, the body gives many clues to scientists.

(Is the body capable of confessing anything?)

Many questions about the body will never be answered, but the body does give scientists many clues.

Recovering from her "rematriculation" shyness, her pace of two courses per semester suited her.

(Her pace was shy?)

She was still recovering from the anxiety of returning to school, so the pace of two courses per semester suited her.

She is driving a Chevy Suburban, and she tries to pull in behind us, but since she is so big, she is still sticking into traffic.

(So who's going to tell her not to stick out in traffic?)

She is driving a Chevy Suburban, and she tries to pull in behind us, but since the van is so big, it is still sticking out in traffic.

The following misplaced modifiers come from a Northwestern University law professor, Steven Lubet, who collects misplaced modifiers as some people collect Elvis memorabilia.

The late astronomer Carl Sagan *began researching the origins of life in the 1960s.*

Sen. Richard Durbin (D-Ill.) *pledged to work for increased gun control in his campaign.*

Lubet notes that a foundation advertises that it has been "working to make economics understandable for 50 years." He says he'd be happy "if someone would make economics understandable for half an hour."

Another list of misplaced modifiers comes from *The Suspended Sentence* by Roscoe Born:

From Fortune magazine: *Hewlett-Packard has just introduced a $4,995 personal computer for engineers with a nine-inch electro-luminescent screen.*

From the Los Angeles Times: *In 1935 he joined the embryonic Basie Group and remained with what many consider the greatest jazz organization until 1948.*

From the Boston Globe: *As lead singer Paul Redman pranced on the stage, a woman, perhaps 70, smiled and watched, her hair drawn back in a tight bun and dressed in a widow's black.*

From the Detroit News: *Feikens is to make a final decision on how the contractors, Vista and Michigan Disposal Inc., can continue to haul Detroit sludge in a meeting next Monday with their lawyers.*

Writing Directly, without Apology: Avoiding Tiptoe (or Weasel) Words

As the pompous writer loses the trust of the reader, so too does the subservient reader. If writers can't or won't communicate with readers at eye level, one human being to another human being, they risk losing those readers.

Pomposity turns off readers for obvious reasons. Few people like to be preached at, or told they aren't as good or as erudite as the writer. The writer who is subservient to the reader sends a message that is more subtle, but no less damaging. That message says, "I am afraid to be honest with you, so I'm going to sort of tiptoe." Sometimes the writer has no choice, and words like *sort of* accurately describe a degree of similarity, but not often. The honest writer writes directly to the reader, without apology.

We'll talk more about honesty—and the appearance of honesty—in Chapter 7. But here are some examples of how not to use tiptoe words, or weasel words:

Teachers need to be motivated to teach a little better than they are doing.
Teachers need to be encouraged to teach better.
Or
Teachers need a reason to teach better.

The wind came from the North. It almost seemed to dance through the tree branches.
The North wind danced through the tree branches.

The lawn mower seems to have created its own sculpture with its uneven movements.
(Note the misplaced modifier. According to the writer, the sculpture is moving.)
The mower's uneven movements have created their own sculpture.

Compared with her neighbors, she is relatively new to the West.
Compared with her neighbors, she is new to the West.

The National Weather Service predicts showers around 100 percent likely on Friday.
(I guess bettors of sure things wouldn't want to risk their money on something that was "around" 100 percent. By the way, "around" is a geographic term. If a word is necessary to measure a quantity, "about" works better.)
The National Weather Service says it is 100 percent sure Friday will bring showers.

She says she is a little nervous.
(Just "nervous" will do, unless "a little nervous" is a direct quote.)
She says she is nervous.

She kind of shelved some of the hopes she had.
(Did she or didn't she?)
She shelved some of her hopes.

Other tiptoe words: *aspect, area, numerous, probably,* plus cute versions of "a little"—a *tad,* a *skosh,* a *hair,* a *wee bit.*

Replenishing the Word Supply

As we noted in Chapter 1, the huge vocabulary that English carries can be the language's curse, because it gives pompous, dishonest or sloppy writers so much opportunity to misuse it. But if you have the opposite problem—your vocabulary runs toward lean—then work to strengthen it, don't feel alone. Here are some examples of imprecision collected by instructors I know:

> *And Jesus healed the leopards.*
> *The governors kept the king on his thrown.*
> *Fans pay exuberant sums of money to watch NBA games.*
> *The hurricane reeked haddock.*
> *He was at her every beckon call.*
> *… the trill of victory*
> *Only your tows are touching the mat.*
> *A woman may choose abortion if she finds out that the baby she's carry-*
> *   ing has a genital defect.*
> *Many pro-life supporters believe that life begins at contraception.*
> *The strict dress code was the one stat chute he didn't regularly abide by.*
> *   Often dawning the torn slacks and wrinkly undone cotton dress shirt,*
> *   he appeared to be dressed in the fashion of characters in Oliver Twist.*

You can indeed do something to improve your practical vocabulary. Develop a meaningful relationship with a dictionary and place a copy of *Roget's Thesaurus* within reach of your keyboard.

I would add an additional piece of advice. Get in the habit of working crossword puzzles. Start with easy ones. Solving crossword puzzles isn't an efficient way to add to your vocabulary— among the words you learn will be dozens you'll never use—but it will make you more skillful in coming up with the right word on demand. And as many copy editors will tell you, crossword puzzles provide excellent language calisthenics.

We'll be doing some more fine-tuning of deathless prose in Chapter 9. In the next chapter, however, we'll deal with two special ways of writing with strength, economy, clarity and integrity: the use of active voice and action verbs.

Exercises

A. Wordiness. Edit or rewrite these sentences to eliminate un-needed words.

1. The ice has melted and the water has taken on the kind of bright blue color that is more likely to be seen in the South Pacific.
2. We are starting to approach the library, which I notice is quite a large building.
3. We can see that whether or not you feel like adding salt to the pot of soup, the salinity level will be more than we need to establish that sodium poisoning can be a possibility.
4. She made the decision to vote in favor of the liquidation of the corporation.
5. She is in fact interested in the broadcast media; this idea came about by a stray remark made by one of her high school teachers. She felt high school was "definitely" a place that this all started when the teacher said, "You have the nicest voice I've ever heard."
6. He has often been giving reviews of movies.
7. He does not believe that many people think that language skills are of much value.
8. I would like to call your attention to the fact that, in spite of the fact that this mountain highway is curving, your car is in the process of going straight.

Sometimes wordiness and redundancy amount to the same thing. Here are a couple of examples for you to edit or rewrite:

9. They are considering San Antonio as a possible home for the future.
10. Dr. Malone is currently at the hospital, where he is engaged in the delicate surgery involved in removing a patient's tonsils.

B. Misplaced modifiers. See if you can straighten out these sentences and place the modifiers where they belong.

1. Lighting a cigarette, a small prop plane passed overhead.
2. Two people, including a 15-year-old boy who was in critical condition, were shot as they walked along an Atlanta street Thursday.

3. Turning the corner, the jackhammer grew louder and louder until we were hit by a shattering crescendo.

4. Single, no children, age 28 is thinking of children at a later time in her life.

5. Since 1927, it's been illegal in Maryland to shoot waterfowl under the influence of drugs or alcohol. (Source: the Chesapeake Bay Maritime Museum, St. Michael's, Md.)

6. Once defrosted, we add pumpkin to the other ingredients.

7. The late Carl Sagan began researching the origins of life in the 1960s.

8. While touring the Louvre, the paintings of several French impressionists came into his view.

9. U.S. Sen. Mitch McConnell (R-Ky.) pledged to fight campaign finance reform during his campaign.

10. In 1935, he joined the embryonic Basie group and remained with what many consider the greatest jazz organization until 1948.

C. Redundancies. Edit or rewrite these sentences or phrases to eliminate redundancy.

1. Some of these projects include:

2. The Defense Department spokeswoman said the Army is not sure at this stage how it will integrate the new tank program.

3. She lived overseas for five years and crisscrossed Europe and Asia as well.

4. She says she hopes to eventually own her own magazine in the future.

5. Walking by the alley, he got the unpleasant smell of garbage.

6. He has obtained both a bachelor's degree at Pepperdine University as well as an MBA at the University of Michigan Graduate School of Business.

7. He grew up in Salt Lake City throughout his lifetime.

8. A circuit court judge set a $900,0000 bond Wednesday for an 18-year-old man charged with killing two men dead and wounding another.

9. In addition, he also edits the sports pages.

10. Not only is the play still showing in London, it is also on tour around the United States.

Suggested Rewrites or Edits

A. Wordiness

1. The ice has melted and the water has taken on a bright blue more likely to be seen in the South Pacific.

2. We approach the library, a large building.

Or

We approach the imposing library.

3. Your soup already has enough salt to induce sodium poisoning.

4. She decided to vote to liquidate the corporation.

(*Note: "She voted to liquidate" would change the meaning.*)

5. She says her interest in the media began in high school when a teacher made a stray remark: "You have the nicest voice I've ever heard."

6. He often reviews movies.

7. He believes most people place no value on language skills.

8. This mountain highway is curving but your car is going straight.

Or

Watch out for that curve!

Or

Stop!

9. They might move to San Antonio.

10. Dr. Malone is at the hospital removing a patient's tonsils.

Or

Dr. Malone is at the hospital performing a tonsillectomy.

(*Note: "At the hospital" is not redundant. Dr. Malone could perform the operation at a clinic or a M*A*S*H unit.*)

B. Misplaced modifiers

1. As she lit a cigarette, a small prop plane passed overhead.

(*Note: Since the exercise taker doesn't know who lit the cigarette, any personal pronoun will do.*)

2. Two people were shot as they walked along an Atlanta street Thursday night. One of them, a 15-year-old boy, is reported in critical condition.

3. Around the corner, the jackhammer grew louder until it reached a shattering crescendo.

4. She is single, 28, and someday she might want children.

5. Since 1927, it's been illegal for anyone under the influence of drugs or alcohol in Maryland to shoot waterfowl.

6. Once the pumpkin is defrosted, we add it to the other ingredients.

7. During the 1960s, Carl Sagan began researching the origins of life.

8. As he toured the Louvre, he saw the paintings of several French impressionists.

9. During his campaign, U.S. Sen. Mitch McConnell (R-Ky.) pledged to fight campaign finance reform.

10. In 1935 he joined the embryonic Basie group and remained with it until 1948. Many consider the group the greatest jazz organization.

C. Redundancies

1. These projects include:

2. The Defense Department spokeswoman said the Army is not sure how it will integrate the new tank program.

(*Note: Avoid the temptation to write "not yet sure." That assumes the Army will someday figure out how it will integrate the program and, even though that is likely, the reporter's job is not to assume.*)

3. She lived in Europe five years and crisscrossed Europe and Asia.

4. She says she wants to own a magazine.

5. As he walked by the alley, he smelled garbage.

6. He earned a bachelor's degree at Pepperdine University and an MBA at the University of Michigan Graduate School of Business.

(*Note: Most readers should know that "MBA" stands for Master's of Business Administration.*)

7. He has lived all his life in Salt Lake City.

8. A circuit court judge set a $900,000 bond Wednesday for an 18-year-old man charged with killing two men and wounding another.

9. In addition, he edits the sports pages.

Or

He also edits the sports pages.

10. Not only is the play still showing in London, it is on tour in the United States.

The voice of the people is the voice of God [Vox
populi vox dei.]
—Alcuin, *Letter to Charlemagne*

God is a verb.
—R. Buckminster Fuller, *No More Secondhand God*

6 Active Voice,
Action Verbs

The use of active voice in English might well be
the least understood element that most people think they understand. Students understand even less when they get the use of active voice confused with the use of action verbs. And many do.
I've even known editors who can't keep them straight.

Fact is, they aren't even related. They just sound as if they are.
A sentence written in active voice can include a "being" verb.

Assam is an Indian state.

And a sentence written in passive voice can include an action
verb.

Nicholas O'Herlihy was named after his maternal grandfather, a Russian.

Active voice and action verbs do have one thing in common.
They contribute to strong, honest, direct writing.

Active Voice versus Passive Voice

If the subject of a sentence creates the action, the sentence is
in active voice. Active voice is the exact opposite of the sentence-

wrecker known as passive voice. Here's an example of active voice:

The train struck the truck.

The train is the subject of the sentence. The train is doing the action. Therefore, the sentence is in active voice. Here's the same sentence in passive voice:

The truck was struck by the train.

Now the subject has switched roles. No longer is it creating the action. The truck has become the subject, but it is not doing the action. It's receiving the action. That's passive voice.

Notice that passive voice has forced the addition of a verb, *was*, and a preposition, *by.* Together they have made the sentence longer, 40 percent longer. This is not an unusual result of passive voice, and it is one reason good writers avoid passive voice when they can. But at least two other reasons exist for using active voice.

Take a convoluted sentence that seems to start off in several directions and ends up going nowhere. Now, take a close look at it. Chances are, the writer began writing the sentence in passive voice. Few other forms of sloppy writing produce such muddiness.

> *Working on newspapers even allowed him to open up other opportunities, such as being a reporter nominated by his teacher for a news company to the Republican National Convention the year it was held in Philadelphia, where he has grown up.*

This sentence does begin in active voice, but it falters in the second clause. Try it this way:

> *Working on newspapers allowed him other opportunities. A teacher nominated him to report the Philadelphia Republican National Convention for a news organization.* (Here it would have been helpful if we knew which news organization, or even which news medium.) *Philadelphia was where he grew up.*

Another reason to use active voice is that it is more honest. It takes responsibility. Passive voice is a way to avoid responsibility.

At least two recent U.S. presidents—Ronald Reagan, a Republican, and Bill Clinton, a Democrat—have used the identical phrase in passive voice in an attempt to deflect criticism and embarrassment and to avoid responsibility:

Mistakes were made.

What it means is, "It wasn't my fault. I didn't do it. Some other [unnamed] official in my administration did it."

Lauren Kessler and Duncan McDonald offer two situations in which passive voice must be used. First, passive voice is justified if the receiver of the action is more important than the creator of the action. They use this example:

A priceless Rembrandt painting was stolen from the Metropolitan Museum of Art yesterday by three men posing as janitors.

In this case, the Rembrandt should remain the subject of the sentence even though it receives the action. The painting obviously is more important—more newsworthy—than the three men who stole it.

Kessler and McDonald's second reason for using passive voice is if the writer has no choice. That's when the writer does not know who or what the actor, the creator of the action, is. The example they use:

The cargo was damaged during the trans-Atlantic flight.

Air turbulence? Sabotage? Was the cargo strapped in properly? The writer doesn't know, so the voice must be passive.

One final, note, a specialized one: When you're reporting a police or court event during which someone is charged with a misdemeanor or felony, you usually must deliver the word *charged* in passive voice. It is possible to say police charged a woman with murder, but it usually is not accurate, because it isn't the police who are doing the charging. Charging is a process that involves prosecutors—in the United States, district attorneys or state's attorneys or their assistants. Since the journalist most often does not know exactly who is doing the charging, it is considered proper to say, "The woman was charged with first-degree murder"—even though the sentence is in passive voice.

Use Active Voice

Yes, active voice is direct, active voice is honest, active voice is economical. But mostly, active voice is considerate of readers, of their limited amount of time and of their need for clear, concise information. Passive voice is one reason many people swear off how-to books on computing, carpentry or cooking.

> *First, a pair of chopsticks is placed on top of a pot of water. Then, the asparagus is put inside a wicker basket and the basket is placed on top of the chopsticks. The water is brought to a boil, and the asparagus is steamed for no more than 10 minutes, so a slight crunchiness is retained.*

It seems to take so long to get it out. But when you turn these instructions into commands, using active voice, they become much more crisp and clear. The writer addresses the reader directly, with "you" implied.

> *Place a pair of chopsticks on top of a pot of water. Put the asparagus inside a wicker basket and place the basket on top of the chopsticks. Bring the water to a boil and steam the asparagus for no more than 10 minutes, so it retains a slight crunchiness.*

Here are some more examples of how active voice creates clarity:

> *After my clothes were on, I drove to the firehouse.*
> After I put my clothes on, I drove to the firehouse.

> *State lotteries are used to fund education.*
> State lotteries support education.

> *When examined in independent university studies with other leading cellular industry products, its high-efficiency design has been scientifically proven to reduce dropped calls and failed call attempts.*
> Independent university researchers compared it with other leading cellular products. They proved that its efficient design reduced dropped calls and failed call attempts.

You're driving to work, and it is announced on the radio that the com-
  pany you work for is completely breaking apart.
("Completely" is redundant. See Chapter 5.)
You're driving to work, and the radio news reporter announces that the
  company you work for is breaking apart.

Nothing but his heavy breathing can be heard by him, and only the dis-
  tant oaks can be seen in the darkness.
He can hear nothing but his heavy breathing and he can see only the distant oaks in the darkness.

The previous summer was spent by him at Mobil Corp.
He spent the previous summer at Mobil Corp.

Each week a different musical theme would be supported for a different
  cosmetic brand.
Each week a new musical theme would support a different cosmetic brand.

Passive voice not only robs sentences of clarity and economy, it
buries the subject of the sentence. The reader finds it difficult to
learn who or what is doing the action. It's the writer's job to make
sure the subject is obvious.

By using chemicals and preserving the corpse at low temperatures, the
  necessary tests were conducted.
Pathologists preserved the corpse at low temperatures and used chemicals
  to conduct the necessary tests.

Big words often are used to impress readers.
Writers often use big words to impress readers.

He was called into his supervisor's office.
His supervisor called him into her office.

Action Verbs and Imagery

In Chapters 1 and 3, we made a case for avoiding pomposity
in writing; sneer at your readers and they will make a point of

not reading what you wrote. Well, one super way to write pompously is to drain the energy of your sentences with being verbs, like this:

> *I am hopeful that that solution to your predicament will be an effective resolution.*

What is this writer trying to say? The sentence was in trouble before it appeared on the screen. Look at it. It starts with a being verb and a latinized adjective: *am hopeful.* The writer could easily have replaced it with the action verb *hope.* Then we have *that that.* Grammatically it's all right, but it's awkward. Then we read "will be an effective resolution"—What's that doing there? The writer can say write the sentence much more clearly this way:

> *I hope that solves your problem.*

Technically, action verbs and their opposites, being verbs, don't exist. What writers informally call action verbs, grammarians divide into two categories: *transitive verbs,* which move the action from the subject to the object, and *intransitive verbs,* which sound active but have no object.

Transitive: *He drove the car.*
Intransitive: *He swam.*

And what writers informally call being verbs, grammarians call *linking verbs,* because they link the subject with the object to describe a state of being.

> *You are beautiful.*

Although it isn't a bad idea to become familiar with the nuances of transitive, intransitive and linking verbs, it is enough for the practical writer to know that action verbs do things, but being verbs simply are. Since action verbs add energy to sentences and being verbs often sap sentences of energy, good writers prefer action verbs—transitive or intransitive.

Being Verbs

Being verbs are, or they were or they have been. But they simply won't do. Here's an example:

> *Major League Baseball was the first sports organization to institute the concept of free agency for its players.*
> (This sentence is also wordy.)
> Major League Baseball created free agency first.

Action verbs serve no greater service to English than when they replace a noun that just sits there as the reflection of the subject and the beneficiary of a being verb. (Grammarians call such nouns *predicate nominatives.*) Here, the verb *edits* takes the place of the predicate nominative *the editor.* In the process, the writer has extracted another freeloader, the preposition *of.*

> *He is the editor of two magazines.*
> He edits two magazines.

In the next example, "said they are satisfied" has replaced "expressed satisfaction." Granted, we've added two words, but now the sentence is more direct, and it allows a little paring later on.

> *Officials of the Air Line Pilots Association and United Airlines expressed satisfaction Friday with an almost unanimous vote by pilots in favor of a four-year wage agreement.*
> Officials of the Air Line Pilots Association and United Airlines said Friday they are satisfied by the pilots' near-unanimous vote for a four-year wage agreement.

> *She is a self-proclaimed renaissance woman.*
> She calls herself a renaissance woman.

> *Every year, there is a race along the Inca trail.*
> Every year, a race takes place along the Inca Trail. (See "Special Red Flags" in Chapter 9.)

> *She is still in need of instruction and practice.*
> She still needs instruction and practice.

The next example obviously has much going against it, and the use of an action verb won't solve the whole problem. But an action verb, *cite*, can start the editing process. Let's pick through it and see if we can make the sentence make sense:

> *Officials with the Attorney Registration and Disciplinary Committee have said similar representations of tax clients in which city officials opposed the city, even indirectly, have been found against legal ethics.*
> Officials of the Attorney Registration and Disciplinary Committee cite similar cases. When lawyers who hold civic office file legal action against the city, they have been found to violate legal ethics—even if their involvement in the lawsuits is indirect.

But wait. Chapters like this one, Chapter 5 and Chapter 9 are by their nature punitive and restrictive. Taken too literally or thoroughly, they can kill the creativity that even a journalist should be able to call on.

One of the 20th-century's great wordsmiths, H.L. Mencken, put it this way in *A Book of Prefaces*:

> To the man with an ear for verbal delicacies—the man who searches painfully for the perfect word, and puts the way of saying a thing above the thing said—there is in writing the constant joy of sudden discovery, of happy accident.

Such a dictum from a man whose fame derived from the way he wrote editorial columns, not unbiased news reports, might provide a quandary for journalists today. It would seem that good journalism dictates that content reigns, that the "thing said" should always outrank the "way of saying it." But we can take some solace from the fact that rarely do the two collide. Any perusal of Pulitzer Prize–winning articles will convince the reader that fairness and good writing need not compete.

Mencken—who admitted he was not a fair person—is simply saying that writers should never get so picky with their content or their prose that they kill the great joy that can come from writing and discovering that they have indeed developed that elusive thing called style. That's what makes the otherwise toilsome job of writing fun.

Few of the arcane rules of journalism are so absolute that they cannot be ignored or broken. If you do break a rule, though, make it a conscious crime; make sure you know why you're doing it. One definition of professional journalists—or professional anythings—is that they know the rules well enough to know when to break them.

Exercises

A. Passive to active voice. Edit or rewrite the following sentences, changing the voice from passive to active:

1. The suspects were arrested by California Highway Patrol officers.
2. The Oscars were provided by the Academy of Motion Pictures Arts and Sciences.
3. The report concluded that perhaps $10 billion a year is added to the economy by immigrants.
4. Labor unions and advocates for the poor say it would be illegal and unfair for welfare recipients to be forced to work for less than the minimum wage.
5. A soul-infused tone was set by the singer for the evening.
6. Penalties against the New York Knicks were upheld Friday by a U.S. district judge, hours before the Knicks faced the sixth game of their National Basketball Association playoff game.
7. The quality of apples in southern Pennsylvania is helped by the state's soil and climate conditions.
8. The threat of war is often used as intimidation.
9. The operation of a commuter airline has been suspended by the Federal Aviation Administration.
10. A drop of more than 100 points was registered by the Dow Jones Industrial Average as the result of a quarter-percent raising of the rate that the Federal Reserve Board charges the nation's banks.

B. Being verbs to action verbs. Edit or rewrite the following sentences and transform the being verbs into action verbs without altering the meaning of the sentences:

1. The president says he is hopeful that the talks will lead to an accord.
2. Privately, officials are doubtful that the two sides will ever get together.
3. He has been a teacher for 14 years.
4. The blood bank is in need of more donations, especially of "O" negative.
5. He is the self-proclaimed first citizen of the new regime.

6. The forest fire was being contained by smokejumpers from the Oglalla Sioux nation who were flown in. (This one needs active voice as well as an action verb.)

7. It is "more than likely" that there was a conspiracy, according to the prosecutor.

8. County officials are in review of the records of a day-care center where a 10-month-old boy died from what they believe was shaken-baby syndrome.

9. The Atlanta Braves are in anticipation of winning another National League championship, but their goal is bigger than that.

10. Journalists are sworn to say that no matter what goes wrong, it isn't their fault.

Suggested Rewrites or Edits

A. Passive to active voice

1. California Highway Patrol officers arrested the suspects.

2. The Academy of Motion Pictures Arts and Sciences provided the Oscars.

3. The report concluded that immigrants add perhaps $10 billion a year to the economy.

4. Labor unions and advocates for the poor say it would be illegal and unfair to force welfare recipients to work for less than the minimum wage.

5. The singer set a soul-infused tone for the evening.

6. A U.S. district judge upheld penalties against the New York Knicks Friday, hours before the Knicks faced the sixth game of their National Basketball Association playoff game.

7. The soil and climate conditions in southern Pennsylvania help the quality of apples.

8. Countries often threaten war to intimidate other countries.

9. The Federal Aviation Administration has suspended the operation of a commuter airline.

10. The Federal Reserve Board's quarter-percent hike in the rate it charges the nation's banks has caused a 100-point drop in the Dow Jones Industrial Average.

B. Being verbs to action verbs. Edit or rewrite the following sentences and transform the being verbs into action verbs without altering the meaning of the sentences:

1. The president says he hopes the talks will lead to an accord.
2. Privately, officials doubtful the two sides will ever get together.
3. He has taught for 14 years.
4. The blood bank needs more donations, especially of "O" negative.
5. He calls himself the first citizen of the new regime.
6. Smokejumpers from the Oglalla Sioux nation flew in to help contain the forest fire. (This one needs active voice as well as an action verb.)
7. The prosecutor says it is "more than likely" that there was a conspiracy.
8. County officials are reviewing the records of a day-care center where a 10-month-old boy died from what they believe was shaken-baby syndrome.
9. The Atlanta Braves anticipate winning another National League championship, but their goal is bigger than that.
10. Journalists swear that no matter what goes wrong, it isn't their fault.
    Or
    Journalists say no matter what goes wrong, it isn't their fault.

*Beware of false prophets, which come to you in
sheep's clothing, but they are ravening wolves.*
—The New Testament, Matthew 7:15

*The principles of accuracy and fairness stand at the
very heart of journalism.*
—Jay Black, Bob Steele and Ralph Barney,
  Doing Ethics in Journalism

7 An Appearance of Honesty

To many people who are not in the news business—
and to some who are—"journalistic ethics" is an oxymoron, a con-
tradiction in terms. Many of us go after the cheap scoop, especially when we're in pursuit of celebrity melodrama. So readers,
viewers and listeners may be excused if they wonder what reporters give up in exchange for their scoops, and if ethics aren't
at the top of the list of items they give up.

In fact, in the great majority of the mainstream news media,
journalistic ethics do exist, they are spelled out and they are en-
forced. Reporters and editors do lose their jobs if they violate
those ethics. Most good journalists carry a gut-level, regardless-of-
consequences, raw sense of honesty with them. Some carry it to ex-
tremes; people view them as downright rude, and often they are.
(Some manage to be obnoxious without bothering with the un-
derlying honesty that's supposed to be the source of the rudeness.)

It should go without saying that it is important for the reporter
and editor to adopt a strong sense of honesty. But because of a
strange path that logic and reason take, it's even more important
that the writing convey an appearance of honesty. They are not
always the same.

From an ethics point of view, obviously, honesty is more important than the appearance of honesty. But readers, viewers and

listeners have no idea if the writer is honest or not; they can only respond to appearance. So, in that sense, the appearance becomes more important.

What sounds honest sometimes isn't, and history is littered with charlatans who took advantage of people who didn't know the difference. And the charlatans have used clear language—the kind that is encouraged in good writing—to defraud and misguide their followers. Sometimes it isn't even conscious fraud. Many writers and orators don't know the difference themselves, and they have managed to gull themselves along with their followers.

Most recently, such chicanery has found its way into what we call journalism, even though it has not restricted itself to tabloid newspapers or journalism. At its rawest, it is used by supermarket tabloids to trick unsophisticated readers into believing that truth resides in a story about aliens who abducted Britney Spears and invaded Graceland because, as they told O.J. Simpson, Elvis gave them permission. But style can overcome credibility even in the nation's most sophisticated newspapers, and we're not just talking about "attitude" tabloids like the *New York Post*. Even the stately *New York Times* has recently found itself following after the coverage of sensational news by tabloids like the *National Enquirer*, whose "reporters" blanket such stories.

Training people in the art of using language to sound honest is not the same thing as teaching them to be honest. Doing so might be akin to teaching miners how to use explosives, knowing that a few miners might go on to become terrorists. So in that sense, clear, informal, conversational language is a tool, just as explosives are. Honest-sounding words and expressions can be used for good or ill. We know that. But one thing we can be sure of: Pompous, overblown English is a lousy tool for communicating anything, honest or not.

A Passion for Accuracy: Check Facts, Eliminate Typos and Be Specific

More than half a century ago at the City News Bureau of Chicago, a prime training ground for new reporters, a phrase was coined that has since become a newsroom cliché: "If your mother says she loves you, check it out." (Actually, in the interest of accuracy, we must point out that the original version included the words "check on it." Modern usage has replaced the phrase with "check it out.") Most people in the news business take dictums like these quite seriously. Many of us remember instructors—not fondly—who reacted to a single misspelled word by calling it an error of fact and giving a student an F for a whole story. (See "Replenish the Word Supply" in Chapter 5.)

To a professional journalist, few things are more embarrassing than inaccurate copy, and few should be. The key ingredients of accuracy are honesty, specificity and depth of questioning and investigation. The chief opponents of accuracy are dishonesty, exaggeration, overgeneralization and the shallow acceptance of what appears to be factual—most often in pursuit of an unrealistic deadline.

Sometimes inaccurate reports are simply a matter of typographical errors that the computer's spellchecker could not be expected to highlight. For example, one student we know recently referred to a well-known civil rights leader as "Martian Luther King."

Here are some more examples of inaccuracies:

The common cold infects more than 1 billion people a year in the United States.
(Not bad for a country with less than 300 million people.)

Haystacks were a favorite subject of impressionist painter Claude Manet.
(It was Claude Monet. The impressionist with a similar name was Eduoard Manet.)

... Mainz University in Austria.
(Mainz is in Germany.)

In many countries such as Africa, AIDS has become an epidemic.
(If Africa is a country, what continent is it on?)

Gettysburg was the greatest battle ever fought, not only in Virginia, but in the Western Hemisphere.
(Gettysburg is in Pennsylvania.)

Foreign affairs experts call the Cashmere region between India and Pakistan the greatest potential threat to world peace.
(It's the Kashmir.)

The Patriots won the superball.
(Super Bowl)

He has visited several foreign countries, such as Canada, France, Germany and New Mexico.
(If you need help with this one, find a map of the Southwestern United States.)

The New Deal was a populist political and economic plan offered by the administration of Theodore Roosevelt.
(Right family, wrong president. It was Franklin Roosevelt. They were distant cousins.)

A Goodrich blimp flies overhead, advertising Sea World.
(It's the Goodyear Blimp.)

Avoid Generalizations, Assumptions, Pomposity and Overblown Statements

Getting the facts right is only one way to be accurate. To be truly accurate, the presentation of facts must be as concrete as it can be, with as little ambiguity as the writer can squeeze out of the subject. The less specific the subject matter, the more abstract, the more it lends itself to ambiguity.

A political consultant once confided to a reporter that when his colleagues talked with news people they would, as a matter of course, double the estimated size of the crowds that greeted their candidates. Why? Because they knew that skeptical journalists would automatically take their head counts and cut them in half. This particular consultant, however, did not share their enthusiasm.

"That's ridiculous," he said. "What they really should do is not estimate the crowd at 5,000, but go for a specific number, like 4,568. That's more believable, and you guys will accept it."

Moral of the story: Reporters should take their own head count and not rely on political operatives to do their work for them. But the point is still made; the more specific, the more believable. Such is the philosophy that underlies journalistic writing. It shuns the generic and goes for the concrete. Here are some examples that lack the required specificity:

> *He attends Queens University in Ontario, Canada.*
> (Ontario is a province, like a state in the United States. Where in Ontario?)

> *He wrote a freelance story for the local paper.*
> (What's its name?)

> *She began working as a procedure writer for a corporate systems department.*
> (What company? And what, by the way, is a procedure writer?)

> *His basic training was in Texas. Then he was stationed in California.*
> (The writer picked the two most populous states in the union, and both are geographically diverse. Tell the reader where in Texas. Tell the reader where in California.)

> *Tennis players fill the lighted court with activity.*
> ("Activity" is generic. Describe it—with nouns and action verbs, not adjectives and adverbs.)

Be Honest: Avoid Euphemisms

One way to avoid total honesty is to use euphemisms. The *New Webster's Dictionary and Thesaurus of the English Language* defines "euphemism" as "the use of a pleasant, polite or harmless-sounding word or expression to mask harsh, rude or infamous truths."

Journalists are supposed to take pride in avoiding euphemisms, and an inevitable result of that is that journalists are often considered harsh and rude. But it is true that we avoid saying someone "passed away" when what the person did was die. We often find ourselves snickering at those who would be politically correct by referring to the blind as "visually challenged." (I've know some delightful people who cannot see. They call themselves "blind.")

In *The Language of Argument*, Daniel McDonald and Larry W. Burton write about euphemisms, which they call "purr words," as opposed to "snarl words."

For generations, minorities have been insulted with snarl words. They were called *niggers, spicks, broads, queers, fatties, old geezers, retards, gimps,* and so on. To avoid this (and, indeed, to compensate for it), academicians, ethnic voices, and social critics have produced a new vocabulary to discuss minority groups. We now speak of *African-Americans, Hispanics, spokespersons, people of color, alternative life styles, senior citizens, people of size,* and individuals who are *physically challenged or intellectually challenged.*

As a writer, you can expect problems in this area. Of course, you want to use politically correct language where you can. First, because it is the civilized thing to do, and second because there is a broad audience that expects it (as well as a hostile audience that demands it). It's a mistake to offend someone you didn't want to offend.

But don't let political correctness cripple your prose. You still want to write with specific details. You want to sound like a speaking voice. Therefore, you shouldn't write, "At school yesterday, I talked to an African American, a senior citizen, and two people of size. One had a child who is physically challenged." This language calls too much attention to itself, and your reader won't know what you're talking about. You can do better than this.

Political correctness is a worthy goal, but it can be a minefield for writers and persuaders. Walk with care.

(Sexist language is discussed in Chapter 5.)

A fine but fuzzy line exists between being polite and being dishonest. And, as the late S.I. Hayakawa demonstrated in his classic book on semantics, *Language in Thought and Action,* Americans have had a history of keeping the line fuzzy.

Words having to do with anatomy and sex—and words even vaguely suggesting anatomical or sexual matters—have, especially in American culture, remarkably affective connotations. Ladies of the nineteenth century could not bring themselves to say "breast" or "leg"—not even of chicken—so that the terms "white meat" and "dark meat" were substituted. It was thought inelegant to speak of "going to bed," and "to retire" was used instead. In rural America there are many euphemisms for the word "bull"; among them are "he-cow," "cow-critter," "male cow," and "gentleman cow." But Americans are not alone in their delicacy about such matters. When D.H. Lawrence's first novel, The White Peacock (1911), was published, the author was widely and vigorously criticized for having used (in innocuous context) the word "stallion." "Our hearts are warm, our bellies full" was changed to "Our hearts are warm and we are full" in a 1962 presentation of the Rodgers and Hammerstein musical *Carousel* before the British Royal Family.

Hayakawa did find some redeeming social value in verbal taboos, though. He wrote that uttering forbidden words "provides us with a relatively harmless verbal substitute for going berserk and smashing furniture; that is, the words act as a kind of a safety valve in our moments of crisis." (I can say with some authority that Hayakawa obviously never enlisted in the U.S. Navy, where sailors apparently face continual moments of crisis.)

In *Copy Editing for Professionals*, Edmund Rooney and Oliver Witte define euphemism as a "polite expression for an impolite idea." They continue:

> Euphemisms are offenses against plain speech and clear communication, which is why bureaucrats and the politically correct love them.
>
> Only the CIA could make laughable a chilling expression like *terminate with extreme prejudice*. Even *intelligence* is a euphemism for *spying* and perhaps also for *killing*.
>
> When words become polluted, we discard them and move on to pollute new words.
>
> Opposed to war? The United States abolished it a long time ago when the *War* Department was renamed the *Defense* Department. Its mission hasn't changed, but somehow people are more comfortable for what it does. The AP takes a middle position: Don't call it *defense spending*, the stylebook warns; say *military spending*.
>
> Having fouled *Welfare*, we renamed the department *Human Services* and everyone feels good better about giving and receiving *public* assistance.
>
> Perhaps those who have been fired from their jobs would be more accepting if they understood that they participated in corporate *downsizing*. It didn't take long for *downsizing* to acquire a bad name (*down* has an unfavorable connotation), so the term became *rightsizing*.
>
> 1995 marked the year genocide was banished; now it's called *ethnic cleansing*.
>
> Athletes at one university no longer play games; they engage in *athletic competition*, according to mail from the athletic department.
>
> You don't have an obsolete computer; you have a *legacy* computer.

> One of the most common euphemisms in journalism is *passed away* for *died*. The classic retort is, "And what did he pass away of?"

Euphemisms, like clichés, offer clever writers and editors an opportunity for humor, as when one wag described the PC terminology for wholesale firings as a progression from downsizing to rightsizing to capsizing.

Don't Embellish Your Prose with Fudge Marks

Embellishing your copy with **boldface**, <u>underlining</u>, *italics*, ALL CAPS and exclamation points!!! are sure ways to get the reader to doubt your sincerity. Instead of persuading readers that what you have to write is important, you're telling them, "I'm too lazy to come up with the precise word that will communicate the exact idea, concept, opinion or emotion I want to convey, so I'm going to dress my message with words that shout at you." Such usages are akin to going to war in cardboard tanks. It is the way you put words together, not their ornamental embellishments, that determines the strength of your copy.

A more practical reason exists for the journalistic prohibition of two of these devices: underlining and italics. In the days before computers, it was impossible to convey such embellishments in Morse code or, later, on the limited keyboards available on Teletype machines. And even now, they are not available on all typesetting equipment.

Another way to lose your readers is by misusing quotation marks. Quote marks are for quotations, or to highlight terms that the writer is pretty sure the reader is not familiar with. Any other use of quote marks tells the reader that you're trying to be "cute." Or they tell readers that you don't really mean what you're saying. Retailers are especially fond of misusing quote marks. The phrase "We Aim to Please," embellished with quote marks, means we really don't aim to please, but we're just saying that, or we're quoting someone else who is saying that.

Yet another way to persuade readers that you don't know what your talking about is to use some form of et cetera; "etc." or "and so on and so forth" or "and stuff." By adding an appendage of this sort to a list, you're telling the reader, "I can't think of anything more, but I can fool you into thinking I can."

Opinion and Ethics: The Elusiveness of Truth and Objectivity

We journalists often take ourselves too seriously and, when we do, we talk about our mission to communicate the truth and our duty to report with objectivity. Truth, however, is elusive. Because truth deals with conclusions and values, each of us has a different interpretation of what truth is and what it isn't.

It is journalism's job to provide facts, concepts, ideas and emotions—as we sense them—but not conclusions. Conclusions are what the reader, listener or viewer comes to.

Objectivity, which is supposed to be the soul of journalism, simply does not exist. The moment a reporter uses his or her sense of newsworthiness to decide what to keep in a story and what to leave out, objectivity has vanished. What passes for objectivity becomes the reporter taking the job of a tape recorder, methodically taking down what was said and making no effort to check its veracity. Nor does such a "reporter" make any effort to get another point of view.

Better that we, as journalists, pursue attainable goals: accuracy, balance and fairness without bias. That we can do. Not only can we; we must.

There is, however, a place in a newspaper (and sometimes a magazine or a newscast) for honest opinion. In most newspapers, opinion takes three forms. The opinions of the publisher, editor or editorial board become editorials, typically four- or five-paragraph statements of what this newspaper believes. Often on the same page, letters from opinionated readers find their way into print. And opposite the editorial page (on the *op-ed* page) are columns, local and nationally or internationally syndicated, staff-written and freelance, that might or might not agree with the newspaper's own opinions.

But only the most biased or irresponsible publications allow their opinions to slop over into the news pages. In the examples of feature profiles in the next section, even the well-meaning cheerleading is opinion. They don't belong in news copy.

Don't Editorialize unless You Are Writing a Column or Editorial

> *Anyone who has been to the State Driver's License Bureau suspects that this is where the winners of both political parties have deposited loyal supporters who were not qualified to do anything else.*

(Quite an assumption, and in some cases it might be true. But it isn't the reporter's job to make assumptions of any kind. Better that he or she get such a quotation from someone who has just walked out the Driver's License Bureau door; then get someone in the bureau to refute it.)

> *Whether in trading, public relations or marketing, she will do fine. She has youth and perseverance on her side.*

(Seasoned journalists will tell you it's dangerous to predict anything—she could get hit by a truck tomorrow. The folly is compounded in this case by a writer who had just met his subject and could not have known if she will do fine or not.)

> *During the past few months, a gaggle of corporate executives have succeeded in their attempt to encourage the investing public to turn their backs on Wall Street. Today, the machinations of yet another have emerged.*

(First, "gaggle" is a gathering of geese. Although many a corporate executive might have earned the epithet "silly goose," using "gaggle" has convicted them all. And to imply that even the most avaricious of the executives accomplished their nefarious deeds because they wanted to discredit Wall Street is crazy. The slick ones among them count on people believing that the investment community is incapable of wrongdoing. Finally, by using a loaded word like "machinations," the reporter has played judge and jury by convicting the most recent reported wrongdoer. Not the reporter's job.)

However—and this is a big however—don't be afraid to provide some analysis if you're covering a complicated issue. Just be sure, first, that you truly understand the issue and, second, to back your analysis up with assertions from people you've interviewed.

Here's a solid analytical lede from *USA Today*'s Jim Drinkard and Kathy Kiely:

WASHINGTON—Under a withering lobbying campaign that included calls from some of their biggest donors, Senate Democrats on Thursday shelved an attempt to tighten rules on the accounting treatment of stock options.

(Without showing bias, Drinkard and Kiely put two facts together that apparently belonged together. The first was that lobbyists, including big donors, were busy working on Senate Democrats. The second was that the Senate majority party backed off from rules that might restrict the actions of such donors. Notice that the reporters refrained from writing that one caused the other; that's a conclusion they left up to the reader.)

Sometimes editorializing doesn't so much display the writer's opinion as it does assume that all oh-so-cool people—writers and readers alike—think the same. And aren't we clever? The implication here is that anyone who doesn't think this way is obviously of a lower social order.

Hollywood's newest power couple Cruised—or is that Cruzed?—the red carpet at last night's LA premiere of the new World War II romance "Captain Corelli's Mandolin." The erstwhile Mr. Kidman arrived with his gal pal, "Corelli" ingénue Penelope Cruz. The two gleefully embraced and flashed miles of smiles to a wildly cheering crowd. And Cruz's onscreen leading man Nicholas Cage created a stir of his own, meeting up with his rumored new squeeze, Lisa Marie Presley." It's a little weird and kind of unnecessary," said Oscar winner and age buddy James Coburn ("Affliction") of all the love-life hoopla. "But I guess the gossip people and all those magazines just love this kind of stuff."

(The biggest problem here is that the writer doesn't report, she gushes. Cruised and Cruzed? Oh my, we do so enjoy impressing the world with our pun-making. "The erstwhile Mr. Kidman," for those who can't possibly know, refers to Tom Cruise's ex, Nicole Kidman. They "flashed miles of smiles." [See Chapter 8.] And now we have the opportunity to breathlessly gush over two more celebrities, Nicolas Cage and Lisa Marie Presley. At least the writer showed an awareness of the plastic in her own profession with the Coburn quotation.)

Perhaps soon he will realize that it is never too late for an education.

(The "perhaps" automatically turns reporter into speculator. And then what he ends up saying is such a truism that even a rabid supporter of education would have difficulty caring.)

A view on relationships: that they consume you, and tend to take the
focus away from the self. This seems to be contradictory, but really
is not, for only a person attuned to the self can really help others.
(Huh?)

Don't Tell the Reader What to Think; Don't Write Down to the Reader; Don't Draw Conclusions for the Reader

Making judgments and leading with conclusions can have a deadly effect on your writing as well as your reputation for fairness and balance. Citing examples from his generation, Hayakawa wrote that hasty judgments induce a temporary blindness.

> When, for example, a description starts with the words, "He was a real Madison Avenue executive" or "She was a typical hippie," if we continue writing at all, we must make all our later statements consistent with those judgments. The result is that all the individual characteristics of this particular "executive" or this particular "hippie" are lost sight of; and the rest of the account is likely to deal not with observed facts but with stereotypes and the writer's particular notion (based on previously read stories, movies, pictures and so forth) of what "Madison Avenue executives" or "typical hippies" are like. The premature judgment, that is, often prevents us from seeing what is directly in front of us, so that clichés take the place of fresh description.

Here are some more examples of conclusions unnecessarily drawn for readers:

It is clear that while her career has been very challenging, it has also
been extremely demanding.
(Give examples and let the reader decide how challenging and demanding it is.)

American confidence is more than a state of mind; it is a muscle, a west-
ward ho-ing, atom-splitting, moon-landing muscle, and Osama bin
Laden's autumn ambush, designed to break it, seemed only to make it
stronger. The markets reopened within a week after Sept. 11, swooned
and then revived, and even as the fires still burned downtown and the

soldiers headed off to war, more Americans said they believed the country was on the right track back in October than felt that way last week. Is it possible we could do to ourselves what our worst enemies did not manage?

The corporate criminals among us, the swindlers and the profiteers, are now described in language once saved for bin Laden's legions. Business professors are staggered by the suicidal audacity of top executives—did they really think they would not be caught?

(Here, the conclusion begins the story. The reader gets the feeling the writer is trying too hard to come up with an enticing lede. Rhetorical questions help soften the writer's conclusions, but it's obvious what she and her magazine believe.

This sensitive, intuitive, people-person feels that she has a creative side that isn't being fully utilized.

(The writer had not met the interview subject before the interview took place. For all he knew, she kicked the dog when she arrived home at night. He should have quoted her and let the reader decide.)

People become disoriented from their friends due to their preoccupation with their significant others when they should be preoccupied with relationships with friends. It shifts to concern about their significant others' unhappiness as well as their own happiness.

(What does it mean? Here's a case in which the writer's attempt to draw conclusions led only to confusion.)

His education includes a number of noteworthy accomplishments.

(Tell the reader what they are and let the reader decide if they are noteworthy.)

She made the bold decision to quit her job and pursue academics full-time.

(The reader can assume the decision was bold unless she won the lottery first.)

Tragically, her father died when she was 3.

(The reader can figure out that a father's death is tragic.)

There are 12 people playing tennis and, surprisingly, all are male.

(A dozen people are playing tennis. All are male. Why is that surprising?)

Students wander by. They have athletic builds, suggesting a fitness-
   minded generation.
(It also suggests a writer who belabors the obvious.)

The law school has a strange-looking blue piece of artwork in its lobby.
(Describe it in detail and let the reader decide if it's strange.)

She has dabbled in things that few of us would even think of.
("Try me," the reader responds.)

Do Make Sure the Reader Knows What You're Talking About

There comes a point at which many reporters begin speaking
a language that is not shared by the audience. This seems to happen most frequently with reporters who cover beats like the police or politics for a long time. They begin to adopt the language
of the people they are covering, a bureaucratic idiom that makes
sense to them but few others. (See "Using Jargon" in Chapter 8.)
   Here are lede paragraphs from the normally crisply written
Washington Post. You might want to read it over more than once.

The FBI's inquiry into the leak of intercepts related to the Sept. 11 attacks
   began to focus on members of Congress after a government agency told
   the FBI that news reporters had claimed to have received the informa-
   tion from lawmakers, according to sources close to the investigation.
When FBI agents visited one national security agency several weeks ago,
   officials provided detailed accounts of conversations they had had
   with at least two reporters who, officials said, revealed their sources
   to be members of Congress. The government agency, which insisted it
   not be named, gave agents copies of phone records that confirmed the
   date and time of day these conversations took place.

Granted, reporting the doings of two bureaucracies plus some
members of Congress cannot be easy, and the task isn't made any
easier when the reporter is forced to name unnamed sources.
(The *Post* says it adheres to a policy that requires confirmation by
two independent sources before the newspaper will run an un-
named-source story.) But the least the two reporters who wrote

this story could do was to define for poor, ignorant readers what a "leak of intercepts" is.

It isn't until 10 paragraphs later that the terms are explained, sort of:

> *The leaked information, parts of which had been reported in The Washington Times in late September 2001 and then again by other news outlets in mid-June, contained snippets of conversation intercepted by the NSA on Sept. 10 in which people, speaking in Arabic, said "The match is about to begin" and "Tomorrow is zero hour."*

The size of that sentence alone is an indication of the fogginess that permeates this story. Its most serious problem is that it is potentially a compelling story. Somehow it links members of Congress to information that, if translated and processed in time, might have helped prevent the actions of September 11. Yet, the reader is not sure if it's compelling or not, because the reporters did not bother to explain what they were talking about.

Here are some shorter examples by writers who assumed the reader knew what the reader might not know:

> *He is another who exists simply to manage this seemingly unstoppable tsunami of regulations, who was to be fired by Bush.*

(Don't assume the reader's command of the Japanese language includes the word for "tidal wave." Also, the sentence is wordy.)

> *The lawn is cut in a circular moiré pattern.*

(I had to look up "moiré" in the dictionary. And then I found out I was pronouncing it wrong.)

> *He was a bar back at a local bar.*

("Bar back" apparently is an Eastern U.S. regional usage. It means a bartender's assistant.)

> *The press today is often accused of being liberal. He would agree with that assessment.*

(That the press is too liberal? Or that the press is accused of being too liberal?)

*Dreams of summers in Rangoon eating freshly cooked chipmunk and
other various luxuries he will most likely enjoy, as well as a more
concentrated focus on God. Have him and his future further the testament which he placed down doing various actions that define who
he is.*

(I just don't know.)

Quotations and Attributions

One thing that distinguishes journalistic writing from most
other forms of writing is the use of the direct quotation, the word-
for-word repetition of what the subject said. Quotes make the
story appear more honest. They take the onus off the reporter—
"I didn't say it; the subject of my story said it."

As in a research paper, direct quotations can be citations of
written statements, but most often journalistic quotes are spoken.
Journalists use them much more often than other kinds of writers, except maybe those of chatty fiction.

Newspaper writing, which remains at the core of all journalistic writing, has developed certain traditions about how to deal
with quotations or "handle a quote." (Broadcast writing handles
them differently. See Chapter 10.)

Usually, in first reference, use *according to* or *says* or *said*, followed by the name and title of the source. After that, in second
reference, the name comes first, followed by says or *said*. The attribution most often comes at the end of *the* quoted sentence or
at the end of the first quoted sentence in the paragraph. And a
direct quote usually begins a new paragraph.

*The crash was vivid, according to Sam Jones, curator of the Museum of
Demolition Derbies.*
*"The smell of rubber sure was awful," Jones said. "It was even worse
than that time in Talladega when four cars all came together."*

Striving to find a new way to attribute a quotation can make the
writer sound silly. So attributions usually are a prosaic *said* or *says*
(depending on tense), not *cited, stated, averred, opined, noted, enthused, reflected* or *chortled*. If sticking with *says* or *said* sounds monotonous, that's because you're the writer. The reader rarely notices.

He cited that he liked children.
He said he liked children.

She opined that the good old days just aren't what they used to be.
She said the good old days are gone.

"This is going to absolutely be the best time we ever had," she enthused.
(The words she used make it obvious she's enthusiastic. You don't even
    need to emphasize them with an exclamation point.)
"This is going to be the best time we ever had," she said.

Sometimes attributions add a tint of color or bias that the
writer had not intended. In *The News Business,* John Chancellor
and Walter Mears provided two examples:

> Substitute "claimed" for "said" and the verb casts doubt on the state-
> ment being quoted. Substitute "declared" and you may have elevated
> the statement, perhaps more than you intended. "Declared" is overused,
> and should be saved for formal statements and occasions.

Here are more examples of how such words can be misused:

"I went into medicine because I love people," she claimed.
(Using "claimed" makes it sound as if she really went into medicine because
    she liked poking people with needles and listening to them squeal.)

"Good writers all start somewhere," our young writer admits.
(What did he do wrong?)

Exceptions do exist. If a prisoner confesses in court, it is more
precise to use "he *confessed*" or "he *admitted*" than "he *said.*" Back
to Chancellor and Mears:

> Verbs can be character assassins. Unless it is the specific or accurate
> word, don't write that someone admitted, insisted, argued. Those are
> valuable words, but they've got to be kept in their place. Otherwise you
> risk unconsciously slanting the story.

Sometimes writers will try to get around what they think is the
monotony of using *said* by substituting *pointed out.* The problem

is, once you have said, "She pointed out that the whole world agrees with her," you've automatically acknowledged the apparent truth of what she said. She pointed it out, and there it was.

One solution is to change *pointed out* to *pointed to*—now you're simply acknowledging the direction in which she is pointing. Or "She *noted* that …," but that comes mighty close to affirming that she spoke the truth. Better yet, go with *said*. The reader rarely notices.

Yet another rule with attributions: The end quotation mark comes after the final comma, period or question mark.

"The ballot is stronger than the bullet," Lincoln said.

Don't Mind Read: Use Attribution

If an interview subject states an opinion, expresses an emotion or reports a perception of the senses, the quotation, direct or indirect, needs to carry an attribution. Otherwise, the reader can accuse the writer of mind reading—"The subject felt sad?" the reader asks. "How did the reporter know that?"

The reporter was likely to have done one of two things, listened to the subject or reported how the subject looked or acted. But since no apparent reporting took place, the reader is resigned to believe the reporter is mind reading.

She hopes to find a career that would offer her both the financial rewards and personal satisfaction she is looking for.
(How does the writer know what her hopes are? The interview subject must have told her. So the writer needs an attribution.)

She enjoys the occasional trash novel.
She says she enjoys the occasional trash novel.

She finds great fulfillment in her volunteer work.
She says she finds great fulfillment in her volunteer work.

After living in New York City a couple of years, he was concerned about moving to Chicago, a city with substandard cultural offerings.
(Says who?)

Her abundant enthusiasm and thirst for knowledge forces her to move on.
(The writer can report her apparent enthusiasm; that's observable. But
   her thirst for knowledge is a matter of opinion. It must carry an
   attribution.)

Look for the Interesting Quotation

There is no particular reason to make a direct quote from a
mundane informational statement—"I was born in a hospital in
Tacoma, Washington"—but if the quotation has some life to it,
try to get it verbatim. Each of the following examples indicates
what the direct quote might have been.

He likes argumentative, meaningful conversation.
"I like argumentative, meaningful conversation," he said.

Although he has no plans for the future, he hopes to see the world. He
   would also like to attend graduate school, but right now he would just
   like to graduate from college and see where his life goes from there.
(There would be no reason to transform all this into direct quotations, but
   the writer does need to establish that these opinions are those of the
   interview subject, not her own. And it would be nice if one of the sentences was a direct quote.)
Although he says he has no plans for the future, he hopes to see the
   world. "I do hope to see the world someday," he said. "But right now I
   would just like to graduate from college and see where my life goes
   from there."

She has stories about nearly being eaten by a lion and some baboons. She
   is the only person she knows who has been urinated on by a leopard.
"I could tell you stories about how I was nearly eaten by a lion and some
   baboons," she said. "And I'm the only person I know who has been
   urinated on by a leopard."

After Sept. 11, it's been perplexing for him to witness nothing but blind
   patriotism smeared throughout America's media and political bodies.
"Since Sept. 11, it's been perplexing to witness nothing but blind patriotism smeared throughout America's media and political bodies,"
   he said.

She is very athletic and enjoys jogging, even though she recently
sprained her ankle while running in Lincoln Park.

She says she is very athletic. "I enjoy jogging, even though I just
sprained my ankle," she says. "I was running in Lincoln Park when it
happened."

When he was a high school senior, he was fortunate to experience
one of the coolest moments of his life. The event was a tour of
Air Force One.

"When I was a high school senior, I experienced one of the coolest moments of my life, a tour of Air Force One," he said.

He has spent a tremendous amount of time in the scientific and medical
research field.

"I've spent a tremendous amount of time in science and medical research," he said.

Sometimes a quotation is good because it's bad. Many journalists make a point of collecting not-meant-to-be-funny quotes,
holding up as prizes those that come from prominent people.
One such quote, from New York Yankees great Yogi Berra, has
been repeated so often that it has become a cliché. Many people
who say it, and then giggle, have no idea where "It was déjà vu all
over again" came from. Berra also is credited with saying, "You
can observe a lot by watching" and "The game ain't over 'til it's
over." But Berra by no means is alone.

During the infamous 1968 Democratic convention, during
which police went after political activists with little restraint,
Chicago's first Mayor Daley, Richard J. Daley, said this in a fit of
pique: "Get this straight once and for all. The policeman isn't
there to create disorder. The policeman is there to preserve disorder."

Former Vice President Dan Quayle: "We are now ready for any
unforeseen event that may or may not occur."

The late film magnate Samuel Goldwyn: "Anybody who goes to
see a psychiatrist ought to have his head examined."

Former President Gerald Ford: "If Lincoln were alive today,
he'd roll over in his grave."

Keep the Interviewer Out of the Story

The reporter's role as a conduit means most of the time he or she should remain invisible. Sometimes the writer feels the need to report that a response came in reaction to a question. Often, that can be accomplished by beginning with a rhetorical question.

> *When asked how he handles the financial uncertainty of freelance writing, he says, "The first rule is to have a spouse with a steady job."*
> How does he handle the financial uncertainty that is part of freelancing? "The first rule is to have a spouse with a steady job," he says.

Often, however, you don't need any such device; the interview subject's answer implies what the question was.

> *When questioned as to the immediate benefits of such a course, other than increasing his ability to write concisely, he found little or no connection to his current occupation as a sales representative.*
> Except for increasing his ability to write concisely, he said he finds little to connect writing with his occupation, sales.

> *When asked what writer inspired him, he said it was Joseph Conrad. Regarding Conrad, he said, "I am struck by the way he put words together."*
> He said his favorite writer is Joseph Conrad—"I am struck by the way he put words together."

> *On this balmy summer evening, I had the pleasure of interviewing Ms. Miller and I must say I received more than an interview. I received a trip through her childhood to her present state.*
> (Not only did this writer insert herself needlessly into the story, her writing is gratuitous and cloying.)
> Miller looked out at the balmy summer evening and began reciting a trip that began with her childhood and ended with who she is now.

Exercises

A. Find the inaccuracies in the following statements and correct them. (People with a mild awareness of the world should know all of these items. American journalists should have at least a mild awareness of the world around them so they don't commit ludicrous errors of fact.)

1. The ambassador then introduced the speaker of the U.S. Senate.

2. Since it was attacked, the grounds of the New York World Commerce Center have become a shrine to those who lost their lives on Sept. 11, 2001.

3. Hurricanes most frequently cut a swath through a territory that extends from north Texas through Oklahoma and Kansas.

4. In 1997, the 99-year British lease on Taiwan expired and the colony reverted to being a province of China.

5. Theodore Roosevelt was confined to a wheelchair throughout his presidency.

6. President George W. Bush appointed former Maine Sen. George Mitchell to direct the nation's homeland security.

7. In the Galapagos Islands, now a territory of Ecuador, Alfred Russel Wallace began to develop the idea that would lead to the Theory of Evolution.

8. Since the demise of the Soviet Union, Stalingrad has reverted to its original name, St. Petersburg.

9. Despite protests from Utahans, their state has been designated as the place to bury spent nuclear fuels.

10. Several languages have influenced the development of English, but the main three have been Anglo-Saxon or Old English, ancient Greek and Norman French.

11. The Battle of Gettysburg in Virginia is considered the turning point of the U.S. Civil War.

12. Canada is, at least in theory, bilingual. The two primary languages of Canada are English and Spanish.

13. Al-Jazeera, an organization of militant Islamists, claims credit for the Sept. 11 attacks.

14. The stock market was mixed today, as the tech-heavy Dow Jones Industrial Average lost 5 points and the blue chip NASDAQ gained 8 points.

15. President Bush spent the early part of his presidency trying to figure a way to oust his father's most troublesome world leader, Iran's President Saddam Hussein.

16. Only Liverpool, England, could have created the personalities of John Lennon, Paul McCartney, George Harriman and Ringo Starr, who as the Beatles changed popular music forever.

17. The capital of Mexico is Monterrey.

18. The capital of Tennessee is Memphis.

19. Many of Britney Speers' fans are preteen girls.

20. The State of Washington shares borders with two states: Oregon and Montana.

B. Rewrite these statements so they contain no reference to the interviewer or reporter.

1. When asked about strife between the East and West, philosopher Martin Buber said, "The real struggle is not between East and West, or capitalism and communism, but between education and propaganda.

2. I asked poet Carl Sandburg if he thought slang corrupted the language. To my surprise, he answered, "Slang is the language that rolls up its sleeves, spits on its hands and goes to work."

3. When asked what effect language had on him, V.S. Pritchett said, "I am under the spell of language, which has ruled me since I was 10."

4. I asked mystery writer Agatha Christie what compelled her to avoid clichés in her writing. For one thing, she replied, clichés aren't always accurate. As an example, she cited "Necessity is the mother of invention.

"I don't think necessity is the mother of invention," she said. "Invention, in my opinion, arises directly from idleness, possibly also from laziness. To save oneself trouble."

5. When I asked Stevie Wonder what he thought of me, he answered, "You are the sunshine of my life. That's why I always stay around."

Correct Answers and Suggested Rewrites

A. Find the inaccuracies.

1. The ambassador then introduced the speaker of the U.S. House of Representatives.

2. Since it was attacked, the grounds of the New York World Trade Center have become a shrine to those who lost their lives on Sept. 11, 2001.

3. Tornados most frequently cut a swath through a territory that extends from north Texas through Oklahoma and Kansas.

4. In 1997, the 99-year British lease on Hong Kong expired and the colony reverted to being a province of China.

5. Franklin Delano Roosevelt was confined to a wheelchair throughout his presidency.

6. President George W. Bush appointed former Pennsylvania Gov. Tom Ridge to direct the nation's homeland security.

7. In the Galapagos Islands, now a territory of Ecuador, Charles Darwin began to develop the ideas that would lead to the Theory of Evolution. (Wallace introduced the theory about the same time as Darwin, but it was Darwin who visited the Galapagos.)

8. Since the demise of the Soviet Union, Leningrad has reverted to its original name, St. Petersburg.

9. Despite protests from Nevadans, their state has been designated as the place to bury spent nuclear fuel.

10. Several languages have influenced the development of English, but the main three have been Anglo Saxon or Old English, Latin and Norman French.

11. The Battle of Gettysburg in Pennsylvania is considered the turning point of the U.S. Civil War.

12. Canada is, at least in theory, bilingual. The two primary languages of Canada are English and French.

13. Al-Quaeda, an organization of militant Islamists, claims credit for the Sept. 11 attacks.

14. The stock market was mixed today, as the tech-heavy NASDAQ lost 5 points and the Dow Jones Industrial Average gained 8 points.

15. President Bush spent the early part of his presidency trying to figure a way to oust his father's most troublesome world leader, Iraq's President Saddam Hussein.

16. Only Liverpool, England, could have created the personalities of John Lennon, Paul McCartney, George Harrison and Ringo Starr, who as the Beatles changed popular music forever.

17. The capital of Mexico is Mexico City.

18. The capital of Tennessee is Nashville.

19. Many of Britney Spears' fans are preteen girls.

20. The State of Washington shares borders with two states: Oregon and Idaho.

B. Rewrite these statements.

1. "The real struggle is not between East and West, or capitalism and communism," Buber said, "but between education and propaganda."

2. A poet like Carl Sandburg must think that slang corrupts the language. But Sandburg disagrees. "Slang is the language that rolls up its sleeves, spits on its hands and goes to work," he says.

3. "I am under the spell of language, which has ruled me since I was 10," Pritchett said.

4. Christie illustrated her distrust of clichés.

"I don't think necessity is the mother of invention," she said. "Invention, in my opinion, arises directly from idleness, possibly also from laziness. To save oneself trouble."

5. "You are the sunshine of my life," Stevie Wonder sang. "That's why I always stay around."

Hackneyed phrases ... come into the writer's mind as danger signals ... because what he is writing is bad stuff, or it would not need such help.
—Henry Watson Fowler and Francis George Fowler,
  A Dictionary of Modern English Usage

An empty bag cannot stand upright.
—Benjamin Franklin, *Poor Richard's Almanac*
  (Note: Paper bags didn't exist in Franklin's day.)

8 On Being Original

Words get tired. Or people get tired of words and expressions that have lost their meaning because they are worn out. Others were empty of meaning to begin with. When writers, especially journalists, find themselves becoming rhapsodic, searching for that one modifier that is going to send the audience into a swoon, they are approaching danger. Soon any originality will be released into the air.

When William Shakespeare wrote "parting is such sweet sorrow," the words were as fresh as the play from which they came.

When Benjamin Franklin first penned "a penny saved is a penny earned," the phrase must have struck his fellow colonials as the ultimate in pith, innovation and wisdom. It might even have impressed a few British, to whom the language rightfully belonged.

When Winston Churchill coined the term *iron curtain*, the term was lively enough to be used by journalists and politicians across the English-speaking world.

It has been more than half a century since Churchill uttered his words at Westminster College, in Fulton, Missouri, and the iron curtain has gone the way of the Soviet Union. Two and one-half centuries have passed since Franklin created pithy sayings for his *Poor Richard's Almanac,* and most of them have lost their pith. Four hundred years separate us from "Romeo and Juliet," and our parting from many of the tired lines has proved more sweet than sorrowful.

Avoid Empty and Trite Statements

Read the following lede and listen to it with your mind. There's nothing particularly wrong with it, but it represents wasted space. It adds nothing to what most people already know.

> *KANSAS CITY, Mo.—More and more Americans are recognizing the importance of community-level action in order to improve the health and well-being of their communities and countries.*

You can hear the reader saying, "Yeah, so what's the point?" In this case, the point was that 120 national organizations had formed a coalition dedicated to improving the health of communities across the United States. But readers had to get through the empty lede first, and not many could have hung around long enough to learn what the story was about.

So how about reporting what happened?

> *KANSAS CITY, Mo.—Members of 120 national organizations met Monday to try to improve the health and wellbeing of communities across the United States.*

Rhapsodic utterances generally make for poor journalism and most other forms of writing. They haven't made for good writing in general since the Romantic Age of the early- to mid-19th century. Here are some more examples:

> *Nothing is more beautiful than a fall evening in Chicago. Fall is a wonderful time of the year. It indicates the end of summer and the beginning of a new season. Seasons are a part of city living.*
> (Grand revelations, all.)

> *One look into the soulful eyes of a Basset Hound will tell you that dogs are a man or woman's best friend. The noble and loving dog is eternally devoted to you and wants to be with you forever. Even when a dog is scratching him or herself or when he or she is working on*

gnawing at a bone, he or she is always thinking of you, the master or mistress of your earnest and lovable canine companion.
(I love dogs and have owned several Basset Hounds, but prose like this might make me change my mind.)

Our employees are the true professionals who have exhibited dedication and commitment to the highest level of expertise in their respective areas.
(As opposed to the untrue professionals, of course. See "Business Jargon" later in the chapter.)

Clichés: Always a Better Way to Say It

Many writers believe that if a cliché describes what you want to say, then use it—if the cliché fits, wear it. A couple of problems come with that belief, though.

No matter how well the cliché fits, readers, listeners and viewers are likely to have heard it so often that they're tired of it. By blocking it from their minds, they miss its meaning. A second problem results from the perception that the writer has not bothered to find a more original way to communicate the fact, concept, idea, opinion or emotion. The intelligent reader perceives that as a put-down.

Some clichés live long enough that they get recycled. Some of the meaty sayings in the King James Bible seem to be on their way back. For example, during a time when personal sniping, nuisance lawsuits and petty exposés get more and more public, "judge not lest ye be judged" is finding a new audience.

Other clichés make the journey from freshness to triteness in record time.

It was as recently as 2001 that President George W. Bush first used the phrase "axis of evil" to describe Iran, Iraq and North Korea. Now the phrase is often used sarcastically, a good indication that it is developing cliché status.

It hasn't been all that long since it became fashionable for a public official, corporate executive or athletic coach who faced imminent dismissal to say "I have resigned to spend more time with my family."

Not more than 10 years ago, "Think outside the box" was a command to avoid clichés of thought. Now it has become a cliché itself.

The point is, whatever the message—no matter how apt the cliché sounds—there is always a better way to say it. (And this is one of the few times in this book you will see the word *always*.)

Clichés to Avoid

Common clichés include:

*Not only did the taxi driver overcharge her but, **adding insult to injury**, he left her at the wrong address.*

*We try to give you the training you need but, once on the job, it's **sink or swim**.*

*The U.S. soccer team scored 7 minutes into the match, but the goal turned out to **be a drop in the bucket**, and the Mexico team won 5-2.*

*We're behind you **110 percent**.*

*She was **catching some z's**.*

*Finally the astronaut faced **the moment of truth** as she opened the hatch and began her space walk.*

***A chill ran down his spine** as he looked down and saw an underground river 50 feet below.*

*When she met adversity, she just **kept plugging away**.*

*The team that Enron assembled appeared to be the industry's **cream of the crop**.*

He's history.

Rome wasn't built in a day.

Has the cat got your tongue?

The sky's the limit.

You can't teach an old dog new tricks.

The early bird gets the worm.

That's how the cookie crumbles.

Follow your heart.

Rise and shine.

*The ever-delightful **like** at the beginning of each sentence, phrase or clause, often followed by **you know**.*

Revisions or comments accompany these cliches:

*This is no time to **play it safe**.*
This is no time to hold back.

She could not decide if the job's benefits would outweigh its liabilities.
   *Finally, her husband said to **go for it**.*
Finally, her husband said to take a chance.

*Party leaders said it was **a little late in the game** for the president to be*
   changing his position on sanctions against China.
Party leaders said it was too late for the president to change his position
   on sanctions against China.

*He **has a way with words**.*
He is articulate.
(Better yet, quote him and let the reader decide if he's articulate.)

*The new Miss America **has it all**.*
(List her qualities, and let the reader decide.)

*There was an unbelievable **hustle and bustle** along 42nd Street.*
(Describe the activity in detail, with strong nouns, action verbs and a
   minimum of modifiers, including "unbelievable.")

*Our Introduction to Psychology course must **inculcate** into the students*
   the principles of Freud, Jung and Adler.
("Inculcate" is an academic favorite. According to Webster, it means "to
   teach and impress by frequent repetitions or admonitions.")

*… **a typical Joe Blow**.*
(I once knew a man whose last name was Blow, and he was anything but
   typical.)

Where the Fun Never Sets
(A tourism industry favorite.)

Knowledge is power.
(This might be true, but figure out a less-stale way of stating that
   truth.)

Winning isn't everything. It's the only thing.
(Here's a case in which the late Vince Lombardi took a cliché
   and refreshed it, only to have his refreshing line itself become
   a cliché.)

An apple a day keeps the doctor away.
(This is so old it harkens back to a time when physicians routinely made
house calls.)

Don't give up the ship.
(A cliché since the War of 1812, when Captain David Lawrence uttered it
during the Battle of Lake Erie.)

The more things change, the more they remain the same.
(A cliché in two languages. It originated in the French—or maybe
Romans said it first.)

No problem!
(Often offered in reply to "thank you," as a substitute for "your welcome.")

Whoa! (Another cliché that's made it in record time. It means something
like "Wait a minute!" or "I sure didn't expect that.")

Attitude
(As in "He's got attitude"—he's arrogant.)

Sheer can refer to stockings or cliffs, but it's a cliché if you're referring
to a state of mind. If you write ***sheer idiocy, sheer lunacy, sheer folly***
or ***sheer madness***, it's a cliché.

Some clichés make no sense:

*The marathoners have been **drinking water like it's going out of style**.*
(If it was going out of style, stylish marathoners wouldn't touch the stuff.)

*He **could care less**.*
(The cliché should be "he could***n't*** care less.")

Here are some more clichés:

a meaningful relationship
a meltdown situation
a sad state of affairs
ahead of the game
any port in a storm

back on track
busy as a bee
chocoholic or workaholic
dear to your heart
empowerment
flew the coop
full speed ahead
humungous
industrial strength
... or whatever.
runs the gamut
All was not lost.
Avoid clichés like the plague.
Been there, done that.
Give credit where credit is due.
He was at a crossroads in his life.
He's right on target.
I'm outta' here.
Necessity is the mother of invention.
Out of sight, out of mind.
She had her head squarely on her shoulders.
She's losing it.
She was cut out for ...
The answer is yes to all of the above.
There's no stopping him.

Some clichés arise from the fact that a particular modifier almost always precedes the same one or two nouns, prepositional phrases or set of synonyms. For example, *fraught* is almost always followed by *with peril*. The same is true with *one fell swoop. Fell,* in this sense, used to be an adjective that applied to anything that was dread or deadly, but now it is almost never used with any noun except *swoop. Whirlwind* almost always brings with it the nouns *tour* or *campaign.* (See "Journalese" later in the chapter.)

Some clichés, when taken literally, don't even make sense; for example, *viable candidate.* As John Chancellor and Walter Mears put it in *The News Business,* "Taken literally, that means that the candidate has developed sufficiently to live outside the womb."

Another example of these prefabricated clichés can be interpreted as racist, even if the writer didn't mean it that way.

Inscrutable Oriental or *inscrutable* (American) *Indian* refers to an outward stoicism that many Caucasians interpret as a cultural trait. But such labels also can be interpreted as a cultural over-simplification. Further, many Americans whose roots come from the Western Pacific prefer to be called Asian-Americans, and many American Indians prefer to be called Native Americans.

Apprentice Clichés—They'll Soon Be Clichés If They're Not Already

In his book, *The Suspended Sentence*, Roscoe Born asks why we who are so eager to denounce clichés are so apt to keep on using them. He concludes that students make a mental note of the list of clichés they have read, but do not remain on guard to avoid new clichés.

In the first edition of this book, I offered some recent sayings that were rapidly on their way to either becoming clichés or being forgotten completely. During the four years since, some have graduated: *Attitude; been there, done that; industrial strength; I'm outta' here; chocaholic or workaholic; she's losing it; a meltdown situation.*

Others appear to be dying without ever attaining the level of a true cliché: *Get out* or *get out of town* (as in "you don't say," or "you're kidding"); *oh please!* or *puh-leeze!* (in reaction to a suggestion that sounds ludicrous); *chill!* or *chill out!; show me the money; get a life; go figure; wake up and smell the coffee.*

In one special category, which I called "almost anything from the movie *Wayne's World*," *party on* appears to have graduated to a full-blown cliché, but the practicing of adding *not!* to something that sounded positive appears to have died out. But the chances of my being wrong are reasonably high.

Since 1998, some new apprentice clichés have crept into the vocabulary of young men and women. I vouch for none of these, but here are a few recent examples from students and faculty members:

as cool as cancer
I'd rather chew broken glass.
Check yourself before you wreck yourself.

That's so quality.

good stuff (another way of saying "That's so quality")

Sweet! (pronounced "swe-e-e-t"; a synonym, with perhaps more enthusiasm, of "cool")

phat (synonym of "cool")

sick (not a negative; synonym of "cool")

hot (not a negative; "cool")

slammin' (not a negative; "cool")

bangin' (not a negative; "cool")

fly (not a negative; "cool")

blazing (smoking an illegal substance)

bling bling (an adjective apparently describing a rap artist who wears a
great deal of jewelry)

my bad ("my fault" or "my error")

keeping things on the DL or keeping things down low (keeping things
shady or sketchy)

She's so shorty. (She's "hot" or she's "fly"—even if she stands six feet.)

I've been googled. (Men and women have been known to go to the
Google search engine to learn something about someone they're interested in dating.)

That's so gay. (Not a reference to sexual preference. It means "That's so
stupid" or "That's so silly.")

I'm bouncing. (I'm leaving this place.)

Investors are reluctant to *catch the falling knife*. (They don't want to hang
onto stocks during a *bear market*. See "Business Jargon" later in the
chapter.)

She's been *borked*. (Derived from Robert Bork, a Reagan nominee to the
U.S. Supreme Court whose confirmation was turned down by the U.S.
Senate.)

Born offers this warning:

The cliché factory works around the clock. A writer with any
pride—and there are no real writers without it—will brace himself
constantly against some other writer's trick phrase or odd use of a familiar word. A phrase that a writer admires may, indeed be worthy, but
he must resist the temptation to adopt it as his own, first because it
would be a shameless theft, and second because a thousand other imita-
tive writers are sure to do the same. That is the way to avoid clichés.
And the writer who shuns the fashionable will always be in style.

Using Jargon

One sure way to avoid being original is to get caught up in the jargon of the business or profession you're in. As do clichés, jargon provides a comfortable escape for the lazy writer. Just parrot the expressions you hear each day, and you need not waste brainpower and energy thinking up new ways to say things. The trouble is, intelligent readers know flat, jargon-riddled copy when they see it, and they have ways of getting back at you. They have that irritating habit of moving on to something else if the copy doesn't keep their interest.

As we mentioned in the first chapter, jargon does play a legitimate role among colleagues in the same industry or profession. It helps professionals communicate with a great deal of precision, because the originator and consumer of the message both recognize exactly the same definition for each word of jargon. To two physicians, a shinbone is a *tibia.* It simply cannot be defined as a lower leg bone. If they continue calling it a tibia as they make repairs on it, it lessens the chances that they might accidentally be working on the *fibula,* that other lower leg bone, instead.

It's when professionals use jargon on people who aren't among the privileged of the profession that they get in trouble as writers and, generally, as communicators. Nowhere is this more true than in the realm of business, especially big corporate business.

Business Jargon

Big corporations employ many Americans who spend at least half their waking hours behind a desk in a cubicle, so it becomes tempting for them to assume that just about everyone shares their language and their—cliché on the way—corporate culture.

What results if business jargon goes unchecked and travels beyond the corporate door are reports like this one concerning the merger of two broadcast holding companies:

> *The sales are consistent with the station divestiture and portfolio optimization initiatives being undertaken in connection with the formation of the media corporation. At the time of the merger and acquisition agreement were announced, the two companies indicated that they*

would sell stations in markets where the combined entity exceeded
current Federal Communications Commission ownership limits.

Aside from the unnecessary use of passive voice, this paragraph glistens with jargon: "optimization initiatives," "merger and acquisition" (It's usually one or the other; where they come together is usually in the department of a corporate law firm.) and "the entity" or, in this case, the "combined entity."

Comic value aside, it was exactly this kind of language that covered up creative accounting and hid true revenues from stockholders in several corporations during 2002. As we have painfully learned since then, financial reports need to appear transparent so shareholders and bondholders can see how the numbers were put together. And that requires writing that uses as little jargon as possible.

Another way to misuse jargon is with business euphemisms, a term which itself has been used as a euphemism for business lies. By now, we've lived through a couple of decades of corporate writing that first used *downsize* to describe massive layoffs. Then, as downsizing was used to the point that it became a dirty word, corporate writers replaced it with *restructuring*, then *re-engineering*. Both of those terms have legitimate definitions, but neither is an adequate substitute for massive layoffs. True re-engineering is accomplished surgically, with a scalpel; downsizing is done with a meat cleaver.

Then, when restructuring and re-engineering began to acquire an odor brought on by misuse, corporate writers came up with *rationalizing the workforce*, another way of saying—you guessed it—conducting massive layoffs.

Some elements of business jargon are benign, though. Sometimes business jargon is simply a matter of wordiness. For example, "The list of bidders for the project are as follows" can easily be replaced by "Here are the bidders on the project" without changing the meaning at all.

Some additional nuggets of business jargon are:

Enclosed please find ...
She's on the fast track.
the bottom line
as per your request

a sudden downturn
move up the ladder
repropose
state of the art
infrastructure
paradigm
in the event of
corporate meltdown
best-of-breed
window of opportunity
access (as a verb)
dynamic (as a noun)
impact (as a verb)
implement (as a verb)
service (as a verb with an object, usually a customer or an account. "Serve" or "maintain" works much better.)
freefall (a noun describing stock prices in a bear market)
cutting edge or leading edge or bleeding edge (Someone suggested I call this whole section "Cutting Edge Clichés.")
initiate (legitimate, but overused)
scalable (What's wrong with "measurable"?)
turnkey (This usage began as an imaginative way to define an entire working system that came in a single package—all you had to do was turn the figurative key to make it work. But overuse has turned the concept into a cliché.)

The business world and, increasingly, nearly everyone's world, includes the widespread usage of a couple of words that normally are not clichés or jargon. But corporate technology has pushed *system* and *program* to the point that they are, if nothing else, overused.

In addition, here's a usage common in business that should not be used outside of business, but it is—frequently: CEO, or *chief executive officer.* (Since the collapse of so many companies to bad accounting, it seems that everyone knows what CEO stands for.) The CEO can be the chairperson of the board or the president or both. That distinguishes the top executive from the chief operating officer, or COO (who can also be the president); the chief financial officer, or CFO; and the chief information officer, or CIO. But chief executive officer is redundant.

In any publication or medium that does not cater exclusively to a corporate audience, the corporate leader should be simply the *chief executive*. That is, after all, what we call the President of the United States. But I don't see this happening any time soon.

In journalistic copy, by the way, the chairman is not referred to as the chairman of the board or even the board chairman—simply as chairman or chairwoman. "Of the board" is assumed.

Another by-the-way: In the continuing campaign to eliminate sexist language, many writers refer to a chairman or a chairwoman simply as a chair. But I can't imagine that too many shareholders would be happy knowing their company is being run by a piece of furniture. If the board's leader is a woman, call her a chairwoman; if a man, stick with chairman.

Cop and Criminal Lawyer Lingo

Reporters on the police beat and those who cover the courts are notorious for their ability to pick up the bureaucratic jargon of law enforcement. Someone being apprehended no longer is a person, or even a suspect or a defendant. He or she becomes a "subject" or an "individual" or an especially ungainly "citizen." If charged with a violent crime, that person gains the all-purpose tag of "offender." Because they want to observe the rules of fairness, the cops and the courts both modify their suspect's action with *alleged* or *allegedly*, an adjective or adverb that has a particularly sluggish sound to people who like their English crisp and fresh.

Most often, journalists don't need such a modifier at all. All they need do is quote police or prosecutors, directly or indirectly. Instead of writing "Wilson allegedly stole $500 from an Arlington bank," you can simply write "Prosecutors accuse Wilson of stealing $500 from an Arlington bank." If you must use an adjective or adverb, make it *reported* or *reportedly*.

In many police stories, hit-and-run drivers never drive away from the accident site. They *flee the scene* of the accident. But the *scene* of an accident or crime demonstrates a catchall quality that makes all such stories sound generic. Generic is easy. Original it isn't.

These usages appear in the deliberately bland, presumably unbiased report language of the police officer. They find their way into the prose of many young police reporters and, regrettably, that of many veteran journalists who started out on the police beat. Suspects or witnesses seem to lose their humanity when they get referred to as *citizens, subjects* or *individuals. Residents* seems to work better, but not much.

An unknown suspect appears not only guilty but awkward when he or she gets referred to as the *offender* or the *shooter*. For some reason that is beyond me, it seems better to refer to an unknown perpetrator of a violent crime as an *assailant*. (If English always made sense, it would be a science, not a form of expression.)

One common usage turns out to be comical. "The suspect turned himself into New Jersey police" turns out to be quite a feat, especially if the suspect didn't attend a New Jersey police academy first. To avoid this misplaced modifier, try "The suspect surrendered to police" or, to make it clear that the surrender was voluntary, "the suspect surrendered himself to police." It sounds redundant, but it isn't. (See "Your Antecedents Are Showing" in Chapter 5.)

Journalese

Yes, we do it ourselves. The resulting *journalese*, as William Zinsser puts it, is "the death of freshness in anybody's style." And as columnist Paula LaRocque says, we journalists are in no position to complain about someone else's jargon. LaRocque takes her own digs at what she calls *mediaspeak*:

> It's flat and overused and long ago lost any real meaning. We're talking here about verbs such as *spawned, spurred, sparked, fueled* or *targeted*. Or adjectives such as *burgeoning* or *skyrocketing*. Or words and expressions such as *amid, worst-case scenario, level the playing field* and *in the wake of*.

At seminars she conducts across the country, LaRocque offers a long list of examples of journalese. Here are a few—but by no means all—of the words on her list:

strife-torn
witch hunt

heated exchange
chilling effect
a steep decline
beleaguered
resonate
a whirlwind tour
spiraling inflation
firestorm of criticism
escalated
stunning
rising tide
political football

"No," LaRocque says. "Nobody talks this way."

Not to be outdone, Paul Harral, news vice president for the *Star Telegram* of Fort Worth, Texas, offers what he calls a journalist's toolbox for reporters, especially television reporters, who need a quick, handy phrase and don't believe they have time to come up with anything original. The journalist's toolbox first appeared in an Internet chat room called the "downhold," populated by former employees of United Press International. Some examples, accompanied by Harral's comments:

- *Iceberg tips*, as in, "Investigators say the scandal uncovered today is just the tip of the iceberg." A popular item.
- *Sighs of relief.* "New Yorkers breathed a sigh of relief today as Hillary Clinton finally announced she is running for the Senate." This is a handy phrase.
- *Wrong place, wrong time.* "An innocent bystander was shot to death during a gang battle on the West Side tonight. John Jones was in the wrong place at the wrong time."
- *Cudabens.* "Police report 25 people were killed but it could have been worse." A wonderful all-purpose tool.
- The *nightmare* card—often played by the knowing journalist. "A dream vacation turned into a nightmare tonight for the Spinola family."
- *Brutal murder* tags. Very effective in separating brutal murders from sensitive and gentle homicides.
- *Deadly* labels. They modify any event in which there is a death. Deadly accident, deadly shooting.

- *All-purpose closers.*
  - A. This one is suitable for deadly accidents, brutal murders, weddings, tornadoes, hurricanes and the return of a life savings, found on the seat of a bus, to a little old lady: "This day is one they'll never forget."
  - B. This one is heavily used in Washington stories: "One thing's for sure; nothing is certain here."
- *Full-blown investigation.* Larger than a somewhat-blown investigation but of less intensity than an inquisition.

Other former Unipressers (known as downholders because UPI was chronically strapped for funds and editors were constantly asked to downhold their budgets) added these items to subsequent chats:

- *Completely destroyed or, better yet, almost completely destroyed*
- *Mass exodus*
- *"We don't know anything right now, but here's what we know."*
- The drug bust that is inevitably the *biggest* in the history of whatever agency did the busting
- The explosion or tornado that *"sounded just like World War II,"* although that one is obviously going out of style, and somehow "sounded like the Gulf War" hasn't really replaced it.
- Let us not spare those who insist on modifying or qualifying "unique": *sort of, nearly,* even *very*
- *Conducting an ongoing investigation*
- *Most every.* Has *almost* been stricken from the dictionary?
- The victim was shot six times in the back, so *"police suspect foul play."*
- Fires that *gut* buildings, as if the buildings were fish.
- *Perfect* 10. We never hear of anyone scoring an *imperfect* 10.
- *Rescuers are sifting through rubble.*

Trying Too Hard to Be Original Can Hurt You

The following list was emailed to dozens if not thousands of people. It carried the label "No Traceable Attribution." It compiles the efforts of writers who have hurt themselves by trying too hard:

He spoke with the wisdom that can only come from experience, like a guy who went blind because he looked at a solar eclipse without one of those boxes with a pinhole in it and now goes around the country speaking at high schools about the dangers of looking at a solar eclipse without one of those boxes with a pinhole in it.

She caught your eye like one of those pointy hook latches that used to dangle from screen doors and would fly up whenever you banged the door open again.

The little boat gently drifted across the pond exactly the way a bowling ball wouldn't.

McBride fell 12 stories, hitting the pavement like a Hefty bag filled with vegetable soup.

From the attic came an unearthly howl. The whole scene had an eerie, surreal quality, like when you're on vacation in another city and "Jeopardy" comes on at 7 p.m. instead of 7:30 p.m.

Her hair glistened in the rain like nose hairs after a sneeze.

Her eyes were like two brown circles with big black dots in the center.

Her vocabulary was as bad as, like, whatever.

He was as tall as a six-foot, three-inch tree.

The hailstones leaped from the pavement, just like maggots when you fry them in hot grease.

Her date was pleasant enough, but she knew that if her life were a movie, this guy would be buried in the credits as something like "second tall man."

Long separated by cruel fate, the star-crossed lovers race across the grassy field toward each other like two freight trains, one having left Cleveland at 6:36 p.m. traveling at 55 mph, the other from Topeka at 4:19 p.m. at a speed of 35 mph.

The politician was gone but unnoticed, like the period after the Dr. on a Dr. Pepper can.

They lived in a typical suburban neighborhood with picket fences that resembled Nancy Kerrigan's teeth.

John and Mary had never met. They were like two hummingbirds who had also never met.

The thunder was ominous-sounding, much like the sound of a thin sheet of metal being shaken backstage during the storm scene in a play.

The red brick wall was the color of a brick-red Crayola crayon.

His thoughts tumbled in his head, making and breaking alliances like socks in a dryer without Cling Free.

Exercises

Replace the following clichés without altering their meaning.

1. It looks as if Inmate Smith *flew the coop.*
2. The company's success is the result of its ability to *stay ahead of the game.*
3. *There's no stopping him.*
4. After suffering eight losses in a row, the Tigers find themselves in a *meltdown situation.*
5. A corporate spokeswoman said managers are prepared *in the event of a strike.*
6. Acme researchers appear to be at *the leading edge* of their field.
7. The administration hopes the talks will provide some relief for *strife-torn* Afghanistan.
8. It became obvious by the end of the second period that the Mighty Ducks were history.
9. The effects of the flood continue to *resonate* through the river communities.
10. The mayor's staff is trying to deal with *a rising tide* of criticism.

Suggested Rewrites

Replace the following clichés.

1. It looks as if Inmate Smith has escaped.
2. The company's success is the result of its ability to stay ahead of its competitors.
3. He is constantly in motion. He appears unbeatable.
4. The Tigers suffered eight losses in a row. It was becoming obvious that nothing was working for them.
5. A corporate spokeswoman said managers are prepared if a strike occurs.
6. Acme researchers appear to be far ahead of anyone else in their field.

7. The administration hopes the talks will provide some relief for Afghanistan, which has had so little relief until now.

8. It became obvious by the end of the second period that the Mighty Ducks were not going to win this game.

9. The effects of the flood continue to be felt throughout the river communities.

10. The mayor's staff is trying to deal with increasing criticism.

Nature speaks in signals and signs.
—John Greenleaf Whittier, to Charles Sumner

… truth itself does not have the privilege to be employed at every time and in every way; its use … has its circumscriptions and limitations.
—Michel de Montaigne, *Essays to the Reader*

9 Red Flags and Not-evers

Experienced writers and editors work hard to develop mental files of words and expressions that might belong in their copy, but usually don't. It's useful to think of them as red flags. As soon as they appear, they wave themselves in front of the writer, giving the writer the chance to stop and ask, "Is this word necessary? Is there a better way to say this?" The writer should take advantage of that chance, every time.

Some words and expressions simply do not belong in journalistic copy, and it is likely they don't belong in most other forms of writing. These don't need a red flag, they need elimination; these I call *not-evers*. They should never appear unless in a direct quotations.

Red Flag Words: Is This Word Necessary?

More often than not, the red flag words below are not needed. They often contribute to wordiness and sometimes redundancy. Take *located*, for instance.

> *A computer controls the Flexliner from a booth located in the passenger cars at the end of the train.*
> ("Located" plays no role in this sentence. Take it away, and the sentence loses none of its meaning.)

If it's used as a verb, *located* performs a legitimate function but, even then, the Anglo-Saxon verb *found* does a better job. (See "Avoiding Wordiness" in Chapter 5.)

> *Finally, after six attempts during a period of 8 hours and 32 minutes, a helicopter located the shipwreck survivors.*
> Finally, after six attempts during a period of 8 hours and 32 minutes, a helicopter found the shipwreck survivors.

Another red flag word, *extremely*, along with its cousin, *very*, can kill the impact of the words they are modifying. *Very* is so overused that it merits its own disease.

> *He delivered an extremely striking portrayal of Willy Loman in Death of a Salesman.*
> (Better yet, describe the portrayal in some detail, and let the reader decide if it was striking or even extremely striking.)

The *very* disease:

> *The war in Afghanistan is a very unique war.*
> (No degrees of uniqueness exist; something or someone either is or it isn't. If it is, describe how it's different and maybe the reader will reward you by concluding the war is unique. See "Don't Tell the Reader What to Think" in Chapter 7.)

> *That was very awesome.*

> *She is very pregnant.*
> (She either is or she isn't. If you mean she is well-along in her pregnancy, then say so, or say how many months she's been pregnant.)

Using *get* or *got* or *get out* or *got out* usually does nothing more than give the writer an excuse to be wordy.

> *The Environmental Protection Agency plans to spend $22 million to get the hazardous wastes out of the site.*
> The Environmental Protection Agency plans to spend $22 million to eliminate the hazardous wastes from the site.

Hold or *held* is often misused, and sometimes it is redundant. You *hold* something in your hands or you *hold* a degree or a bank *holds* your savings, but you *conduct* a meeting or *sponsor* a cake sale.

I attended the meeting that was held at the Moose Lodge.
I attended the meeting at the Moose Lodge.

Some other red flag words:

all
also (also worthy of its own disease)
both
everyone
everywhere
interesting (when you can't think of anything complimentary to
    say)
obtain (Here, "get" or "got" is acceptable.)
over (when you use it in place of "about" or "around")
overall

The Big Red Flag: *That*

That might be the most overused word in the English language. Sometimes it is needed, but usually it represents nothing more than a verbal form of throat clearing.

In one special way, *that* should never be used except in a direct quotation. Writers should never use *that* as a pronoun for a human being. I'm amazed at the number of grammarians who spend paragraphs writing about the fine art of determining when *who* or *whom* should be used but shrug when someone points out that a *that* is not a proper identification of a person. Even humanists, secular or religious, let a *that* slip out when they're describing the representatives of humanity whose cause they are so fond of espousing.

Despite the fact that journalistic stylebooks use *that* for animals, I prefer *who* or *whom*. But, then, I like animals.

He spotted some parents and children that were out walking.
He spotted some parents and children who were out walking.

She recently completed a writing class taught by a teacher that the whole student body adored.
She recently completed a writing class taught by a teacher whom the whole student body adored.
(What was the teacher's name? If the teacher was that good, he or she deserves credit. But it is doubtful that every student, without exception, adores any teacher.)

Special Red Flags: *There Is* and Similar Usages

One way to add novacaine to a sentence is to begin it with a form of *there is* or *there are*. Try replacing them with action verbs.

There are many trees that cast their enduring shadows over us.
(Shadows are not noted for their endurance.)
Many trees cast their shadows over us.

There was a mix of people smiling, laughing, frowning and some were nondescript.
People smiled, laughed and frowned. Some wore blank expressions.

There is a cooling winter breeze coming across the courtyard.
A cool winter breeze wafted across the courtyard.

There is a string of popcorn on the tree.
A string of popcorn adorns the tree.

There is the slightest yellow beginning to show on the leaves.
The slightest yellow begins to show on the leaves.

There were few smiles, just looks of steely determination.
They displayed few smiles, just looks of steely determination.

There were four or five people jogging along the lake.
Four or five people jogged along the lake.

Always a Red Flag: *Feel*

Don't get *feel* confused with *think* or *believe*. *Feel* refers specifically to emotion or sensory information. If it involves thought, *think* or *believe* is more accurate. To avoid any hint that the writer is making it up, *says* or *said* might be more appropriate. (See "Don't Mind Read" in Chapter 7.)

She feels that this war is not going to end with Afghanistan, Israel and Iraq.
She says this war is not going to end with Afghanistan, Israel and Iraq.

Some people feel athletes who play contact sports must be missing part of their brains.
Some people think athletes who play contact sports must be missing part of their brains.

He feels his youth was interesting and fun.
He says he enjoyed growing up.

She feels that the pursuit of a future either in writing or interior design has equal appeal.
She says she might pursue either writing or interior design.

He feels that the overall atmosphere is both physically hard and abusive.
He says the atmosphere is physically hard and abusive.
Or
He says the atmosphere feels hard and abusive.

Red Flag Tenses: Perfect Doesn't Always Mean Good

Beware of the so-called perfect tenses, past perfect and present perfect. Both add an auxiliary "being" verb to a verb that already is on the job doing the work. The perfect tenses usually create imperfect sentences that are weak and wordy.

Our ally is seeming to be supporting the other side.
Our ally seems to support the other side.

See how the soccer ball is eluding the goalie.
See how the soccer ball eludes the goalie.

He is enjoying a busy life in Cincinnati.
He enjoys a busy life in Cincinnati.

She discontinued her studies because she was traveling across the country.
She discontinued her studies because she traveled across the country.

She wants to be one of those lawyers who are representing the poor.
She wants to be a lawyer who represents the poor.

The congressman said he is hoping that these corporate accounting scandals will not reflect badly on the administration around election time.
The congressman said he hopes these corporate accounting scandals will not hurt the administration around election time.
Or
"Come election time, I am hoping that these corporate accounting scandals will not reflect badly on the administration," the congressman said. (If that's what the congressman actually said.)

While she is pursuing her academic career, she should be watching out for colleagues who are making catty comments about her.
As she pursues her academic career, she should watch out for colleagues who make catty comments about her.

I was watching cars pass by when Ed McMahon walked up the steps, but all he wanted was a cup of sugar.
(In this case, the past perfect "was watching" is the correct tense because it indicates something that was in the process of happening when something else occurred.)

Not-ever Words and Usages: Don't Use Them unless They're in a Direct Quotation

Good writers use red flags if they know why they're using them and have given themselves permission to use them (at least this once). But they know that some words and usages simply do not belong in journalistic copy or most other forms of writing. Unless they take the form of a direct quotation, not-evers shouldn't exist. Usually, all they add is extra syllables or words and often they are redundant.

Here is a list of not-evers:

due to
per se
alot (It's either "a lot"—a great amount—or "allot"—apportion)
etc. (See "Don't Embellish Your Prose with Fudge Marks" in Chapter 7.)
hopefully ("She hopes" maybe, or "I hope")
in order to ("to")
one (as a personal pronoun. In American English, it sounds stiff.)
ongoing (Use "continuing" if you must.)
prior to ("Before" works nicely.)
upon ("On" means the same thing.)
utilize ("use")

Special Not-evers: *Currently* and *Presently*

Currently and *presently* are almost always redundant. The only time *currently* is not redundant is when you want to make a distinction in time, such as "She was in high school; currently she is in college." *Now* has two fewer syllables and six fewer letters.

Presently is almost always misused. It doesn't mean now; it means soon. Since it's used as a synonym for *currently*, it has become an artificial replacement for something that is already artificial.

And Another Thing: Rules to Write By?

If you think journalism students get tired of going through the arcane rules of their chosen profession, so do working journalists.

Because journalists often chafe under such rules, they are eager to read things like the following satire on grammar rules, and what they went through to get to the pages of this book.

In *The News Business,* John Chancellor and Walter Mears took a list of special rules from Harold Evans, in his book *Newsmen's English* (the title of which has been changed to *Essential English for*

Journalists, Editors and Writers). Evans in turn got the list from a bulletin board at Denver's *Rocky Mountain News.*

Anyway, here it is, written by an anonymous copy editor or group of editors:

1. Don't use no double negatives.
2. Make each pronoun agree with their antecedents.
3. Join clauses good, like a conjunction should.
4. About them sentence fragments.
5. When dangling, watch your participles.
6. Verbs has to agree with their subjects.
7. Just between you and I, case is important too.
8. Don't write run-on sentences they are hard to read.
9. Don't use commas, which aren't necessary.
10. Try to not ever split infinitives.
11. It's important to use your apostrophe's correctly.
12. Proofread your writing to see if you any words out.
13. Correct spelling is esential.

Over the years, the list has been expanded by an informal network of donors, including a few of my former students, who send examples to each other on the Internet. Here are some additional examples:

1. Prepositions are not good words to end sentences with.
2. Be sure to use adjectives and adverbs correct.
3. Parenthetical remarks (even when relevant) are distracting.
4. Avoid unnecessary redundancy.
5. Foreign words and phrases are not apropos.
6. Be more or less specific.
7. Watch out for irregular verbs that have creeped into our language.
8. Who needs rhetorical questions?
9. Above all, writing should be sincere, whether you mean it or not.
10. And the ever-popular "Avoid clichés like the plague."

Exercises

A. Eliminate the unneeded *that*'s, *there is*'s, *there are*'s, *there was*'s and *there were*'s from the following sentences. Rewrite if you have to.

1. There are half a dozen vintage airplanes standing in the foreground of the museum.

2. Police officials said that there was a 13 percent decrease in drunk-driving citations on the state's highways, roads and streets last year.

3. There was a surgeon working intently on a prone figure.

4. The president said that welfare reform should include safeguards for people who cannot find jobs.

5. Around the world, there are millions of children that are starving.

6. There are three things that can happen when you pass the ball, and two of them are bad, according to Woody Hayes, who coached the Ohio State Buckeyes football team for years.

7. The police officers had a warrant and they wanted to inspect the home for weapons or drugs, but there was a Pit Bull keeping them from entering the front door.

8. The late Harry Caray said that "the more games you play, the more chances you have to break a record."

9. Her grandfather said that "many a damned fool went to college."

10. The ambassador said she wanted to know why there were not enough limousines waiting for the members of her delegation.

B. Edit the following sentences to find a more direct tense and to replace red flag words.

1. Every day while I am gardening, I am chatting with the neighbor that is hanging over the fence.

2. The mayor feels that the members of the legislature do not understand the city's needs.

3. Prior to the meeting, he is holding a news conference.

4. She feels that her journalistic skills are much better on account of her having taken two classes last summer.

5. In order to utilize the computer adequately for his assignments, he is taking a course in word processing.

6. Due to her ongoing struggle with lung cancer, she is resigning her post as chief executive of the tobacco company.

7. The car he is offering for sale is very broken down.

8. She has been testifying that the man she saw that was wearing a gray hat limped a lot.

9. The district attorney feels that the outcome of the trial is a forgone conclusion due to the confession of the suspect.

10. The meeting will be held at 10 a.m. and will end prior to when the ceremony has begun.

Suggested Rewrites

A. Eliminate the unneeded *that*'s, *there is*'s, *there are*'s, *there was*'s and *there were*'s.

1. Half a dozen vintage airplanes stand in the foreground of the museum.

2. Police said drunk-driving citations decreased 13 percent on the state's highways, roads and streets last year.

3. A surgeon worked intently on a prone figure.

4. The president said welfare reform should include safeguards for people who cannot find jobs.

5. Around the world, millions of children starve. (Note: Even if the "that" were needed, it should have been replaced by a "who.")

6. Woody Hayes, who coached the Ohio State Buckeyes football team for years, said three things can happen when you pass the ball, and two of them are bad.

7. The police officers had a warrant to inspect the home for weapons or drugs, but a Pit Bull prevented them from entering the front door.

8. The late Harry Caray said, "The more games you play, the more chances you have to break a record."

9. "Many a damned fool went to college," her grandfather said.

10. The ambassador said she wanted to know why too few limousines awaited her delegation.

B. Edit to replace red flag words.

1. Each day as I garden, I chat with the neighbor who hangs over the fence.

2. The mayor says the legislature does not understand the city's needs.

3. Before the meeting, he is to conduct a news conference.

4. She says two journalism courses she took this summer have helped her improve her skills.

5. He is taking a word processing course so he can use his computer more effectively.

6. Her continuing battle with lung cancer has forced her to resign as chief executive of the tobacco company

7. The car he offers for sale is broken-down. *Or* The car he offers for sale is a wreck.

8. She testified that the man who was wearing a gray hat limped.

9. The district attorney said the suspect's confession makes the outcome of the trial a foregone conclusion.

10. The meeting will begin at 10 a.m. and will end before the ceremony takes place.

How dreary—to be—Somebody!
How public—like a Frog—
To tell one's name—the livelong June—
To an admiring Bog.
—Emily Dickinson, *No. 288*

The medium is the message.
—Marshall McLuhan, *Understanding Media*

10 Those Other Media

During the late 1960s and early 1970s, the above quotation from Marshall McLuhan, a Canadian pioneer in media studies, became a cliché. Not only was it a cliché, it became a glib explanation for a rainbow of communication phenomena to which I'm sure McLuhan never meant to apply his five little words. But even the quotation's most glib interpretation carries some meaning. If the medium is not the message, then it certainly has the power to alter the message or its importance.

Medium versus Message: When the Visual, the Entertaining and the Newsworthy Conflict

Take for example a common news story and look at how two news media treat it. A fire consumes a large building, but it injures or kills no one. The story might make page 4 of the second section of the local newspaper. But on an average news day, it will be at the top of the newscast. Why? Because it carries such visual impact, and TV is nothing if not visual.

Using the newsworthiness criterion of "need to know," few stories are more newsworthy than a story about changes in a tax formula, because the great majority of Americans pay taxes. So what could be more significant to the average American?

If we use entertainment as a criterion of newsworthiness, though, a tax story falls to the bottom of the list. An important tax story usually will make the front page of a normal *broadsheet*—that is, *not tabloid*—newspaper. Its sidebars, or auxiliary stories, might grace the business pages. And it will attract the deepest thoughts of the editorial and op-ed pages of the *New York Times, Wall Street Journal, Christian Science Monitor* and *Washington Post.* Further, it will dominate the appropriate sections of *Time, Newsweek* and *U.S. News & World Report* as well as most business magazines.

If the story does make a broadcast news show, it will be written differently. Here's an example of a state tax story lede as it might appear in a newspaper:

> *In an attempt to increase state contributions to local school districts and decrease per-pupil disparities between rich districts and poor districts, Gov. James B. Carlson proposed a plan Thursday that would decrease local property taxes by 10 percent and increase the state income tax by 12 percent, with added state revenues going directly to the school districts.*

Here's a broadcast version of the same lede:

> *Governor Carlson says he wants to do something about the big difference between the amount of state money that gets spent on pupils in rich school districts ... and those in poor districts. What Carlson wants to do is raise the state income tax 12 percent. But he also wants to decrease property taxes 10 percent. The governor says he wants the extra money the state gets from taxpayers to go directly to school districts.*

No matter how skillfully written, though, chances are that the tax story is going to be relegated to a paragraph in someone's broadcast news summary. A murder, even in a major metropolitan news market, is likely to nudge ahead of a tax story in a radio newscast. And on television the murder story will be superseded by a fire story—any fire story. We know a tax story has no entertainment value. Now we learn that it has no visual value either.

Radio news is not concerned about visual value any more than a newspaper is (unless a dramatic picture accompanies the newspaper story). But radio does like background noise, an audio "atmosphere" that makes listeners sense that they are in the middle of the story. There isn't much chance that a tax story will generate noise, not unless the groans of legislators count. So what you might get on the radio is a 30-second overview of the tax story, simplified enough for the listener to understand it—but providing no real understanding.

One reason a tax story plays better in print is this: If readers don't understand a sentence the first time they read it, they can read it again. (Maybe they wouldn't need to if the reporter was a better writer.) But no such option exists for viewers or listeners, so the writer must not pack too much detail into the story.

Because television news relies so much on visual, it's easier for its producers to devalue stories of significant importance if they have little visual value. A recent newscast on CNN Headline News demonstrated how visual news and sensational news can dominate the newscast of even a reasonably responsible television news service.

The newscast led with the fate of a helicopter crew that was sent to rescue some hikers from a glacier on Mount Hood in Oregon. Three of the hikers had died, but the thing that put this story at the top of the newscast was that the helicopter crashed and rolled down the mountainside—as a video camera was pointed at it. No one was killed or seriously hurt in the crash, but the visual apparently riveted the Headline News staff, because they continued to run it at the top of each 30-minute newscast.

The second story had no visual; it simply was reported by the anchor. Sharks attacked swimmers in California. No one was seriously hurt, but the combination of sharks and California seem to always send the story toward the top of television newscasts. If CNN had been able to get some video footage, it might have beat the helicopter crash for first in line.

The third story was about Seattle's attempt to add a tax to espresso coffee; definitely an item for the 18-35 age group, which advertisers dream of harnessing. And it is, I suppose, an unusual story. But as the third story of a national newscast?

That story was followed by one reporting that the Federal Bureau of Investigation was relaxing some of the restraints, born of civil liberties, that have hampered agents in their quest to find terrorists after September 11. A good story to ponder but not heavily visual.

The final story before the first commercial break was about the threat of terrorists using old shoulder-held surface-to-air missiles to shoot down U.S. airplanes. A scary thought, and certainly newsworthy. But the report went on to say that most of these missiles were so old that the gas used to propel them had corroded the missiles beyond repair.

Now, at this same time, India and Pakistan were busy trying to escalate their conflict over the Kashmir region into a war. And that was newsworthy because such a war could evolve into the world's first reciprocal nuclear war. But apparently the network had no fresh visual footage, so the potential war would have to wait to make it among the newscast's top five. On this particular day, viewers had to wait until after the first commercial break.

Comparing the Media

Perhaps someday the forces that shape the Internet will find a way to bring the immediacy of the broadcast media together with the depth that the print media can and sometimes does provide. Until that union occurs, though, the journalist is stuck with different ways to write copy for each medium.

They do have something in common. Good journalists subscribe to the tenets of integrity—accuracy, fairness and balance—regardless of medium. Their tone is informal and conversational; in broadcast, downright chatty. They like short sentences; shorter in broadcasting, longer in most magazines, but with the "no wasted words" dictum still intact. They thrive on active voice and action verbs. They like quotes, but each medium handles them differently. They all try to describe in detail, but the better ones make use of what fits their medium best.

One element they treat quite differently is the lede. A good unfluffy feature might adhere to the *Wall Street Journal* formula of leading however you want to as long as the payoff comes in the "nut graf," three or four reasonably short paragraphs into the story. (See "Using the Nut-Graf Approach" in Chapter 3.) A good magazine article might spend that long just developing the landscape, describing the environment and atmosphere with strong nouns and action verbs.

By contrast, broadcast news stories have no ledes, not in the sense that the print media use them. The closest thing to a lede in most broadcast newscasts is the introduction, or *intro,* which an anchor reads and then "throws" the story to a street reporter, who carries the story from there. Or maybe television or radio viewers won't see or hear the street reporter right away. They first might get a *sound bite*—an audio or video quote. Or the radio listeners might get some natural sound up front. Examples of a broadcast sound cliché are the sound of the clanging of a cable car in a story about San Francisco, the noise of a cash-register computer in a story about the retail industry, or the sounds of jet engines on a runway in a story about an airport.

In television, the opening videotaped footage should be dramatically or artfully visual—"vision" is after all the medium's last name. It might include the sound of the reporter's voice accompanying the video (called a *voice-over*), or the voice of the interview subject. It isn't unusual for a field producer to begin a longer story on, say, the environment with 15 seconds of natural sound emerging from some gorgeous natural footage before the reporter speaks the first words.

Writing for Broadcast

Writing for broadcast means writing for the ear always and the eye sometimes. All general rules of broadcast writing apply to both the audio and video media, but writing for television and other visual media brings a few extra rules. We will come to them.

In print, it's a good idea for the writer to read the copy aloud during the editing process. In broadcast, the writer simply must read the copy aloud—moving the lips. If the writer fails to catch a flub, the anchor might miss it too, to the embarrassment of the newsreader or anchor and the subsequent verbal abuse of the writer. (Take it from someone who's been there.) Reading the copy aloud ensures the story will retain a conversational rhythm. And, as it does in print stories, reading the copy aloud makes unneeded words and sentence elements obvious immediately.

Reading copy aloud before it's aired also helps eliminate tongue twisters and excessive sibilants like "Since she is said to have seen Sasquatch, she has been surreptitiously seen at a San Jose soda stand, superciliously sipping sarsaparilla through a squiggly straw, so say some sightseers who say they saw her." Such a sentence creates microphone noises that sound awful on the air. And it puts the newsreader in a bad mood.

Broadcast writing is linear. It goes from point A to point B to point C in a straight line, without digression and without explanation. For that reason, it doesn't hurt to repeat a fact or two in case the listener or viewer missed it the first time. In other words, be repetitive or even redundant—just as Chapter 5 tells you not to do.

Writers of broadcast copy thrive on delivering short sentences. What otherwise might be a numbingly repetitious series of subject-verb-object sentences is not unusual. Nor does it create a problem for the newsreader, nor the person listening or watching.

A rule of thumb dictates that a broadcast sentence should not exceed 20 words. I'm tempted to say the 20-word limit discounts the intelligence of the listening or viewing public. But the KISS principle—Keep It Simple, Stupid—must rule.

The fact is, when viewers or listeners are engaged in a newscast, they are often not totally engaged. Other things happen in a house or apartment when the TV set is on, things that require viewer attention. And radio listeners usually are doing something else as they listen to the news. Most often, they're driving. By contrast, readers usually absorb themselves in what they read. Hence the broadcast emphasis on short sentences and repetition.

Here's an example of a couple of paragraphs of a newspaper lede, followed by how the same lede might be written for radio and television. Note how differently the broadcast lede handles detail. First, the newspaper version:

> *Responding to an emergency appeal from the U.N., the United States announced Tuesday it will ship $15 million worth of corn to North Korea to assist children affected by severe food shortage.*
>
> *Nicholas Burns, a State Department spokesman, said the decision was not linked to a North Korean announcement, expected Wednesday, on whether it will accept a U.S.-South Korean proposal to begin peace talks.*

Now the broadcast lede:

The United States has responded to a U-N plea to send 15-Million dollars worth of corn to help starving children in North Korea. State Department spokesman Nicholas Burns says the shipment is NOT linked to any expected announcement from the North Koreans. A North Korean announcement would confirm if they will or won't accept a proposal from South Korea and the United States to begin peace talks.

Note a few changes in basic style. *U.N.* has become *U-N*. The amount of *$15 million* is *15-Million dollars* with a capitalized *M*. (If it were $15 billion, the broadcast version would be *15-BILLION dollars* to remind the newsreader to emphasize the *B*. That's because *M* and *B* can sound the same, and no anchor wants to get a million confused with a billion.) And the word *NOT* is capitalized. That's so the on-mike or on-camera reader does NOT inadvertently make a positive out of a negative.

To understand a big difference between print and broadcast news, notice that the two newspaper sentences, each with dependent clauses, have been transformed into three terse, declarative sentences. And the newspaper method of identifying a subject, *Nicholas Burns, a State Department spokesman*, has been replaced with the broadcast-style *State Department spokesman Nicholas Burns*.

Another newspaper example:

BOSTON—In his first public court appearance since the clergy sexual abuse scandal surfaced in January, Cardinal Bernard F. Law testified today in defense of the Boston archdiocese's decision to back out of a $30 million dollar settlement with 86 alleged victims of convicted pedophile and ex-priest John F. Geoghan.
Law said under oath that the settlement had not yet gone into effect because it had not been signed by all parties and there was not enough money to pay for it.

A broadcast version:

In Boston, Cardinal Bernard Law says there was no agreement to back out of. That's because NOT all parties signed a 30-Million-dollar agreement between the archdiocese and several dozen people who say they were sex-abuse victims. The cardinal says the 30-Million dollars was too expensive anyway. That's why he says the Boston archdiocese will NOT pay 86 people who say they were victims of ex-priest John Geoghan (GAY'ghen). Geoghen is the convicted pedophile whose actions opened up a clergy sex abuse scandal last January. Cardinal Law denied the archdiocese reneged on an agreement in testimony in Suffolk Superior Court.

The broadcast lede teases the listener into the story by mentioning an agreement without identifying it in the first sentence. But it is detailed in the second sentence and *agreement* is repeated. The middle initials of Law and Geoghan are eliminated. Again, the dollar amount is spelled out and the *NOT* is capitalized. The exact number of plaintiffs isn't clear until the second reference to them. First it was *several dozen*, now it's *86*. And the ex-priest's name carries a phonetic "pronouncer." The emphasized syllable is capitalized and carries an apostrophe, and an *h* is added to the second syllable to make sure the newsreader uses a hard *g*, not a *j* sound.

In second and third reference, Law is referred to as *the Cardinal* and *Cardinal Law*. That's because repetition and redundancy, so despised by good newspaper and magazine writers, fulfill a needed role in broadcast. A cliché of sorts has developed among broadcast news people: "Tell'em what you're going to tell'em, tell'em, and then tell'em what you told'em. And do it in 30 seconds or less."

All right, so now you've fashioned a short, declarative sentence, the essence of direct, clear broadcast journalism. But what if you want to add a clause? Sometimes you must. The general rule is this: Separate the clause from the sentence by placing an elision (three dots) ... where a comma or a semicolon might be in a print story. That way, the newsreader knows he or she must end the main part of the sentence with the voice up ... then stop for half a beat before reading through the rest of the sentence. But don't overdo it. Short sentences work best.

The broadcast media are the media of immediacy—not deep but certainly timely. So the tense of preference is the present tense, just as it is in a print feature in which the writer wants readers to feel as if they are right there. The exact time when the story took place is not as important as it is in print. A broadcast story has the most impact when the time is "now." And that means the word *today* isn't nearly as important as it is in newspapers. In broadcast copy, if you insert the word *today*, you shove the sentence into past tense.

But sometimes present tense sounds funny, like a stilted television attempt to imitate a newspaper headline. Suppose you write "The governor endorses a news education package" without referring to when the governor made such an endorsement. Well, this is when the broadcast newswriter resorts to tenses that print reporters are supposed to shun, past perfect and present perfect.

> *The governor has endorsed a new education package.*
> *Or*
> *The governor is endorsing a new education package.*

Some Broadcast Style Pointers

Whole books are written about how to write for broadcast, and we make no attempt here to compete with them. But here are a few suggestions (more are in Appendix C):

- Numbers one through eleven get spelled out. (In print journalism, it's usually one through nine). The reason "eleven" gets spelled out is that 11 can be misinterpreted as the Roman numeral II—two.
- Usually you avoid using middle initials unless you are referring to someone named James Smith or Robert Johnson who was killed in a neighborhood where there might be a dozen James Smiths or Robert Johnsons. Or unless the middle initial is a part of a recognized name like George W. Bush, George M. Cohan or Johnny B. Goode.
- Quotation marks cannot be seen in broadcast copy, so what might be good print journalism—quoting accurately, word for word—simply gets lost on viewers and listeners. That's one reason so many broadcast quotes take the form of sound bites. If the on-air reader is quoting, though, make sure he or she uses the attribution first: Not *"Why can't we all just get along?" Rodney King asked*, but *Rodney King asked ... in these words ... "Why can't we just get along?"*
- In broadcast copy, today is today, not Sunday or Tuesday or Thursday. And yesterday is yesterday and tomorrow is tomorrow.

Weekday names are used only for dates that occurred up to a week ago (*last Sunday* if today is Sunday) or a week from now (*next Sunday*). Any other day that is more than seven days before or after today is designated by its date. And it isn't April 12 or the 12th of April, but April 12th. The first eleven dates of the month are spelled out—September first, August fifth or December eleventh, but February 25th.

- Use hyphens (or single dashes) freely to help the announcer, especially with compound words or words with prefixes and suffixes: *co-opt, pre-empt, count-down, school-children, re-election, man-slaughter, with-hold* and the like.

- Help the anchor as much as you can with pronunciations of strange-sounding words. Do it with simple phonetic "pronouncers"—anything that can be constructed out of the often-inadequate 26 letters of the English alphabet. For example, Duke University basketball coach Mike Krzecziewski is pronounced (Sheh-SHEHF'skee). Some others: former French President Giscard D'Estaing (ZHEE'-kahr Deh-STANG'); Birmingham (BER'ming-um), England (as opposed to BER'ming-ham, Alabama); or Cairo (KEH'roh), Illinois (as opposed to (KYE'roh, Egypt). (The newsreader should already know that the *s* in Illinois is silent.)

The Demands of Airtime

When a newscast includes not only a newsreader but a reporter, the newsreader then becomes an anchor and he or she is required to set up any story that involves that reporter. The set-up is called a *lead-in*, and it serves somewhat different purposes than a print lede.

Lead-ins serve two purposes. As a lede does in print, the lead-in sets up the story but, unlike the print lede, it also introduces the reporter—sort of an audio byline. Often, the reporter writes the lead-in as if he or she is introducing the story and then turns it over to a news editor along with an audiotape or videotape of the reporter reciting the rest of the story, including any sound bites. The editor then incorporates the story into the newscast, complete with a time estimate. The total package rarely exceeds 90 seconds and usually it is under a minute.

National Public Radio news people take some pride in digging into a story more than the average commercial broadcast or cable news operation would, so their stories tend to be a little longer. For their regular newscasts, reporters write their own scripts and record them, as their commercial competitors do. But in NPR's in-depth news programs, "Morning Edition" and "All Things Considered," they take a little extra time for an informal dialogue between the anchor—or "host"—and the reporter.

Here's a recent example in which anchor Renee Montagne, subbing for the regular host of "Morning Edition," Bob Edwards, introduces the story.

MONTAGNE: *Iraqi opposition leaders are in Washington today for talks with State and Defense Department officials about the future of Iraq. The Bush administration signaled again this week that no invasion is imminent, but the opposition leaders say they believe it will happen. They want to know how they can help and what kind of role they might play afterwards if President Saddam Hussein is overthrown. N-P-R's Mary Louise Kelly is covering the meeting today, and she joins me now.*
Good morning.

MARY LOUISE KELLY reporting: Good morning.

MONTAGNE: *Tell us about these opposition leaders. Who are they?*

KELLY: *Well, the most prominent is Ahmed Chalabi. He's the leader of the Iraqi National Congress. It's an umbrella group that claims to represent a number of exile groups, and this is the group that the U-S government is openly funding. But there are five other groups in Washington today. They include Kurdish groups from the north of Iraq. They include Shiite Muslim groups, and the leadership of those groups is based in Iran. And there's the Iraqi National Accord. So there's six groups total.*

These groups, in the past, have not always gotten along, to put it mildly. And so the challenge now is: Can they put their differences behind them? Can they convince the Bush administration that they are really capable of helping to lead some sort of transition to a democratic Iraq? And the other big question is how much support any of them actually command in Iraq. A lot of these people, with the exception of the

Kurdish groups, have been outside the country for many years, so how much support they have there, how good are their contacts anymore, it's not clear.

MONTAGNE: *So what's expected to come out of the meetings today?*

KELLY: *Well, this is a chance for the Bush administration and the opposition leaders to look each other over. This is probably the highest-level, the most broad-based group with which the administration has met. The meetings this afternoon are at the undersecretary level, so that's a notch down from Secretary of State Colin Powell. But it would not be a big surprise if more senior people ended up talking with them. There are reports that tomorrow the vice president, Dick Cheney, will talk to them from a video linkup from where he's spending the month of August, at his home in Wyoming.*

MONTAGNE: *Speaking of Vice President Cheney, both he and the president have been out talking about Iraq this week. But are they toning down the rhetoric?*

KELLY: *I think it's fair to say that perhaps they are. Both the president and vice president gave speeches in the past couple of days stressing, again, no decision has been made. But there's a tiny shift. Some people are pointing to perhaps a subtle signal. Both talked about listening to other views on Iraq; the president in particular promised to be deliberate, promised to be patient, said he would consult with Congress and with allies. So this is being seen as an effort from the Bush administration to reassure people, "We are not about to go out and do anything rash. We will take other views into account before making a decision."*

MONTAGNE: *And is this in response to opposition in the rest of the world, which seems to be growing, to a U-S invasion of Iraq?*

KELLY: *Hard to say. It may be intended just as much for the U-S Congress, to reassure Congress "We will consult with you before deciding what to do." But it's certainly true, as you say, that opposition is hardening. Saudi Arabia this week said the U-S cannot use its territory to launch any operations against Iraq. Jordan's King Abdullah has repeated that, in his view, an attack would have disastrous consequences. And we're hearing this from Europe, too; in particular, this week from*

Germany, Chancellor Gerhard Schroeder delivered quite a strong speech opposing U-S military action in Iraq.

MONTAGNE: *And Saddam Hussein is out giving speeches, not exactly conciliatory.*

KELLY: *That's right. Saddam yesterday went on Iraqi T-V and warned people that if they attacked his country, they would be "digging their own graves," his words. U-S officials dismissed it. Yesterday the State Department called it "bluster from an isolated dictator." So it does not look like the speech has changed any minds in the Bush administration.*

MONTAGNE: *Thanks very much, N-P-R's Mary Louise Kelly.*

With its unscripted dialogue, this story took three minutes and forty-six seconds. In broadcast notation, that would appear as 3:46. In almost any other newsroom, a report that long would be rare. Time is the dictator in the broadcast newsroom. An understanding of the demands of airtime goes a long way toward explaining the strange rules of broadcast writing.

Variations for the Visual Media

The emphasis on the visual in television is so powerful that sound and even words take a distant second or third place. What appears visually (on-screen) occupies its own place in a television script, which is divided vertically. On the left side, taking up about one-third of the page, is space for a few notes. They include visual descriptions, audio notations and directions to the studio director and the technical director, whose job it is to punch the right buttons among the myriad on the TV console.

The right two-thirds of the TV script includes the copy of a story that involves no outside reporter or the lead-in of a story that does. If the reporter's story is on tape, the lead-in will end with something like "Here's Mike Morrison with the story." At this point, on the right side, the notation might include a "V/O," meaning the reporter's taped narration is a "voice-over" the visual story; an *incue*, the first words on the tape; an *outcue*, the last words the reporter spoke on the tape; and a total tape time and "sound under," indicating that natural background sound will accompany the reporter's narration:

> *V/O RUNS :45 SOUND UNDER*
> *INCUE: "The car was caught between two trucks ... "*
> *OUTCUE: "... Morrison, Channel 6 News."*

The format varies, depending on network and local station rules.

If the reporter is live, he or she is introduced with a scripted "throw" from the anchor, something like "Here's Mike Morrison live on the scene," and a scripted end to the story, something like "Mike Morrison ... reporting from the Farragut Freeway."

To combine the anchor's copy with videotape, the newswriter can write the script first and then work with the video technician or tape editor to get the raw footage, selecting segments that will match the script. But usually it works the other way around. The most dramatic video segments are electronically spliced together and then the newswriter writes the script to match. Most often, the anchor intro is written first, the video is edited and put together, and only then is the script written. Using the right two-thirds of the script, two lines of 12-point copy equals about five seconds.

For a reporter's voice-over, the newswriter writes the intro and then collaborates with the tape editor to match video with audio. Then the writer adds the time, incue and outcue and sends it to the newscast's producer.

Writing for Magazines

Forty or 50 years ago, there existed a category called *magazines*, and it was reasonably well-defined. It included feature magazines with names like *Life, Look, Collier's, The Saturday Evening Post* and *The New Yorker.* (*Life* and *The Saturday Evening Post* still exist but in an abbreviated state. *The New Yorker* remains one of the strongest general-readership magazines.) The category also included weekly news-magazines—*Time, Newsweek* and *U.S. News & World Report* are still going strong—as well as specialized consumer magazines that ranged from *Popular Mechanics* to *The Ladies' Home Journal, Argosy, Better Homes & Gardens, Field & Stream, True Romance,* and *True Detective.*

As it does now, *Parade* came along with a newspaper in nearly every market of any size, and most larger newspapers printed their own Sunday magazine. Few magazines came under the heading of "trade publications." Industries weren't nearly as self-conscious as they are now, and there seemed to be a stronger sense of "Why should I tell my competitors?"

The Reader's Digest took up, and still takes up, a category unto itself. The *Digest* reprints, in an abbreviated form (with permission, of course), articles from other magazines or from newspapers and specialty publications. And it publishes some original articles.

Now, however, the magazines category includes many of the older magazines and a magazine for nearly every special interest, geographic area, political persuasion, age group, and every variety of "how-to." Airline in-flight magazines have taken up some of the general-readership slack left by *Look, Collier's,* and *The Saturday Evening Post.* So today, the required writing styles vary nearly as much as the variety of magazines available.

As an example, take one specific group of magazines that caters to corporate business. *Fortune* or *Forbes* might take an approach considered "typical magazine style," whatever that is. It usually means the lede will be more languid than you might find in a newspaper; certainly more languid than anything you see or hear on radio or television, unless perhaps it's an in-depth report you're hearing on National Public Radio's "Morning Edition" or "All Things Considered" or a documentary you're watching on television.

The business magazine article might strive to provide the reader with a mood or an environment. It might begin with an anecdote that somehow illustrates the point of the article. Or it might begin by launching into a state-of-the-industry article, with a synopsis of how the industry has grown or withered or changed during the past five or 10 years. Another magazine, *Business Week,* might imitate the clipped, often snappy, sometimes snide style of one of the general weekly newsmagazines.

Once a corporate magazine finds itself playing only to a specific industry audience, though, the writing style might be less important than how specific the content is to the audience.

For instance, the subcategory of corporate computing appears overrun with niche publications, most in magazine formats. Two weekly publications dominate. One is actually a newspaper, *Computerworld*. The other is a newsmagazine, *InformationWeek*.

A third, *Business 2.0*, boasts that it focuses on "business strategies and disciplines, and the integration of the Internet and other technologies into various industries."

Another, *Software* magazine, a monthly, stopped publication for a time but was reborn as a quarterly with an attached electronic newsletter. Either of these could be considered a publication of record for their field. From a somewhat different angle, another magazine, *Upside*, says it focuses on "executives and investors in digital technology companies."

Within the subcategory of corporate computing, several niche magazines perform. One monthly is *Application Development Trends*, obviously aimed at developers of systems that perform specific-user functions (as opposed to systems developers, who concentrate on the systems that in turn provide applications). A competitor is *Enterprise Systems Journal*, which appears only on the World Wide Web.

Two magazines address computer and software security, *Information Security* and *SC Magazine*, which is aimed at top decision makers in corporate Information Technology, or *IT*. These include Chief Information Officers (CIOs), security officers, information-systems managers, network administrators and data processing auditors whose job it is to protect a company's information assets. *Information Security* says it is "an industry trade publication that provides news, analysis, insight, and commentary on today's infosecurity marketplace."

Other niche magazines include those for developers and users of particular computer languages or operating systems, like *Java Developers Journal* or *XML Journal*.

The Long Feature

One thing most magazines have in common is that their feature—or featured—articles are usually longer than those of a newspaper. They involve more interviews with more people, cover a subject with more breadth and depth, and include more of the environment surrounding the story.

Here's a good example of how to set up an environment. In this *Smithsonian* magazine story about England's Stonehenge, David Roberts takes special care to employ the reader's senses as much as possible.

> *Steady rain fell diagonally, driven by a raw wind out of the north, and I narrowed the hood of my parka. With neither tent nor bag, I faced an unpleasant night on southern England's Salisbury Plain. At least my vigil would not be solitary. Around me a boisterous crowd of some 7,000 was camped on the turf at Stonehenge, the enigmatic circle of towering sandstone slabs capped with heavy lintels, whose origins lie in the Neolithic age, some 5,000 years ago. "The most celebrated prehistoric monument in the world," the distinguished archaeologist Sir Colin Renfrew called Stonehenge.*
>
> *In 2000, fifteen years after the British government closed it to large groups of revelers—following desecration of the site and the death by the drug overdose of a young woman in 1984—Stonehenge was reopened to groups, and a long tradition of celebrating the summer solstice resumed. Now, as I huddled in my foul-weather gear, I observed an odd assortment—neo-hippies, self-styled latter-day Druids in white cloaks, Goths in black, New Agers of all persuasions, tattooed bikers, drunken "brew-crew" louts of the sort that have given English football a bad name, along with suburban-looking families with young kids, and elderly couples. For hours, people played drums, zithers, horns and didgeridoos; hugged the stones, eyes shut in beatific trance; kissed each other as they stood inside the trilithons (as the assemblies of uprights and lintels are called); and danced upon the recumbent boulders. There were drugs, drinking and a little nudity, but came a bleak, misty dawn and no one was arrested. The celebrants had even picked up their trash.*

Once Roberts painted this word-picture, he freed himself to go anywhere he wants with his magazine article about Stonehenge. He chose to talk about the great stone circle's influence on a million visitors each year, which brings him to what English composition teachers call his "thesis statement" (I think of it as the payoff sentence of a long lede): "Despite a century of serious archaeology, we still have only the foggiest idea about why and how Stonehenge was built."

I have no idea how many drafts Roberts wrote before it appeared in the *Smithsonian*, but it is the rare full-blown feature that does not require at least one top-to-bottom rewrite. In what often turns out to be a vain attempt to avoid future rewriting, editors require writers to query the magazine with story ideas—even if the writer is a regular employee of the publication. If the editor accepts the story—a big "if"—he or she responds with a detailed outline of how the magazine would like to see the story developing in content, organization and maybe style.

Not necessarily for those reasons, writers should consider their freshly written story not the finished piece, but the first draft. In *Magazine Article Writing*, Betsy P. Graham looks at the draft of an article as a psychological tool, especially for the new writer:

> You'll face a blank sheet of paper or an empty computer screen with less dread ... if you remember that your first draft is indeed private. It doesn't have to be correct, much less artful or brilliant, for no one will see it but you. ... Writing the first draft is simply a matter of putting on a computer screen or paper what you are bursting to say. The stronger the urge to tell someone about your topic the better. Writing it should be no more difficult than telling your best friend about it. You need only make your point, in whatever words tumble out.

Good advice not only for magazine writers, but anyone who faces that demon known as writer's block. Graham provides some more tips:

> Before beginning your rough draft, think once again about your audience and the purpose of your audience. Are you writing to persuade, to entertain, to amuse, or to inform? If you're sure the readers will be keenly interested in getting needed information from the article, the natural mode of writing will be exposition, a clear and logical presentation of facts. Entertainment digressions or embellishments may not be appropriate; in fact, the reader may be annoyed by such distractions. How-to articles, for example, often consist only of a clear set of instructions given in chronological order. No stylistic frills. No amusing anecdotes. If, on the other hand, your purpose is to entertain, ex-

amine your notes for opportunities to use narrative and thus insert anecdotes.

Once the first draft is written, and probably rewritten, the rest should be easy—but rarely is it so. Next comes a period during which the draft usually goes back and forth between writer and editor, especially if they have not worked together before. That's because the writer's conception of the article, seen from a personal point of view, can be at odds with the way the editor perceives it from the broader, better-defined view of the whole magazine.

The lede might change several times. Whole paragraphs and pages are likely to fall out of the article or find themselves next to pages and paragraphs they have never formally met. If the editor is good, he or she will ask the writer to clarify points that are perfectly clear to the writer but, as written, will mean nothing to the reader. On occasion, it's back-to-outline time, to make sure the editor and writer agree on the fundamental reasons to publish the story.

If successful, the writer then carries them through the organization and details of the story. If not, or for reasons that might have nothing to do with the quality of the article but with the internal politics or financial status of the magazine, the story will be killed. If the writer is a freelancer, the magazine might or might not pay a *kill fee*—usually a quarter or half the original agreed-to payment.

Writing for Newsletters

One of the few growth areas in journalism—if indeed journalism it is—is the newsletter. A typical newsletter audience, if such a thing exists, might be an industry or a political group. A typical newsletter might address such an audience with articles that cover less than four paragraphs and are devoted to a highly specific topic. The article's tone is straightforward and conversational but serious, rarely featurish or frivolous.

Such a newsletter article is written with the authority not so much of a journalist covering the field as of one who is an industry or political expert. These newsletters go to subscribers who are willing to part with at least hundreds of dollars a year to get, in return, profitable tidbits that few other people in the industry or the political arena are aware of.

As do all stereotypes, though, this one has plenty of exceptions. Associations have newsletters, companies have newsletters, and people who want your money for philanthropic endeavors have newsletters. As have magazines, newsletters have adopted nearly as many styles as there are audiences to read them; they often reflect the internal politics, and the egos, of whoever is in charge.

"The reality that anything may be subject to the red pencil of the ego-driven superior can be daunting," says Ray DeLong, who has taught newsletter writing at Northwestern Unversity. "Equally deadening is a superior who is spineless. The writer must deal with both."

Regardless of whom a newsletter is aimed at or what the newsletter is about, it generally shares three types of stories with most other newsletters. First, most include at least one short profile of someone—an industry leader, an association maven, a political lion, an employee of the month, or someone who has benefited from the activities of the organization. Second, virtually all newsletters contain, by definition, short news items, often dozens of them. Finally, any newsletter I've ever seen includes a calendar of events.

The writer who can put aside his or her own ego and crank out these often-unexciting tidbits month after month or quarter after quarter might have the most secure job in journalism. Chances are, the writer will become the editor as well. And much of the copy will come from people who are not real familiar with journalistic styles and attitudes—"departmental reporters," DeLong calls them. "The quality of the writing is uneven at best—kind of like small-town stringers for smaller newspapers."

Writing for Wire Services

When United Press International (UPI) was one of the nation's two leading wire services and not the scaled-down version it is now, its staffers took pride in announcing to whomever was listening that if you could write for UPI, you could write for anyone. My first job after college was with UPI, so my assessment of that boast is suspect, but I agree. And although I still retain some nervous tics from that job, I believe no finer journalism boot camp ever existed.

Wire services were invented about the time the telegraph was, hence its generic title. *Agence France Presse* was the first to appear, in 1835. The idea of a news service that served newspapers using the telegraph was developed enough that when the American Civil War began in 1861, separate wire services fed the Union and the Confederacy. In the North, it was the Associated Press (AP), the same AP that today serves thousands of newspapers and broadcasters around the world. In the South, it was the Press Association. It died with the Confederacy.

Most wire services like *Agence France Presse*, Reuters and UPI are businesses; the media they serve are called clients. By contrast, the AP is an association; its outlets are members, not clients. Wire services compete not only with each other but with writing and publishing syndicates that need not worry about being all things to all clients or association members. It is that requirement that makes writing for a wire service more restrictive in style and perspective than any other news medium.

If you're going to write for a wire service, all the rules for newspaper and broadcast newswritng apply, only more intensely. For a wire service, the best style is often no style. Clients or members cover a wide spectrum of editorial and political philosophies, not to mention approaches to journalism and their audiences. Too much of an individual journalistic "voice" in a wire service story is likely to offend someone somewhere. So a wire service newspaper lede can border on being dull.

If editors at a client or member newspaper want to mold a wire service story to a specific style, they are free to do so. But the wire service won't be doing it for them. Clients and members also are free to accept or pass over any item the wire service sends them, and it is entirely up to newspaper editors if they want to run even the bylines of wire service writers.

Another element that distinguishes wire service writing from most other forms is the existence of constant deadlines. Wire services duplicate the hourly deadlines of a radio news department, except that the wire service strives to include more items that can possibly be used in, say, a five-minute newscast. The expanded menu gives radio clients the opportunity to choose which specific stories they want to use in their newscasts. Some client and member radio stations have their own news staff; others feature only an announcer. Before the introduction of computerized telecommunications to the broadcast industry, such stations were known as *rip-and-readers*, because that's what the announcer did. He—and usually the announcer was a *he*—would tear the newscast, spewed onto paper by a Teletype machine, place it beneath his microphone, and read it on the air.

Television deadlines usually became most demanding in midafternoon, but during the past three or four decades, local TV stations have expanded their number of newscasts, so they demand more and more fresh wire copy from the same source the radio stations get theirs. All-day cable networks like CNN, Fox News and MSNBC try to staff as many stories as they can with their own people, but they rely on wire copy as a backup. That comes in handy when a major story breaks and the wire service has something on it before the station or network has a chance to send someone to the site.

A continually breaking story, then, might be followed by several *inserts*, usually between one and half a dozen short paragraphs in length. A significant insert will earn for itself what's known to broadcast news people as a *new top*, an entirely new lede, followed by some restructured body copy.

For newspaper clients, wire services have provided, and some still provide, something similar called a *sub lead*. The sub lead doesn't occur as frequently as a broadcast new top, and it's more formal, complete with instructions on which paragraphs get replaced and where the newspaper might "pick up" copy from the story that is being superseded.

For newspapers, wire services have traditionally met at least two deadlines each day: a night deadline for the following morning's members or clients, known as AMs, and a late morning deadline for afternoon newspapers, or PMs. But the mix has become more complex as larger newspapers have added editions that extend throughout the day. Whole pages might get changed or added during the hour or two between early and later editions.

In addition, wire services of the caliber of AP, Reuters and *Agence France Presse*, all of which are at least bilingual, strive to stay current in each of the world's time zones. Technology has allowed them to make immediate changes to breaking stories. At Reuters, for instance, the operations of adding inserts and applying a new sub lead each time something significant happens has been replaced by rewriting the story each time. The story gets out to all time zones almost as soon as it's rewritten and edited.

Here's how British-based Reuters (pronounced ROI'-terz) handled the September 11 story. The first mention occurred at 14:03 Greenwich Mean Time (GMT), which is 2:03 p.m. London time, in a highlights summary. Reuters copy editors who could not immediately find any other source obviously had television sets on in their offices:

© 2001 Reuters Limited

NEW YORK—Two planes crashed into the towers of the World Trade Center in New York, causing huge explosions and killing at least six people, television said.

New York police frantically began clearing the area around the World Trade Center on fears that a third plane may be approaching, police told a Reuters reporter at the scene.

A New York television station reported that law enforcement officials said the two planes were highjacked flights originating in Boston.

WASHINGTON—The White House ordered an evacuation of the White House complex after a fire broke out in Washington, D.C.

Thirty minutes later, at 14:33 GMT, Reuters issued a World News Digest with ledes from four stories:

NEW YORK—Two planes crashed into the twin towers of the World Trade Center in New York as office workers began work on Tuesday morning, causing huge explosions, eyewitnesses said. TV reports said several people were killed.

WASHINGTON—An aircraft crashed next to the Pentagon on Tuesday, setting off a huge explosion, throwing people off their feet inside the building and setting off a massive fire, U.S. officials and eyewitnesses said.

> *SARASOTA—President George W. Bush on Tuesday condemned what he*
> *called an apparent "terrorist attack" on the World Trade Center and*
> *pledged the U.S. government will "hunt down" those responsible.*

Of the world's wire services, Reuters maintains the most extensive financial reporting system, so it was appropriate that it included this item in the same World News Digest:

> *NEW YORK—Global markets were rocked by reports that two planes had*
> *crashed into the New York World Trade Center on Tuesday, sending in-*
> *vestors scrambling to traditional safe haven assets like U.S. Treasuries.*

Quickly, related items found their way into the Reuters report. At 14:48 GMT, the wire service noted that a Czech airliner bound for New York turned around and went back to Prague. At 14:51 GMT report (2:51 p.m. London time) said the Federal Aviation Administration diverted all incoming transatlantic flights to Canada. At 15:28 GMT Reuters reported that the trading floor of the New York Stock Exchange was evacuated. And at 15:44 GMT, the wire service quoted a top European Union official, Chris Patten, who called the multiple attack the worst attack on the United States since Pearl Harbor.

Then came a news feature about Americans stranded at Toronto's Pearson International Airport after all flights to the United States were cancelled. It is not surprising that in the Reuters Business News Highlights issued at 16:38 GMT (4:38 p.m. London time), all 11 items, including two about halted activities at Wall Street exchanges and banks, were about or were related to the massive attacks.

At 16:18 GMT (4:18 p.m. in London), Reuters sent out a story about tighter security on San Francisco's Golden Gate Bridge. Thirty-seven minutes later, it sent out a full story about Wall Street shutting down. At 17:20, Reuters reported that the U.S. Coast Guard had shut New York's harbor to commercial traffic. And one minute later, it reported that Palestinian President Yasser Arafat had expressed shock at the aircraft attacks and that "he was ready to help Washington hunt down those responsible."

Several more such stories appeared before Reuters reported at 17:43 GMT (5:43 p.m.) that United Airlines had confirmed that two of its planes had crashed with a total of 110 people aboard. At the same time, a shorter story reported that a U.S. official believed Saudi exile Osama bin Laden was responsible for the attacks. Three minutes and two stories later, a Somerset County, Pennsylvania, official said apparently no survivors were among the 45 people on the United plane that crashed there.

After several more stories emerged, at 18:21 GMT Reuters listed a sequence of events from its Washington bureau, this time listing them at the time they happened in Eastern (U.S.) Daylight Time, with the GMT time in parentheses:

8:55 a.m. (1255)—World Trade Center reported burning after plane crashed into it.

9:05 (1305)—Second plane reported to have crashed into World Trade Center.

9:28 (1328)—President George W. Bush issues statement, saying United States will hunt down attackers of World Trade Center.

9:45 (1345)—Third aircraft reported to have hit Pentagon.

9:48 (1348)—U.S. Capitol evacuated.

9:49 (1349)—U.S. Federal Aviation Administration grounds all flights departing from U.S. airports. First ever national ground stop of aircraft.

10:00 (1400)—One of World Trade Center towers collapses.

10:25 (1425)—FAA says all trans-Atlantic flights diverted to Canada.

10:30 (1430)—Second World Trade Center tower collapses.

11:00 (1500)—New York Mayor Rudolph Giuliani calls for evacuation of Lower Manhattan, talks of "horrendous" loss of life.

11:27 (1527)—American Airlines confirms two aircraft lost.

11:29 (1529)—United Airlines confirms plane crashed near Pittsburgh, "deeply concerned" about another flight.

12:33 (1633)—United Airlines confirms second plane crashed at unknown location. Four planes now confirmed crashed by American and United.

12:39 (1639)—Bush makes second statement, vows to hunt down and punish those responsible.

1:20 p.m. (1720)—Bush leaves Barksdale Air Force Base in Louisiana for undisclosed location.

1:26 p.m. (1726)—U.S. officials say some indications people with links to Saudi-exile Osama bin Laden conducted Tuesday's attack.

To get a more detailed view of how a wire service like Reuters covers a continually breaking news story, here is how the wire service covered the Denver trial of Timothy McVeigh two years after the 1995 bombing of the Murragh federal building in Oklahoma

City. The wire service began with a bulletin, in all-caps headline form, at 3:35 p.m., Central Daylight time, June 2, 1997:

MCVEIGH GUILTY OF MURDER IN OKLAHOMA CITY BOMBING—
JURY VERDICT

Then a writer, probably someone called a "rewrite," followed with a 3:38 p.m. lede:

DENVER, June 2 (Reuters)—Gulf War veteran Timothy McVeigh was
found guilty on all counts on Monday in the bombing of a federal
building in Oklahoma City that killed 168 people in the deadliest at-
tack on civilians in U.S. history.
After deliberating for 23 hours over four days, the jury of seven men and five
women found McVeigh guilty on 11 counts of murder and conspiracy.

On the next *take*—what wire services call a page or a full computer screen—the story continued:

The jury must now decide whether to impose the death penalty or life in
prison on the 29-year-old decorated army veteran, whom prosecutors
called a rightwing extremist out to "start a second American Revolution."
Prosecutors said McVeigh bombed the Alfred P. Murraugh building on
April 19, 1995, out of hatred for the U.S. government and rage over
the deaths of 80 Branch Dividian cult members in a confrontation with
federal agents in Waco, Texas. ...

The story continued for two more paragraphs. Then a Reuters reporter rewrote the entire story, this time adding her byline. So 51 minutes after the bulletin, at 4:26 p.m., Central Daylight Time, this 20-paragraph story, covering three *takes*, began to emerge:

By Judith Crosson
DENVER, June 2 (Reuters)—Gulf War veteran Timothy McVeigh was
convicted Monday of blowing up a federal building in Oklahoma City
two years ago, killing 168 people in a crime that stunned Americans.
The panel of seven men and five women deliberated 23 hours before find-
ing McVeigh responsible for detonating a huge truck bomb outside the
Alfred P. Murraugh federal building on April 19, 1995.

Seventeen minutes later, Reuters released an entirely new story, this one written by Ellen Wulfhorst.

Before that, at 3:41 p.m., Reuters had released a three-take chronology of the bombing case, much like the chronology it sent out on September 11, 2001. It began with the Oklahoma City bombing and ended with the conviction.

All this time, reaction stories, known as *reax*, were being reported—of relatives of victims, of President Clinton, of Oklahoma politicians—and mixed in was a sidebar from Wulfhorst about a lucky break that helped convict McVeigh, a truck axle with an identification number amid the debris.

Then, at 6:23 p.m., a correspondent wrapped up the story from a national perspective. Here are the first three paragraphs of that story:

By Michael Conlon

CHICAGO, June 2 (Reuters)—There was applause, tears of relief and demands for vengeance, but little surprise across the United States on Monday at news that Timothy McVeigh had been convicted of blowing up the Oklahoma City federal building.

"Justice prevails," said Mary Ann Dell'Anno, an investment manager in Boston, in a typical reaction. "There's a saying: kill and be killed. They should give him the death penalty."

"It comes as no surprise at all," said Jonathan Leahey, a claims counsel for a reinsurance firm in Overland Park, Kansas. ...

Writing for the Internet

To my knowledge, no set of instructions has yet been published about how to write for the Internet, because the impact of the Internet has yet to be digested by the forces that dictate the course of the language. However, it looks as if the dominant language of the World Wide Web is going to be English, for a while anyway.

Is the language of the Internet going to follow newspaper style, broadcast style, wire service style or book style? Or is it going to evolve into some hybrid that we wouldn't recognize today? Or is the language going to be subservient to the visual, as it is with television now?

In an article in *Writer's Digest,* Steve Outing addresses a few ways that electronic publishing is already changing the way people write:

> ...Writing must adjust to the new media forms that tomorrow's consumers increasingly will use. If the article you wrote for a print magazine also will be published to small digital devices, the form and style that you wrote it in won't be optional. Even when published on the Web, a print-original article often must be tweaked to work online (where users have shorter attention spans than print readers).
>
> Some of your audiences will read your article on personal digital assistants ... with small screens. ...

Outing offers these tips:

Write short. If your audience will be reading your words on small devices ... don't expect them to read all 2,000 words of your magazine piece. ... The same goes for the Web because it's harder on the eyes to read on a computer screen than on a piece of paper—so online users tend to read less.

Write for the presentation medium. Sometimes long is OK, even when writing for digital media. E-book readers are getting closer to becoming mainstream, but these devices aren't just for reading digital versions of books. Increasingly, they will be used for reading magazines and newspaper content. Because they have large screens, the reader experience is similar to print. If your prose is destined for consumption on e-book readers, printlike style and length are appropriate.

Get to the point fast. This applies to most digital media—especially the Web and small portable devices. ... On a Web article, try to present your main point within the first screen—that is, so that it's read without the reader having to scroll down the page. ... On PDAs ... smaller screens mean there's even less space to state your main point and keep it on the first screen.

Write a great headline. *[The journalist should not get this statement confused with the fact that a print reporter almost never writes the headline to a story; an editor does.]* When your writing appears on small digital devices, there's no room for ambiguity. Funny but obtuse headlines don't work as well in enticing readers to scroll on, as do clear ones that quickly explain what an article is about. ...

Speak it to them. Clearly, digital devices will offer more and more content in audio form. It's not that text publications are going anywhere—only that tomorrow's consumers will choose whether they wish to read articles and publications themselves or listen to them. Ergo, tomorrow's writers are advised to get to know how to write for spoken presentation

If Outing's suggestions are any indication of how the world of writing is turning, it looks as if journalists will be more ready than most writers to deal with new media. That's because some of Outing's rules sound like journalistic rules: Use word economy; get to the point, as in the lede of a breaking news story; keep it conversational. Even his advise to write a great headline corresponds to the attention-getting quality of a good lede.

Before Internet users grapple with how they'll communicate with each other, however, they have some more pressing questions to answer. Amid the mass of information indiscriminately scattered among the sites of the World Wide Web is a smaller—but not much smaller—mass of misinformation. If the forces of democracy reign in this most democratic of the media, eventually the voters, the users of the Web—will find a way to demand that information be accurate.

Despite Outing's predictions that good Internet writing is short and economical, in one way the Internet might find itself going long. Ed Bride, a pioneer in the development of corporate computing magazines, says online magazines don't have to worry so much about space limitations, so their articles might run much longer. In the pre-online world, news space was dictated by the amount of advertising a publication sells. Depending on the formula, one page of advertising might yield anywhere from half a page to two pages of editorial copy. But online publications face no such barrier. Sloppier publications might get by without having to even hire real editors. I guess it's up to the online readers to decide if such magazines and newspapers will be worth their time.

Until then, no one is in a position to test the accuracy, fairness and balance of Web-site messages that claim to carry the truth, no matter what the "truth" is, no matter how much sugar you put in the mix, no matter how evil your neighbor appears. No one seems to be warning the information consumer that, in the best journalistic tradition, even if your mother says she loves you, check it out. Whoever cleans up this mess of misinformation—if anyone ever does—might or might not be a journalist. Maybe by then our crusading days will be over. But maybe by then the required attitudes will just happen to be the skills and attitudes that good journalists have today.

It requires no originality to say that the Net will look entirely different 10 years from now than it does today, in form as well as substance. We'll be adjusting to today's technology as we continue to be bombarded by tomorrow's. And the transition to tomorrow is not likely to be pretty.

In a *Columbia Journalism Review* article, *Seattle Post-Intelligencer* reporter Christopher Hanson looks at what might happen now that many newspapers and magazines have gone online. Hanson wrote this in 1997, but his points seem to continue to be relevant:

> Until recently, newspapers had avoided breaking stories online to avoid scooping themselves. But now media reporter Howard Kurtz of The Washington Post predicts that breaking stories will be routine within a couple of years. Today, given the relatively small number of Net users, the main advantages are to ensure getting credit for a perishable exclusive [story] and to have global impact even if one's publication is regional. If Internet readership multiplies and electronic newspapers become profitable, the advantages will proliferate.
>
> Unfortunately, the trend has a dark side. Instant filing may make newspapers more like wire services, and anyone who has ever worked for a wire service knows what that means: an emphasis on getting facts to screens immediately, with little patience for enterprise [reporting] or investigation. Feed the beast. File. Now. Now. Now! If newspapers switch to a twenty-four-hour cyber-cycle, they well take on some of the less desirable traits of today's on-screen news services and net sites. ...
>
> A newspaper that commits itself to the online world is likely to find little energy left over for good writing, clear explanation, in-depth investigation and offbeat approaches that have come to mark the best newspaper journalism.

One thing the Net is likely to do, though, is to return Americans to the written word. Television has been, for us, a vacation of more than 50 years, a vacation from having to use our brains. As a result, many Americans have failed to develop the brain's basic thought organizer, the language that communicates and processes the data, knowledge and information that the brain absorbs and disseminates.

Television has dispensed with the need for the symbols of language: the letters, words, phrases, clauses, sentences, paragraphs and pages that organize, develop and guide facts, ideas concepts and emotions. And television requires nothing in return from the viewer; the viewer is entirely a passive participant. Even radio requires listeners to use their imaginations to envision a scene. TV doesn't even ask that much.

The Internet promises to change all that. Even after voice-recognition hardware and software replaces the keyboard, users still will need to edit their messages. The software will not likely be able to recognize the difference between homonyms like *steel* and *steal*, or if the reader will be *content* with the *content* of the message.

At that point, or by then, the arcane rules of journalism and basic communication will have to be reinvented, to guide Internet users through their new, revolutionary medium. The Internet already has taken care of the passive participant problem. To get, you've got to give.

Now all that needs to be done is to ensure that what gets given will be understood. Hence the need for instruction in the craft of clarity.

Exercises

Turn the following newspaper ledes into broadcast copy. (For the sake of simplicity, "today" is Wednesday.)

1. Connecticut's Legislature Wednesday is considering a major overhaul of its drug laws that would shift the emphasis from punishment toward treatment of drug abuse as a public health problem, in part as an attempt to reduce the cost of imprisonment.

Among the proposals are letting doctors prescribe methadone for patients with a heroin problem, forcing more convicted criminals into drug treatment programs and giving prosecutors the discretion to seek a modest fine for possession of one ounce or less of marijuana.

2. At least some of the universe's missing matter appears to consist of hydrogen and helium gas floating between the galaxies, researchers at Baltimore's Johns Hopkins University reported Wednesday.

In an article in the April 20 issue of the *Astrophysics Journal,* the scientists said the thinly spread gas consisted of atoms of the two elements. These atoms had been stripped of their electrons, or ionized, by intense radiation early in the formation of the universe.

3. The multinational force trying to make aid deliveries safer in Albania grew to 4,000 Sunday as the long-exiled king of this lawless Balkan country returned to his ancestral village of Burgajet to launch a campaign to restore the monarchy.

King Leka was greeted by enormous crowds of cheering supporters before giving his first speech to the public since returning from abroad last weekend. He said it is time for Albanians to put down their guns and work together for peace and order.

"Peace, brotherhood and unity—not fratricide," said Leka, who was two days old when his father, King Zog, fled the country before the invading Italian fascists in 1939.

Suggested Rewrites

1. Connecticut lawmakers are keeping one eye on reforming drug laws and the other on the state budget. They are looking at ways to overhaul drug laws that would shift emphasis away from punishment ... and toward treatment of drug abuse as a public health problem—in part as an attempt to reduce prison costs. Proposals for up-dating Connecticut's drug laws include letting doctors prescribe methadone for heroin users.

2. In Baltimore ... Researchers at Johns Hopkins University say they've figured out what happened to some of the missing matter in the universe. At least some of the missing matter appears to consist of hydrogen and helium gas, floating between the galaxies. The scientists write in a recent *Astrophysics Journal* that ... early in the formation of the universe ... the hydrogen and helium atoms in space were ionized—or stripped of their electrons.

(Note: It's possible that the details are too arcane for a standard broadcast audience. The writer might want to strip away the last sentence.)

3. The number of multi-national troops in Albania grew to four-thousand today. Meanwhile, the long exiled king in the lawless Balkan country has returned to his ancestral village of Burgajet. Enormous crowds of cheering supporters are greeting King Leka as he launches a campaign to restore the monarchy to Albania. The king says it's time for Albanians to put down their guns and work together for peace and order. Leka's father ... King Zog ... fled pursuing Italian fascists in 1938. Zog left the country when Leka was two days old.

Appendix A: Words

Word precision is finding the exact word that says precisely what you want to say, with the exact nuance you intend. Word precision is critical to good writing of any kind, journalistic writing in particular.

In the examples of word choices below, an asterisk denotes sentences with incorrect or less preferred usage.

Accept, except. *Accept*, a verb, means to receive willingly. *Except*, usually a preposition, means "not including." In rare cases, *except* can also be a verb meaning to leave out or exclude. But to avoid confusion, it's better to actually use *leave out* or *exclude*.

I *accept* your criticism, *except* for the statement that I am a waste of carbon.

Access, impact. These are nouns, not verbs. You gain *access;* you feel *impact.* (This is an example of a losing battle for people serious about using good English.)

*I can't *access* my games program.
I can't *gain access* to my games program.

*The cheating by corporate executives and audit firms could not have *impacted* Wall Street at a worse time.
The *impact* on Wall Street of cheating by corporate executives and audit firms could not have come at a worse time.

Adapt, adopt. *Adapt* means to adjust to fit new circumstances. *Adopt* means to take as your own, be it a child or an idea:

If you're going to *adapt* to the demands of journalism, you're going to have to *adopt* a journalistic style of writing.

Adverse, averse. *Adverse* circumstances act against something or in its opposite direction. If you're *averse* to something, you don't like it or you're reluctant to pursue it:

> I'm *averse* to trying anything that comes brings with it an *adverse* environment.

Advice, advise. *Advice* is a noun, the material that is being delivered by an adviser. *Advise* is a verb. It's what the adviser is doing.

> My *advice* is that you *advise* us the next time you decide that going to Tahiti is more important than showing up for work on a Monday.

Affect, effect. *Affect* is a verb and *effect* is a noun—usually. In rare instances, *effect* can be a verb. You can, for instance, *effect* change or *effect* a solution. But most often the two words are used like this:

> The professor gestures for *effect*, and that *affects* the perceptions of his students.

Aggravate, irritate. To *aggravate* is to make more severe. You can aggravate an already irritating problem, but the problem must first exist. *Irritation* needs no help; it can vex or excite someone to anger all by itself.

> You just needlessly *irritated* the boss.
> The boss was already *irritated* with you. Now you've *aggravated* the problem.

Aid, aide. *Aid* as a noun is some sort of assistance. As a verb, it is the act of providing that assistance. *Aide* is someone who's designated role is to render assistance, usually to a boss of some kind:

> A presidential *aide* confirmed that the administration has decided not to provide *aid* to any country that can't pay for it within six months.

All, any, most, none, some. In American English, if we're talking about quantities, these words are treated as singular pronouns.

But if they refer to individual items, they're plural, so they take plural verbs:

> *All* of the moonshine seized during the raid *was* sent to the sheriff's
> office for safekeeping.
> *All* of the troops *were* safely airlifted to Kabul.
> *Any* breathable air we find in this city *belongs* in a museum.
> *Any* of the students who *are* ready to leave class can go now.
> *Most* of the ice cream *was* eaten by the children before the picnic began.
> *Most* of the marathoners *were* dehydrated by the time they reached the
> finish line.
> *None* of the U.N. countries *condemn* the Middle East action, but *some*
> voice their reservations.
> Almost *none* of the oil designated "sweet, light, crude" *comes* from do-
> mestic sources, but *some* of it *comes* from Saudi Arabia.

All together, altogether. *All together* means everything in one place; *altogether* means entirely.

> Now the choir members are *all* together, but the choir director isn't *alto-
> gether* sure they can all sing on key.

Allude, elude, refer. If you *allude* to something, you're referring indirectly to it or hinting at it. (If you're directly referring to something, use *refer*.) *Elude* means something entirely different: to escape or avoid someone or something.

> That embarrassing moment of mine you *alluded* to took place as I was
> trying to *elude* my ex-wife.

Allusion, illusion. An *allusion* is an indirect reference or a hint. An *illusion* is a mistaken idea or visual image.

> You are obviously under the *illusion* that I didn't understand your *allu-
> sion* to my bad habits.

A lot. The expression borders on the colloquial and can usually be replaced with *much, many, a great many* or *a great deal.* But if you do use it or quote somebody using it, it is two words. *Alot* is not a word, and *allot* means to mete out or distribute.

"We've *allotted a lot* of foodstuffs on this rescue mission," the sergeant said.

Alright. This spelling has gained acceptance during the past few decades, but it doesn't really exist as a word. It's two words: *all right.* Not to be confused with *already*, which does exist. So does *all ready*, but its meaning is different:

They *already* told you that they were *all ready* for the game to begin.
Already you think it's *all right* to ask me out, and I don't even know your name.

Among, between. It's a matter of numbers. If you are in the midst of more than two trees or other people, you're *among* them. If, however, they number only two, and you're in the middle, you're *between* them.

Even though I'm *among* the people in the unemployment line, I prefer to believe I am *between* jobs.

Amongst seems to be a word in virtually every English-speaking country except the United States. Here it's *among*, unless, of course, the writer is trying to impress people with high-sounding British words.

Amoral, immoral. The test seems to be just how sinful the subject is. If he is *immoral*, he is morally wrong. If she is *amoral*, she simply doesn't concern herself with morals, morality or immorality.

Amount, number. Amount refers to quantities that can't be counted but usually do take measures like gallons, liters, pounds or grams. *Number* is for things that can be counted.

Use whatever *amount* of *oil* it takes. You're going to be cooking a huge *number* of pancakes.

Actually, it might be simpler to say, "Use *as* much oil as it takes."

And/or. Awkward constructions like this tend to stop the reader cold. Write the concept out. Instead of "The Mighty Ducks expect to win and/or tie the Red Wings," try "The Mighty Ducks expect to at least tie the Red Wings. They could win." (You could eliminate the second sentence. Technically, it's redundant.)

Anxious, eager. It all depends on if the subject is looking forward to the event. If yes, he is *eager.* If no, he is *anxious.*

> The president said she is *eager* for the election to be concluded but *anxious* to learn the results.

Anybody, anyone. Make sure you spell *anybody* as one word unless you're describing a choice in a cemetery, which is what *any body* implies. It can also mean a choice of groups. *Any one* means any single person or thing, not any random person or thing.

> Ask *anyone; any body* like the U.S. Senate can kill *anybody*'s pet project at *any one* time.

Area, nature, oriented. Generally speaking, these terms are too general and are often awkward when they are used as adjectives, and they are usually redundant.

> *She taught in the *area* of physics.
> She taught physics.

> *He was of a pleasant *nature*.
> He was pleasant.

> *Judging from her rhetoric, she appeared to be conservative-*oriented* in her politics.
> Judging from her rhetoric, she appeared to be politically conservative.

As, like. If you're describing a similarity to a noun or pronoun, use the preposition *like.* But if it's an action you're describing, go with the adverb that is introducing a subordinate clause, *as*. In casual conversation, most of us are apt to use *like*, and sometimes using *as* sounds awkward. For these reasons, this is one of the most violated of grammar rules. Nevertheless, if you're going to be correct, you must use *as* when it's called for.

> You are *like* an old English teacher of mine who talked *as* if using "like" when one should have used "as" would bring the end of civilization as we know it.

Aspect, factor. As nouns, these words are usually weak, and they are usually weak because they give the writer an excuse to be wordy and less than specific. (As a verb, *factor*, as in "factor in," can be useful. But it tends to be overused.)

> *Inadequate communication between intelligence agencies is one *as-pect* of the failure to recognize potential terrorists.
> One reason intelligence agencies failed to recognize potential terrorists was that they didn't communicate with each other.

> *Her high school record of extracurricular activities was the biggest *factor* in her successful bid to get into the college.
> The college accepted her mainly because of her many high school extracurricular activities.

As yet. A simple *yet* will do.

> *We don't see the country pulling out of its economic doldrums *as yet*.
> We don't *yet* see the country pulling out of its economic doldrums.

Average, median or mean. Although many reporters use them interchangeably, *average* and *median* are not the same thing. *Average* is the group total divided by the number in the group. The *median* is the figure below and above which there are an equal number of figures. If the annual incomes of five people are $110,000, $50,000, $40,000, $30,000 and $20,000, the average income is $50,000, but the median income is $40,000. *Mean* is a mathematical term for *average*. Technically, they are different, but as practical terms, *mean* and *average* are interchangeable.

Averse, adverse. See *Adverse, averse.*

Awesome. It used to mean inspiring awe, but it has become so overused that now it means no more than "gee, that's nice," or "cool." For some young men and women, *awesome* apparently has become the only adjective they know to modify anything that isn't bad or merely cool or sweet.

Awhile, a while. *Awhile* is an adverb, modifying a verb by describing roughly how long an action might take. *A while* is a noun, an imprecise measurement of time. The key is whether or not it is preceded by a preposition. If it is, then it's *a while.*

> I studied these obtuse journalistic rules for *a while*, and it took me *awhile* longer to understand them.

Bad, badly. *Bad* is an adjective modifying a noun or pronoun; *badly* is an adverb modifying a verb.

> Phydeau is a *bad* dog. (Modifies the noun *dog*.)
> Phydeau acted *badly*. (Modifies the verb *acted*.)

This does not mean, though, that you can't feel bad. *Bad* becomes an adjective that modifies *you.*

Because, since. Don't use *since* when you mean *because*. *Since* refers to the passage of time. When it's used to explain why something happened, it can be mistaken for when it happened.

> *Because* they won the lottery, they have been traveling around the world, and they've been traveling ever *since.*

Because of, due to. *Because of* should always link a cause with an effect. *Due to* is an adjective and a preposition that combine with a linking verb to bring cause and effect together. But if you see them in a sentence, they usually provide an opportunity to tighten that sentence by getting rid of the *because of* or the *due to* and turning the sentence into active voice.

*The flight was delayed *because of* scattered debris on the runway.
Scattered runway debris delayed the flight.

*Authorities appeared to hesitate *due to* the fact that the rock concert
  crowd numbered 50,000, not 5,000.
When authorities learned that the rock concert crowd numbered 50,000,
  not 5,000, they appeared to hesitate.

Being. Often redundant. See if you can say the same thing without using the word.

*She is considered *being* the most astute antique dealer in Pennsylvania.
She is considered the most astute antique dealer in Pennsylvania.

Being as he was the oldest of 12 children, he learned early to take responsibility.
The oldest of 12 children, he learned early to take responsibility.

Beside, besides. *Beside* means next to. *Besides* means as well as or in addition to.

Besides Georgia, only Alabama is *beside* Florida.

Although correct, this sounds awkward. You'd be better off saying
Georgia and Alabama *border, touch* or *abut* Florida.

Between, among. See *Among, between.*

Bi-, semi-. Many people say bi-weekly when they mean it happens
twice a week. *Bi-* means every other time. *Semi-* means half, or
twice during the same period. So:

Semi-weekly means twice a week; *bi-weekly* means once every two
  weeks.
Semi-monthly means twice a month; *bi-monthly* means once every two
  months.
Semiannual means twice yearly; *biennial* (note difference in spelling pattern) means once every two years.

Bring, take. You *bring* something in; you *take* something out.

> Once she *takes* the requisition to the agency, she'll be able to *bring* back the foodstuffs along with a receipt.

Burst, bust. As a verb, *burst* means to fly apart in pieces. It's the same word, past, present or future tense, so there's no such word as *bursted.* The word is also a noun, as in "a *burst* of machine gun fire." *Bust* is a colloquial version of *burst*—usually too colloquial even for informal journalistic writing. *Bust* does have a separate past tense, *busted.* But unless it's in a quotation, don't use it. It also has a noun form, but "the venture was a bust" is rapidly becoming a cliché.

Can, may. *Can* implies ability; *may* implies permission. *May* can also imply possibility, but *might* does a better job of that.

> As far as the editor is concerned, he *may* cover any story he wants. But *can* he?

Capital, capitol. Unless you're talking about finances (capital expenditures), *capital* usually refers to the city in which a state or national government resides. The *capitol* is the building in which lawmakers meet.

> "Can you tell me where I might find the *capitol* in this *capital*?"

Case. An overused word that often defines what has already been defined; redundant.

> *It is rarely the *case* that, in today's baseball, batters try to do anything but hit home runs.
> In baseball today, most batters rarely try to do anything but hit home runs.

Censor, censure. To *censor* means to stop the transmission or publication of written or visual matter considered by the *censor* to be objectionable. To *censure* is to lay blame, and lay it on thickly.

> Anyone who *censors* the media in a democratic society ought to be *censured*.

Chairman, chairwoman, chair, chairperson. For understandable reasons, many readers, viewers and listeners object to the assumption that anyone who chairs a meeting or an organization must be a male. *Chair,* however, sounds as if a piece of furniture is in charge, and *chairperson* suggests a hybrid that is at least strange. Most news organizations simply use the title *chairman* if the person is a male, and *chairwoman* if a female. The same goes for *congressman* and *congresswoman.*

Character. Often unnecessary; redundant.

> *It isn't often that actions of a mild *character* attract this much attention. It isn't often that mild actions attract this much attention.

Cite, site. You can *cite* a source in a research paper or news story, or get *cited* for speeding. But a *site* is a location, even if it's on the World Wide Web.

> The reporter refused to *cite* her sources or tell police the name of the suspect she met at the *site.*

Climactic, climatic. *Climactic,* a derivative of *climax,* describes the peak of a process. *Climatic* refers to the weather.

> At sea level on the equator, almost no *climatic* cycle exists. So unless they travel north or south, residents never experience a *climactic* condition that we would call "the dead of winter" or "the dog days of summer."

Coarse, course. *Coarse* means roughly ground or vulgar. *Course* is a school offering, a direction or part of a transitional phrase between sentences.

> Of *course,* some gourmets like to sprinkle *coarse* red pepper and oregano on their pizzas.

Collision, crash. If two moving bodies come in contact with each other, it's a *collision,* but if only one is moving, it's a *crash.*

> The car *crashed* into a tree, but only after its *collision* with a truck.

Complement, compliment. *Complement* suggests yin and yang—that opposites attract. One thing or person makes another very different thing or person whole. *Compliment* is an expression of approval or courtesy, sometimes an expression of superficial flattery.

> You should be *complimented* on how you have used your creative personality to *complement* your partner's rigid mentality.

Comprise, compose, constitute. If you *comprise* something, you include all of it; literally, you embrace it. The components—the constituents—*constitute* what was being comprised. Something can be *composed* of several other things, but one thing *comprises* all the others.

> Water *comprises* hydrogen and oxygen. Hydrogen and oxygen *constitute* water. Water is *composed of* hydrogen and oxygen.

Congressman, congresswoman. See *Chairman, chairwoman, chair, chairperson.*

Conscience, conscious. If you have a *conscience*, you have a sense of what's right and what's wrong. If you're *conscious*, you might be aware that a difference between right and wrong exists. Maybe not, but at least you're aware of something.

> The only time that politician has a *conscience* is when she is *unconscious*.

Continual, continuous, ongoing. *Continual* means steadily recurring, like the chiming of a clock. *Continuous* means without interruption, like Niagara Falls. Many people say *ongoing* when they mean *continuous*, but *ongoing* is less of a real word than it is a business cliché.

> The space station orbits the earth *continuously*. It is the subject of *continual* additions and improvements.

Could have, could of. See *Of* used as *have.*

Council, counsel. A *council* is an assembly or meeting. A *counsel* is an adviser, often a lawyer. To *counsel* means to advise or give advice.

> The *counsel* to the industry *council* suggested that overt price-fixing
> might not be good for the industry's public image.

Crash, collision. See *Collision, crash.*

Criteria, data, media. Technically, *data* and *criteria* are plural, but almost no one outside of academic or scientific circles says "the data are" or "the criteria are."

Media is not so easy to shrug off. Not many people use it correctly as a plural either, but the fact that we say "the media is" instead of "the media are" helps perpetuate the myth that the news media comprise a monolith or a conspiracy. Fact is, the media are as competitive as they ever were, and we should view them as plural in the extreme.

Currently, presently. Unless it is used to contrast then and now, *currently* is always redundant. If you do use it to contrast, you can use a stronger, punchier word, *now*. *Presently* is one of the most misused words in English. It does not mean now. It means soon.

> *A former professional wrestler, he is *currently* a politician.
> A former professional wrestler, he is *now* a politician.

Dangling modifiers, misplaced modifiers. If you have a modifier—an adjective or adverb—that doesn't modify anything in the sentence, then it dangles or modifies the wrong word.

> *Out of fuel, the rest of the cars passed Jeff Gordon's.
> The rest of the cars passed Jeff Gordon's, which was out of fuel.

Dashes, hyphens. Known as one of the journalism diseases, the overuse of dashes (written as two hyphens) tends to overdramatize copy or imply irony where it might not exist. Use dashes only when the drama or irony is clear, or if you're defining a word or concept in the sentence.

> Samuel Wilkeson Jr.—chief of Civil War correspondents for Horace
> Greeley's *New York Tribune*—left because he didn't agree with
> Greeley that the Confederacy should be appeased. Wilkeson went to

work for Henry Raymond's *New York Times*, but then returned to the *Tribune*—for more money.

Hyphens bring together compound modifiers or take the place of omitted prepositions. (If the first word is an adverb that ends in *ly*, however, eliminate the hyphen.)

Good editors are not satisfied with *pretty-good* copy.

Pro basketball players—and their fans—now endure an *October-June* season. (The hyphen replaces the preposition *through*.)

It isn't that I'm a poor reader, it's that this story is *poorly written*. (No hyphen.)

Data, criteria, media. See *Criteria, data, media*.

Discreet, discrete. They bear no relation to each other. If you're *discreet*, you're letting out no more information than you must; you're doing anything but attracting attention to yourself. *Discrete* means distinct.

I know you're trying to be *discreet* about your feelings, but whether or not you love me is a *discrete* topic for us to talk about.

Disinterested, uninterested. *Disinterested* means impartial; you have no personal interest in how something ends. *Uninterested* means you do not care.

Reporters are often called on to be *disinterested* spectators, even when they might be *uninterested* in the subject.

Due to, because of. See *Because of, due to*.

Each and every. Two words too many. *Every* will suffice.

*Each and every American should remember Sept. 11, 2001.

*Every American should remember Sept. 11, 2001.

Eager, anxious. See *Anxious, eager*.

Effect, affect. See *Affect, effect*.

Elicit, illicit. If you *elicit* something, you draw it out. *Illicit* means illegal or not permitted.

> When you *elicited* support for your campaign 20 feet from the polling
>   place, you did so *illicitly.*

Elude, allude, refer. See *Allude, elude.*

Emigrate, immigrate. It depends on whether you're going or coming. If you *emigrate*, you are leaving a country. If you *immigrate*, you're entering another country.

Eminent, imminent. *Eminent* means distinguished, usually referring to a person. *Imminent* implies threatening, something that could happen at any time.

> I believe a long, boring lecture from our *eminent* professor is *imminent.*

Enthuse. A verb that should go away. A misbegotten form of the noun *enthusiasm*, it tries to take the place of verbs like *encourage, motivate, rhapsodize* and *gush.*

> She *enthused* about the prospect of attending a prestigious graduate
>   school.
> She *talked* about how eager she is to attend a prestigious graduate school.

Etc. A sure way to convince readers that you want them to think you know many examples, but that you can't think of any. A great way to lose reader respect, which writers must earn.

> The alphabet includes a, b, c, *etc.*

Everybody, everyone. Both are treated as singular words, even though nearly everyone seems to ignore the rule in a complex or compound sentence. The use of *every* would seem to imply several or many, but capping the word with a *body* or a *one* makes it revert to the singular.

> *If *everyone* passes the final exam, does that mean *they* will pass the
>   course?

If *everyone* passes the final exam, does that mean *he or she* will pass the course?

Except, accept. See *Accept, except.*

Exclamation point. Save it for quotations in which the person you're writing about is shouting or talking emphatically. Otherwise it not only emphasizes where emphasis is not needed, it detracts from the strength of your words, and it lends itself to editorializing.

> *Here is your change, sir!
> Here is your change, sir.

Factor, aspect. See *Aspect, factor.*

Farther, further. *Farther* implies distance; *further* implies degree.

> The *farther* I drive this gas hog, the *further* it cuts into the money in my wallet.

Feel. A special word that means emotion or reaction to the senses. It should not be used to replace *think* or *believe.* In journalistic writing, it can often be replaced with the more neutral *said* or *says.*

> *He *felt* that some countries are not ready for a system as sophisticated as democracy.
> He *said* some countries are not ready for a system as sophisticated as democracy.

Fewer, less. *Fewer* refers to items that can be counted. *Less* refers to quantities that can't be divided into items.

> We need *fewer* cooks in the kitchen or we're going to get *less* broth.

Figuratively, literally. They are direct opposites, but many writers get them confused. If you're writing about something *figuratively,* you're referring to it symbolically or metaphorically. But if you're treating the subject *literally,* you're telling the reader, viewer or listener that you're referring to it as the word-for-word truth.

When she said she was "*literally* dead with fatigue," she meant it *figuratively*. If she were indeed *literally* dead with fatigue, she wouldn't be able to talk about it.

Finalize. To *end*, to *add up*, to *finish*, to *polish*, to *summarize*—anything, please, but to *finalize*. It's a piece of business-ese that has found its way into pompous people's mouths and memos.

Further, farther. See *Farther, further.*

Good, well. *Good* is an adjective modifying a noun or pronoun. *Well* is an adverb modifying a verb.

> Balzac is a *good* cat. (Modifies the noun *cat*.)
> Balzac sleeps *well*. (Modifies the verb *sleeps*.)

Hanged, hung. A distinction usually ignored. Prisoners who are suspended by the neck from a rope until they die are *hanged*. Anything else suspended has been *hung*.

> U.S. flags *hung* at half-mast after we learned that the guerrillas had *hanged* their American prisoners.

Have, possess. An example of why an Anglo-Saxon usage usually works better than a latinization. Unless you're writing about some supernatural force that takes over a body or a soul, or your car has been repossessed, stick with a form of *have*. It sounds less pretentious.

> You'd think if he were *possessed* by the devil, he'd *have* some wealth to show for it.

Historic, historical. An event is *historic* if it earned a place in history. Research is *historical* if it refers to history.

> Diana Gabaldon based her *historical* novel on the *historic* Battle of Culloden.

Hopefully. If you go with its original meaning, "with hope" or "full of hope," this word usually makes no sense. For instance, if you say, "Hopefully, the truck will start this time," what you're really saying is "The truck hopes it will start this time." But hoping is something a truck almost never does.

But even when you're writing about an entity that is capable of hoping, like a human being, *hopefully* doesn't usually work. For example, if you say, "Hopefully, he'll never have to go through what I've been through," who's doing the hoping? The way the sentence reads, he hopes, but that is not what you meant. If you mean "I hope," write *I hope.*

Horrific. A recent fad word that, it can only be hoped, will fade away as most fad words do. An apparent hybrid between *horrible* and *terrific,* it is an artificial, unnecessary substitute for two perfectly good adjectives, *horrible* or *horrifying.* And the *ic* at the end makes *horrific* sound as if it isn't really horrible, it's only "like" horrible.

Hung, hanged. See *Hanged, hung.*

i.e. It's Latin for *id est,* or "that is." So if your audience speaks English, use English and write *that is* or maybe *in other words.*

If, whether. They sound interchangeable, and sometimes they appear to be, but *if* means in the event that and *whether* offers a choice of alternatives. When you do use *whether,* you can usually eliminate the *or not* that comes after. It's implied.

> He wants to know *if* he will receive the same health benefit *whether* [or not] he retires now or in three years.

If it was, if it were. There is no choice in correct English; it's always "if it were." The *if* means the statement is conditional or hypothetical, and that automatically sends the phrase into the subjunctive mood. And the subjunctive mood verb is *were,* regardless of whether the noun or pronoun is first, second or third person, living or inanimate, or singular or plural.

> If we *were* living 100 years from now, we would not be able to recognize any technology.
> If she *were* a certified angel, I still wouldn't vote for her.

Illusion, allusion. See *Allusion, illusion.*

Immigrate, emigrate. See *Emigrate, immigrate.*

Imminent, eminent. See *Eminent, imminent.*

Immoral, amoral. See *amoral, immoral.*

Impact, access. See *Access, impact.*

Implement. Another clumsy attempt to turn a noun into a verb so the writer can sound impressive. *An* implement is a tool; *to* implement is to carry out, put into practice, make happen, accomplish or simply do. Use plain English. (We say this knowing we're most likely fighting a losing battle.)

> We need to *implement* a new procedure so the system doesn't crash again.

> We need to *carry out* a new procedure so the system doesn't crash again.
> *Or*
> We need a new procedure so the system doesn't crash again.

Imply, infer. Not the same. If you *infer* something, you are drawing conclusions from a set of facts or premises. If you *imply* something, you indirectly suggest something or hint at it.

> Because you *imply* something you obviously know nothing about, I must *infer* that you have not done your homework.

Initiate, instigate. When you *initiate* something, you start it up. (When you write *instigate*, a red flag should go up and you should ask if it might not be better to simply write *start* or *begin*.) When you *instigate* something, you push it forward. *Instigate* often carries a negative connotation.

> How can we *initiate* our reform plan if you *instigate* our removal?

Irregardless. Not a word. The word is *regardless.* But not to be confused with *irrespective, irregular* or *irresponsible,* which are words. In the case of *irregardless,* a negative already is implied by the *less,* so the *ir* is redundant.

Irritate, aggravate. See *Aggravate, irritate.*

Its, it's. *It's* looks as if it should be a possessive, but it isn't. It's a contraction. The possessive is *its,* which looks like a plural, but think of *its* the way you would think of other possessive pronouns: *his, hers, ours,* or *theirs.*

> Now *it's* time for the train to wend *its* way through the Rocky Mountains.

-ize. It's a disease bordering on an epidemic. Although many legitimate words end in *ize,* the suffix is being tacked onto a vast number of nouns to create some incredibly clumsy verbs that usually try to provide a substitute to *make.*

> *You might want to *prosperize* your financial situation.
> I just want my income to exceed my expenses.
> *You might want to *sermonize.*
> I merely want to make my point.
> *You might want to *architize* your edifice.
> I simply want to construct my building.

Kind of, sort of. Unless you mean them literally, as in "licorice is a kind of candy," don't use these in any but the most informal writing to mean somewhat or something like. And even then, *kind of* refers to type of and *sort of* means degree of.

> I left the exam *sort of* tired.
> I left the exam *somewhat* tired.

Lay, lie. In present and future tenses, use *lay* when you require a direct object, and *lie* when you don't. Simple enough until you write in the past tense. The past tense of *lay* is *laid,* but the past tense of *lie* is *lay.*

> When she is ready to *lie* on the couch, she'll *lay* her TV section on the table. At least, that's what she did last time she *lay* there, except that then she *laid* the TV section on back of the couch.

Lend, loan. Although *loan* as a verb has become more accepted in recent years, it is more precise to stick with *lend* as a verb and *loan* as a noun. (Another of those grammatical battle careful writers of English are likely to lose.)

> I know I still owe you for the last *loan*, but can you *lend* me an extra 50 bucks?

Less, fewer. See *Fewer, less.*

Less than, under, more than, over. *Less than* and *more than* refer to quantities. *Under* and *over* are directions.

> *More than* 100,000 people watched the U.S. Navy's Blue Angels fly *over* the stadium.
> It takes *less than* 10 seconds to check to see if there's dirt *under* that rug.

Like, as. See *As, like.*

Like as a refuge for people who cannot express themselves clearly. It's usually spoken, not written, but the overuse of *like* is a symptom of muddled thinking. *Like* is not a punctuation mark, so it does not belong in between every other word or phrase. When people use it that way, they're saying the point they're making really isn't a point, it's only "like" a point. For example, if you say the guy or chic you're dating is "like so cool," you're actually saying he or she isn't really cool, only similar to cool.

> And I *like* told him *like* that's the last time he'll ever *like* stand me up, *like*, you know?

We can infer that she didn't really tell him, and it really isn't the last time, he never really stood her up, and you don't really know.

Literally, figuratively. See *Figuratively, literally.*

Loan, lend. See *Lend, loan.*

Located, location. Usually redundant.

*Hollywood is *located* in Southern California.
Hollywood is in Southern California.

Loose, lose. In common usage, *loose* (pronounced *looss*) is an adjective meaning not well-fastened or free from restraint or obligation. *Lose* (pronounced *looz*) is a verb meaning mislay.

If you wear your cap *loose* that way, you're going to *lose* it in the wind.

Note: You might feel the urge to change *loose* to *loosely,* but if you do, you're actually making a different statement. The adjective *loose* would define the noun *cap.* The adverb *loosely* would define the verb *wear.*

Lot, lots. Use only in the most informal writing. Otherwise, stick with *many* or *much* or a *great deal.*

*A lot of the children said they wanted *lots* more candy with their meals.
Many of the children said they wanted *much* more candy with their meals.

Majority, plurality. A majority of the vote means at least one vote more than 50 percent. A plurality means the most votes cast among three or more candidates, but not most of the vote.

By attracting a *plurality* of 36 percent of the votes, the new governor did not win by a *majority,* but he did manage to beat the other two, each of whom registered 32 percent of the vote.

Mankind. An unnecessary word that carries a connotation of sexism. Try *humans, humankind* or *humanity.*

May, can. might. See *Can, may, might.*

May have, may of. See *Of* used as *have.*

Mean, median or average. See *average, mean or median.*

Meaningful. A word that is less meaningful the more it is used. During the 1960s and 1970s, you could not be blamed if you believed that every college student was in search of a "meaningful" relationship or a "meaningful" course of study. Now, decades later, the word is still overused. Find another way to write it.

> *I do not believe you have contributed in any *meaningful* way to what we have done here.
> I do not believe you have contributed much to anything we have done here.
> *Or*
> I don't believe you've made much of a contribution here.

Media, criteria, data. See *criteria, data, media.*

Median, mean or average. See *Average, median or mean.*

Might have, might of. See *Of* used as *have.*

Misplaced modifiers, dangling modifiers. See *Dangling modifiers, misplaced modifiers.*

More than, over. See *Less than, under, more than, over.*

Nature, area. See *Area, nature.*

Nauseous, nauseated. A distinction that often gets missed: If you feel queasy, you are *nauseated.* If you make someone else feel queasy, you are *nauseous.*

> On our first date, my wife was *nauseated.* I'm surprised she decided to go out with me again, because she now tells me I was *nauseous* on that first date.

None. Whether this pronoun takes a singular or plural noun is a question of amount. If the noun *none* replaces a conglomeration, it takes a singular verb. If it refers to more than one item, the verb is plural.

> *None* of the soup *is* left.
> *None* of the people who said they supported my campaign *were* there for the campaign kickoff.

Number, amount. See *Amount, number.*

Occur, take place. Depends on whether or not the event was planned. If it was, *take place* is appropriate. If it was accidental or unplanned, use *occur* or maybe *happen.*

> "The Exhibitionists" exhibition is to *take place* at 1:30 p.m. Wednesday at the Warhol Memorial Art Museum.
> According to the attending physician, death *occurred* at exactly 3 a.m. on Jan. 14.

Off of. One preposition too many. A simple *off* will do.

> *Kindly get *off of* your soapbox and listen to reason.
> Kindly get *off* your soapbox and listen to reason.

Of used as have. A sloppy adoption from people who use poor diction. Exists only in the most colloquial use of English, and then it's usually spelled with an *a* at the end of a word. For example, when *might have* gets mangled, it becomes *might of,* which translates into writing as *mighta.* From this, we get the popular definition of the subjunctive mood: "coulda, woulda, shoulda."

OK, O.K., okay. In general usage, all are okay, but in print journalism, *OK* is preferred. In broadcast copy, spell it out—*okay.* Use it sparingly, though, and never as a verb unless it's in a direct quotation.

> *The commander conditionally *OK'd* the request to build a club for enlisted personnel.
> The commander conditionally *approved* the request to build a club for enlisted personnel.

> "I'll *OK* your request to build a club for enlisted personnel if five of them volunteer to serve at my wife's reception for the admiral's wife and members of the media," the commander said.

Ongoing. See *Continual, continuous, ongoing.*

Oriented, area, nature. See *Area, nature, oriented.*

Parameters. A burglary of the scientific vocabulary by those who practice the business vocabulary. Webster calls it "an arbitrary constant whose value characterizes a member of a system." Not what a corporate business person means when he or she should have used *boundaries, requirements* or *guidelines* instead.

> *Accountants who get too creative usually work outside the *parameters* of their profession.
> Accountants who get too creative usually work outside the *guidelines* and rules of their profession.

Personally. Usually not needed.

> *Personally*, I don't care if I never see another rerun of that sitcom.
> I don't care if I never see another rerun of that sitcom.

Possess, have. See *Have, possess.*

Presently, currently. See *Currently, presently.*

Principal, principle. A *principal* is a chief executive of a primary or secondary school, a designated leader of a professional firm, a lead in a play or the part of an investment that isn't accrued interest. A *principle* is a rule of law or behavior.

> She was a *principal* in her law firm, and then her *principles* deserted her.

Proved, proven. *Proved* is a verb; *proven* is an adjective.

> The photographic evidence seemed to *prove* that it was the defendant who fled with the cash, but the defense questioned if the pictures had been altered by a *proven* package of computergraphics software.

Quotation, quote. Despite its pervasive use in newsrooms, *quote* is not a noun. It's a verb. The noun is *quotation.* Refrain from using *quote* as a noun in any but the most informal writing (or in writing about journalistic writing).

> He *quoted* the following *quotation* from Joni Mitchell's "Big Yellow Taxi": "They paved paradise and put up a parking lot."

Refer, allude, elude. See *Allude, elude, refer.*

Said, say, state. Most print news stories report something that already has happened. Quotations from such stories should therefore be attributed in the past tense—*said.* As a device to make a print feature or a broadcast story sound more immediate, though, *say* or *says* is appropriate. The verb *state* should not be used in place of *say,* not unless it alludes to a set of beliefs. For example, "He stated his principles."

Semi-, bi-. See *Bi-, semi-.*

Sensual, sensuous. If something like food or sex gratifies the senses, it's *sensual.* If something like art or music pleases the senses, it's *sensuous.*

> The picnic combined the *sensual* gratification of eating with the *sensuous* pleasure of being outdoors.

Should have, should of. See *Of* used as *have.*

Since, because. See *Because, since.*

Site, cite. See *Cite, site.*

Sort of, kind of. See *Kind of, sort of.*

Take, bring. See *Bring, take.*

Take place, occur. See *Occur, take place.*

Than, then. *Than* is used to compare; *then* refers to time.

> Back *then,* most Europeans and Americans of European descent thought they were more intelligent *than* people of other races.

That, which, who. Inevitably, the use of *that* or *which* devolves into a hairsplitting contest, but the distinction is important because it changes meaning. It's impossible to distinguish among them without referring to what grammarians call *restrictive clauses* and what those who define journalistic writing rules call *essential clauses*. In the simplest terms, restrictive or essential clauses use *that* without a comma. Nonrestrictive or nonessential clauses use *which* with a comma. And either type of clause can use *who*, with the comma rules intact.

> *Restrictive* or *essential*: Ships *that* have holes below their waterlines are likely to sink. (Only those ships with holes in them are likely to sink.)
> *Nonrestrictive* or *nonessential*: Ships, which have holes below their waterlines, are likely to sink. (All ships have holes and all are likely to sink.)

> *Restrictive* or *essential*: Americans *who* do not register will not be allowed to vote. (Only those who register will be allowed to vote.)
> *Nonrestrictive* or *nonessential*: Americans, *who* do not register, will not be allowed to vote. (Nobody in the entire country is going to be able to cast a ballot because nobody registers.)

Their, there, they're. The differences should be obvious to a middle-school dropout, but professional writers can get them confused. *Their* is a possessive pronoun. *There* is an adverb that determines location. *They're* is a contraction for *they are*.

> *They're* going *there* to get *their* assignments.

There is, there are, there was, there were. Starting a sentence with any of these phrases should cause a red flag to pop up. Usually, all they do is clutter a sentence and sap it of the strength of its action verbs.

> *There was* a surgeon working intently on a prone figure.
> A surgeon worked intently on a prone figure.

They say. A sloppy way to back up an argument that apparently can't be backed up any other way. Unacceptable in journalism, it should be unacceptable in any other form of writing. Who is this *they*, anyway?

> *They* say the markings were left by aliens.
> Erik von Doniken says the markings were left by aliens.

To, too, two. These get confused often enough that it should be embarrassing.

Our *two* dates were *too* crazy *to* be forgotten.

Toward, towards. *Towards* is acceptable in places like England and Canada, but in the United States, the word is *toward*.

Uninterested, disinterested. See *Disinterested, uninterested.*

Unique. *Unique* carries no degrees of uniqueness; it either is unique or it isn't. So to say something is "most unique" or "very unique" is to say it's uniquer than any other unique thing, which makes no sense.

Upon. Unless you're being poetic, stick with *on.*

Utilize. *Use* works better.

Well, good. See *Good, well.*

Whether, if. See *If, whether.*

Who, that, which. See *That, which, who.*

Whose, who's. *Whose* is a possessive pronoun. *Who's* is a contraction.

If we don't tell *whose* work we plagiarized, *who's* going to know?

Would have, would of. See *Of* used as *have.*

Your, you're. *Your* is a possessive; *you're* is a contraction.

Keep that up and *you're* going to get *your* just desserts.

Appendix B: Various Points of Newspaper Style

This appendix makes no pretense of covering the myriad points that comprise newspaper style, but it does attempt to address those that most frequently arise.

How does newspaper style contrast with generally accepted points of good writing as dictated by, say, the Modern Language Association or the University of Chicago style?

Like most good writing, journalistic style emphasizes word economy, active voice and action verbs. Unlike most, however, newspaper style—the format on which all other journalistic styles were built—concentrates on:

Ledes. Getting a lede that legitimately entices the reader to read on or adequately tells the reader what's important about the story, or both, is about half of what good newspaper writing is all about. And, for the writer, it should help organize the story.

Quotes. As much as 90 percent of journalistic research takes the form of interviewing, and that should result in stories riddled with direct quotations.

Brevity. Without sounding like a *Dick and Jane Have Fun* book, newspaper writing emphasizes short sentences and paragraphs. That does not mean that you should not ever use a compound or complex sentence, but you should default to a simple, declarative sentence.

Paragraphs are shorter. (See *Paragraphs* below.)

Now, in approximate alphabetical order, are some other pointers:

Abbreviations (United States)

United States is spelled out as a noun, abbreviated when it is used as an adjective; for example, *U.S. forces remain in Afghanistan while the United States tries to help Afghanistan develop an infrastructure of services for its people.*

When you write the name of a state, without a city attached, spell it out: *Oregon.* If you include a city or town with it, do *not* use the postal designation. Instead use the system that existed before the postal service altered it 30-odd years ago: *Eugene, Ore.* And unless the state abbreviation ends a sentence, it is flanked by commas: *The University of Oregon resides in Eugene, Ore., which is in the Willamette River valley.*

Here are the state abbreviations (including D.C.) used in most newspapers—note the use of capitals and lowercase letters. (Some states continue to be spelled out.)

Alaska	Alaska
Alabama	Ala.
Arizona	Ariz.
Arkansas	Ark.
California	Calif.
Colorado	Colo.
Connecticut	Conn.
Delaware	Del.
District of Columbia	D.C.
Florida	Fla.
Georgia	Ga.
Hawaii	Hawaii
Idaho	Idaho
Illinois	Ill.
Indiana	Ind.
Iowa	Iowa
Kansas	Kans.
Kentucky	Ky.
Louisiana	La.
Maine	Maine
Maryland	Md.
Massachusetts	Mass.

Michigan	Mich.
Minnesota	Minn.
Mississippi	Miss.
Montana	Mont.
Nebraska	Neb.
Nevada	Nev.
New Hampshire	N.H.
New Jersey	N.J.
New Mexico	N.M.
New York	N.Y.
North Carolina	N.C.
North Dakota	N.D.
Ohio	Ohio
Oklahoma	Okla.
Oregon	Ore.
Pennsylvania	Pa.
Rhode Island	R.I.
South Carolina	S.C.
South Dakota	S.D.
Tennessee	Tenn.
Texas	Texas
Utah	Utah
Vermont	Vt.
Virginia	Va.
Washington (State of)	Wash.
West Virginia	W.Va.
Wisconsin	Wis.
Wyoming	Wyo.

All, everybody, everyone

Let a red flag go up in your head when you find yourself using such words and ask yourself, "Is this accurate?" Usually, it isn't.

Capitalization

Unless it would be capitalized anyway, as would *English* or *Japanese,* a college major is not capitalized. If it is the formal title of a department, however, it is: *the Psychology Department.*

Dates

It is either May 20 or the 20th of May. In newspaper copy, it is never May 20th. (That is the accepted form, however, in broadcast copy.) And when you add a year, you set it off with commas: *Sept. 11, 2001, will always be remembered.*

This century, in newspaper style, is the 21st century. It is not spelled out unless the number itself begins a sentence: *Twenty-first century technological devices will have to wait at least 50 years before they become antiques.*

Weekdays are spelled out.

Month names are spelled out when they stand alone—but most are abbreviated in dates: *Jan. 1 begins the New Year.* Here are the abbreviations as well as which ones continue to be spelled out:

January	Jan.
February	Feb.
March	March
April	April
May	May
June	June
July	July
August	Aug.
September	Sept.
October	Oct.
November	Nov.
December	Dec.

Names

In first reference, use the first and last name, sometimes a middle initial. Do not use a title in first reference. If the subject is charged with a crime, use the full middle name. In second reference or beyond, most newspapers use the last name only. A few, including prestigious ones like *The New York Times, The Christian Science Monitor* and *The Wall Street Journal,* use Mr. or Ms., but not in first reference. You use Dr. only if the subject is a physician (not a Ph.D.).

Numbers

Generally, numbers from one to nine are spelled out; all above nine are written in Arabic numerals. **Exceptions:**

- If a number starts a sentence, it is always spelled out: *Twenty-five years ago, my father graduated from college.*
- Unless they begin a sentence, percentages are always expressed in Arabic numerals, followed by the word *percent* spelled out: *Mormons make up 2 percent of the U.S. population.*
- Age. It usually follows the subject's name and is in Arabic numerals: *Tracy Smith, 9, won the third-grade spelling bee.*

If a number is less than a million and it does not begin a sentence, Arabic numerals will do, with commas in the appropriate places (114 or 12,342 or 100,000). If it's more than a million, use an Arabic numeral followed by *million, billion* or *trillion*, but any fractions follow a decimal point and usually they are rounded off (3 million or 979 million or 1 billion or 1.673 trillion—not 1,672,886,000,000). In normal print copy, dollar figures are rounded off too, so the cents almost never appear: $2.034 million instead of $2.033,540.56.

OK in newspapers (but don't overdo it)

Newspaper copy should be tightly edited *but* sound conversational. Believe it or not, the two are not mutually exclusive, and the best journalistic writing does both. Some forbidding grammar rules are not forbidden in journalism. You may:

- Begin a sentence with a conjunction.
- End a sentence with a preposition.
- Use contractions.

Paragraphs

Newspaper paragraphs are usually short. Two reasons: Newspaper columns are narrow, about half the width of a typewritten page, so long paragraphs tend to make a story look vast and gray. And short paragraphs lend themselves to energetic, punchy writing. They often are one sentence; sometimes one word. In addition, direct quotes are usually separated from narrative to form their own paragraphs.

Punctuation (commas in series)

In journalistic copy, the *and* in a series of three or more items takes the place of a comma, so the final comma is not needed:

The Spanish crew sailed in the Pinta, the Nina and the Santa Maria. (No comma after Nina).

Punctuation (comma-quotation mark placement)

At the end of a quotation, the quote mark follows the comma: *"That was one fine gosh-durn tractor that hit that deer," Myers said.*

Quotations (attribution)

Usually in newspaper copy, unless you have a good reason not to, make the attribution at the end of the first sentence of a quote. If you're introducing the person you're quoting to the reader, give a full title after the name, in lowercase:

> *"Fourscore and seven years ago, our fathers brought forth on this continent a new nation, conceived in liberty and dedicated to the proposition that all men are created equal," said Abraham Lincoln, president of the United States.*

If the paragraph extends to a second sentence, simply continue the quote with no attribution:

> *"Fourscore and seven years ago, our fathers brought forth on this continent a new nation, conceived in liberty and dedicated to the proposition that all men are created equal," said Abraham Lincoln, president of the United States. "Now we are engaged in a great civil war, testing whether that nation or any nation, so conceived and so dedicated, can long endure."*

If you're quoting the same person later on in the story, after he or she has been introduced, attribute with the last name only, followed usually by *said* or *says*:

> *"We are met on a battlefield of that war," Lincoln said. "We have come to dedicate a portion of that field for those who here gave their lives that the nation might live."*

If you're continuing the quote into another paragraph, lose the last quotation mark and continue the quote. Then follow with the attribution; the last name, usually followed by *continued*:

"Now we are met on a battlefield of that war," Lincoln said. "We have come to dedicate a portion of that field for those who here gave their lives that the nation might live.

"Yet, in a larger sense, we cannot dedicate, we cannot consecrate this hallowed ground. The brave men, living and dead, who perished here, have dedicated it far beyond our power to add or detract," Lincoln continued.

Quotations (attribution verbs)

Usually stick with *says* or *said,* depending on whether the story is in present or past tense. It looks monotonous to the writer, but the reader usually doesn't notice, and it sure beats reaching for verbs like *stated, exclaimed, remarked, averred, declaimed, noted, contended* or *indicated.* Be careful using *claimed;* it usually implies that the reporter doesn't believe what the subject says. And *feel* should refer only to the sense of touch or to emotion; *believes* or *thinks* is better, but the reader might wonder if the reporter is making it up. *Says* puts the onus where it should belong, on the subject of the story. **Exception:** If the verb is more specific or more accurate, then verbs like *conceded, replied, explained, recalled, warned* or *admitted* might be more apt. If that is indeed what the subject did, then *says* or *said* is less precise.

Titles

When the title comes after the subject's name—which it usually does in newspaper copy—it is written in lowercase: *The crowd waited for Tom Ridge, former governor of Pennsylvania.* If it comes before the name—which it usually does in broadcast copy but occasionally in newspaper copy as well—its first letters are capitalized: *The crowd waited for former Pennsylvania Gov. Tom Ridge.*

Time of day

Unless it begins a sentence, virtually all references to time of day begin with an Arabic numeral followed by a space and a.m. or p.m.: *4 a.m. or 11 p.m.* Notice that on the hour, you simply have the hour, without colon and zeroes. But they are included if minutes are added to the hour: *4:27 a.m. or 11:45 p.m.* The only times the Arabic numerals are omitted are at noon and midnight, which are called simply *noon* and *midnight.*

Appendix C: A Short Guide to Broadcast Style

Like print writing, broadcast style emphasizes word economy, active voice and action verbs. But its sentences are even shorter and its style is more conversational. Those two requirements sound as if they conflict, but they don't; not necessarily.

Here is a short alphabetical digest of broadcast writing rules. In no way does it pretend to cover all such rules, only those that seem to arise most often:

Abbreviations

First-letters are hyphenated unless they are pronounceable acronyms: *U-S, F-B-I, L-S-D* (the drug), *G-M* (for General Motors), *P-B-S* (Public Broadcasting System) or *the E-C* (European Community). *AIDS* is spelled with all caps, as it is in print. Also as in print: *Mr., Mrs.* and *Dr.* (As in newspapers, Dr. applies only to physicians; Ph.D.'s go only by their last names in second reference, as does everyone else.) Nearly everything else gets spelled out in broadcast.

Alliteration and tongue twisters

Read your copy aloud before it goes on air to make sure there aren't any. Alliteration is the repetition of consonants, especially at the beginning of words or syllables. They can add spice to print copy, but in broadcast they can get an anchor into real trouble. Tongue twisters should be for newsreader training only.

Attributions

Instead of ending a quotation with "according to J.P. McDonald, the company's controller," as you might in print, put the title in front: *Company Controller J.P. McDonald said . . .* (See *Quotations.*)

251

Days and dates

It's yesterday, today or tomorrow, or the day of the week if it's no more than seven days before or after "today." Dates comprise the month and an ordinal number, spelled out if it's less than twelve: *March 23rd, July sixth, October 19th, May ninth.*

Elisions (dot, dot, dot)

Infrequently, you have no choice but to add a clause to a sentence. When you must, put in an elision where a comma or a semicolon might go in a print story.

Hyphens

Hyphens are broadcast-writing workhorses. Use hyphens, or single dashes, freely to help the announcer, especially with compound words or words with prefixes and suffixes, words like: *co-opt, pre-empt, count-down, school-children, re-election, man-slaughter* or *with-hold.*

Lead-ins

Anchors use lead-ins to tell the audience who and what is happening and to introduce the "street" reporter. They are often written by the reporter and co-opted by the anchor, legitimately.

Middle initials

Don't bother using them unless they belong to someone with a common last name like Smith, Johnson, Jones, Robinson, Williams, Wilson, Jackson or Martinez. Sometimes the middle initial is part of a prominent person's recognized name; then you should use them.

Numbers

Spell out numbers one through eleven. Eleven is easily confused with the Roman numeral II—two. That's why it is included even though in print it usually is not.

Present tense

Present tense is the tense of preference in broadcast news, because it gives listeners and viewers a feeling of immediacy, of being right there.

Pronouncers

Do the newsreader a favor and provide a phonetic version of a word whose pronunciation might not be clear. Make sure the phonetics are simple—anything that can be constructed out of the often-inadequate 26 letters of English: French President *Jacques Chirac (Zhahk Shih-ROCK')*; gastronomic delicacies *tournedos (TOUR'neh-doz, not tor-NAY'-doz)*; *Louisville (LOO'-uh-vihl)*, Kentucky, as opposed to *Louisville (LOO'ihss-vihl)*, Colorado; the late United Farm Workers leader *Cesar Chavez (SAY'zar CHA'vehz, not SEE'zur shuh-VEHZ')*.

Quotations

Direct quotations mean little in written broadcast copy because the viewer or listener can't see the quotation marks that set off direct quotes. And all a sound bite needs is an attribution. If you do need to make sure the audience knows the subject said it, not the newsreader, it's a good idea to first write something like "he said ... in these words ... " or "as she put it ..." (See *Attributions*.)

Reading copy aloud before airing

This is something broadcast writers must do. The practice of reading your copy aloud helps you catch mistakes, maintain conversational rhythm, eliminate unneeded words and sentence elements and spot tongue twisters and unnecessary sibilants.

Repetition and redundancy

These are not the sins that they are in print journalism. Because broadcast is a linear medium, listeners and viewers can't go over a sentence they didn't hear the first time, so it's OK to repeat some of the facts.

Short sentences

Show that you care about your anchor's or newsreader's breath supply. Avoid complex and compound sentences.

Sibilants (s sounds)

Go easy with them. They tend to produce a hissing sound in microphones and they lend themselves to tongue twisters.

Tongue twisters and alliteration

See *Alliteration and tongue twisters*.

References

Bennett, Martyn. 1992. *Illustrated History of Britain*. North Pomfret, Vt.: Trafalgar Square Publishing.

Black, Jay; Steele, Bob; and Barney, Ralph. 1993. *Doing Ethics in Journalism*. Greencastle, Ind.: The Society of Professional Journalism.

Bliss, Edward, Jr., and Patterson, John M. 1978. *Writing News for Broadcast*, 2nd ed. New York: Columbia University Press.

Block, Mervin. 1987. *Writing Broadcast News—Shorter, Sharper, Stronger: A Professional Handbook*. Chicago: Bonus Books.

Born, Roscoe. 1986. *The Suspended Sentence: A Guide for Writers*. Ames: Iowa State University Press.

Cabrera, Luis. March 1, 2001. "Earthquake Rocks Northwest. Seattle Panics, But Escapes Catastrophic Damage." *The Patriot-News* (Harrisburg, Pa.), p. 1. From the Associated Press.

Carey, John, ed. 1987. *Eyewitness to History*. New York: Avon Books.

Chancellor, John, and Mears, Walter R. 1983. *The News Business*, 1st ed. New York: Harper and Row.

Chandrasekaran, Rajiv. March 18, 2001. "Restriction-bound Orators Shun Singapore's Soapbox." *The Washington Post*, p. A23.

Colum, Padraic. 1948. *Anthology of Irish Verse*. New York: Liverwright Publishing Corporation.

Conrad, Barnaby. May 1993. "The Four Deadly Sins of Description." *The Writer*. Vol. 106, pp. 9-12.

Coverage of plane crashes and the bombing of the World Trade Center and the Pentagon. September 11, 2001. Reuters.

Cowell, Alan. April 30, 1997. "Sarajevo Orphans Return to Bleak Future." *The New York Times*, p. 1.

Davies, Norman, 1999. *The Isles: A History*. New York: Oxford University Press.

Drabble, Margaret, ed. 1990. *The Oxford Companion to English Literature*, 5th ed. Oxford, England: Oxford University Press.

Emery, Edwin, and Emery, Michael. 1978. *The Press in America: An Interpretative History of Journalism*. Englewood Cliffs, N.J.: Prentice-Hall.

Fox, Ben. April 19, 2002. Story on high school shooting in El Cajon, Calif. Associated Press.

Fox, Walter. 1993. *Writing the News: A Guide for Print Journalists*, 2nd ed. Ames: Iowa State University Press.

Garlock, David, ed. 1998. *Pulitzer Prize Feature Stories*. Ames: Iowa State Press.

Gibbs, Nancy. July 14, 2002. "Summer of Mistrust. Scamming CEOs have accomplished what Osama bin Laden could not—denting our spirit. Can anything restore our faith in the markets?" Time.com.

Goldstein, Norm, ed. 1996. *The Associated Press Stylebook and Libel Manual*. Reading, Mass.: Addison-Wesley Publishing Company, Inc.

Graham, Betsy P. 1993. *Magazine Article Writing*, 2nd ed. New York: Harcourt, Brace, Jovanovich.

Hanson, Christopher. May/June 1997. "The Dark Side of Online Scoops." *Columbia Journalism Review*, p. 17.

Harrigan, Jane T. 1987. *Read All About It! A Day in the Life of a Metropolitan Newspaper*. Chester, Conn.: The Globe Pequot Press.

Hayakawa, S.I. 1978. *Language in Thought and Action*, 4th ed. San Diego: Harcourt, Brace, Jovanovich.

Hough, George A., III. 1988. *News Writing*, 4th ed. Boston: Houghton Mifflin Company.

Johnson, Gene. March 2, 2001. "Quake Damage Estimates Rise to $2 Billion." *The Patriot-News* (Harrisburg, Pa.), p. A5. From the Associated Press.

Joyce, James. 1959. *Finnegan's Wake*. New York: Viking Press.

Kessler, Lauren, and McDonald, Duncan. 1996. *When Words Collide*, 4th ed. Belmont, Calif.: Wadsworth Publishing Company.

Kiberd, Declan. 1979. *Synge and the Irish Language*. Totawa, N.J.: Rowman and Littlefield.

Kilpatrick, James J. April 13, 1997. "It's All Very Relative When Dealing with These Two Words." *Chicago Sun-Times*. Universal Press Syndicate.

Kilpatrick, James J. June 1, 1997. "Nouns, Adjectives and Verbs that Go Clunk in the Night." *Chicago Sun-Times*. Universal Press Syndicate.

Klaus, Mary. March 24, 2001. "W. Hanover Twp. Feline Hospice Overrun with Rabbits." *The Patriot-News* (Harrisburg, Pa.), p. B1.

Knight, Robert. June 25, 1998. "The Gettysburg Battlefield Controversy." Reuters.

LaRocque, Paula. February 1996. "Journalese: Annoying Practice Falls Short of Clarity, Communication." *Quill*, Vol. 83, No. 2, p. 31.

LaRocque, Paula. July/August 1996. "Quest for Perfect Lead May Turn into Disaster for Writer." *Quill*, Vol. 83, No. 6, p. 51.

Lederer, Richard. May 2001. "Can't find the Right Word? Keep Looking." *Writer's Digest*, p. 36.

Levin, Bernard, *Enthusiasms*. 1984. London and New York: Crown Publishers.

Lindeman, Ralph D. The Renaissance. Unpublished lecture.

Lubet, Steven. April 23, 1997. "Stalking the Misplaced Modifier." *The Chicago Tribune*, p. 17.

MacNeil, Robert. 1989. *Wordstruck*. 1990. New York: Penguin Books.

Marcus, Amy Dockser. April 19, 1997. "Egypt Quickly Turns an Investment Famine into Times of Plenty." *The Wall Street Journal*, p. 1.

Martin, Andrew, and O'Brien, John. October 13, 1996. "Alleged Drug Hub Didn't Fit the Area, North Side Boutique Seemed out of Place." *The Chicago Tribune*, p. 1.

McAdam, E.L., Jr., and Milne, George. 1963. *Johnson's Dictionary: A Modern Selection*. New York: Random House.

McArthur, Tom, ed. 1992. *The Oxford Companion to The English Language*. New York: Oxford University Press.

McCrum, Robert; Cran, William; and MacNeil, Robert. 1986. *The Story of English*, 1st American ed. New York: Viking Penguin, Inc.

McDonald, Daniel, and Burton, Larry W. 1999. *The Language of Argument*, 9th ed. New York: Longman.

McMahon, Patrick. March 1, 2001. "Quake Shocks Seattle: 6.8-magnitude Temblor 'Hits You in the Stomach.'" *USA Today*, p. 1.

McMahon, Patrick. March 2, 2001."Northwest Taking Quake in Stride: Natural Disaster Comes with the Territory, Many Unfazed Residents Say." *USA Today*, p. 3A.

McPhee, John. "The Search for Marvin Gardens." September 9, 1972. *The New Yorker*, pp. 45-62. Reprinted in 1976 in *The John McPhee Reader*, edited by William L. Horwath. New York: Viking Penguin Inc.

Mencken, H.L. 1995. *The American Language*, 4th ed. New York: Alfred A. Knopf.

Montagne, Renee, and Kelly, Mary Louise. August 9, 2002. "Latest on Possible War Against Iraq." "Morning Edition," National Public Radio, Washington.

Myers, James P. 1999. *Writing Irish: Selected Interviews with Irish Writers from the Irish Literary Supplement*. Syracuse, N.Y.: Syracuse University Press.

Ousby, Ian, ed. 1988. *The Cambridge Guide to Literature in English*. Cambridge, England, and London: Cambridge University Press and the Hamlyn Publishing Group, Ltd.

Outing, Steve, June 2001. "Write to Fit the Times." *Writer's Digest*.

Priest, Dana, and Dewar, Helen. August 2, 2002. "Security Agency Led FBI to Capitol Hill. Probe Into Leaks of Sept. 11 Warning Implicates Lawmakers Who Reportedly Called Journalists." *The Washington Post*, p. 2.

Roberts, David. July 2002. "Romancing the Stone." *Smithsonian*, pp. 86-96.

Rooney, Edmund J., and Witte, Oliver R. 2000. *Copy Editing for Professionals*. Champaign, Ill.: Stipes Publishing.

Rubenstein, Steve. March 10, 2001. "Plain Speaking Also Falls Victim to Cisco's Ax." *The San Francisco Chronicle*, p. D2.

Spalding, Rachel Fischer. August 14, 2001."The Tom Tom Club. Cruise and Cruz appear in public Together. EW.com catches up with America's new power couple at the premier of her 'Captain Corelli's Mandolin.'" *Entertainment Weekly*'s EW.com.

Strunk, William, and White, E.B. 1979. *The Elements of Style*, 3rd ed. New York: Macmillan & Company.

Synge, John Millington. 1982. *Collected Works*, vol. 1. Buckinghamshire, England: Colin Smythe, Ltd.

Tebbel, John. 1969. *A Compact History of the American Newspaper*. New York: Hawthorn Books.

Thomas, Dylan. 1968. *Quite Early One Morning*. New York: New Directions Publishing Corporation.

"Transplant Network to Share Resources." June 24, 2000. *USA Today*. From the Associated Press.

Zinsser, William. *On Writing Well*, 5th ed. 1995. New York: HarperCollins.

Index